IF NOT NOW, WHEN?

IF NOT NOW, WHEN?

GREG SEARLE

MACMILLAN

First published 2012 by Macmillan

This edition published 2016 by Macmillan
an imprint of Pan Macmillan
20 New Wharf Road, London N1 9RR
Associated companies throughout the world
www.panmacmillan.com

ISBN 978-1-5098-2935-4

PICTURE ACKNOWLEDGEMENTS
Page 1, middle and bottom, courtesy of Chris Brant.
Page 2, bottom; page 3; page 4, top; and
page 6 © Peter Spurrier/Intersport-Images.
Page 4, top © Popperfoto/Getty Images.
Page 5, bottom; page 7, top and middle; and page 8,
top left and bottom © Getty Images.
All other images are courtesy of the author.

A CIP catalogue record for this book is available from
the British Library.

Printed and bound by CPI Group (UK) Ltd, Croydon, CR0 4YY

Visit **www.panmacmillan.com** to read more about all our books
and to buy them. You will also find features, author interviews
and news of any author events, and you can sign up for e-newsletters
so that you're always first to hear about our new releases.

To my family,
without you my dreams could never have become a reality.
You are the most important people in my world.

Thank you.

Jonny, Mum and Dad in 1992.

Jenny, Josie and Adam in 2012.

CONTENTS

PROLOGUE

BE A LEGEND

'Hey, Greg. You spoke at my school when I was fifteen and I loved your story.'

'Greg Searle. I want to buy you a shot. You're a total legend!'

It sounds good and should feel great, so why doesn't it? I don't feel much of a legend.

It's 30 August 2009 and I am at a party hosted by Siemens for the British rowing team on the final evening of the World Championships in the Polish city of Poznan. The team manager, David Tanner, would probably prefer an 'outsider' like me wasn't here, but one of the few members of the team that I know has put me on the guest list. The GB rowers have done well. They deserve to have a big night. I don't. I've become one of those slightly past-it 'hangers-on' who should probably be having a civilized meal in the local city centre square rather than in here necking the free Polish beer and being bought shots by someone half my age.

I'm in Poznan as colour commentator for the official governing body FISA's coverage of the championships, and I have to ask myself, have I been acting like a legend since I arrived in Poland? I've mixed up the names of a couple of the British women rowers, I've been given a lecture by my co-commentator for cutting in and I've turned up for work unprepared. How legendary is that?

As I move from group to group in the Polish brewery, the venue for the party, I wonder why I'm here. With the beer loosening tongues I've heard various stories of how I spoke at schools or clubs a dozen years earlier and helped inspire various members of the team to take up rowing. It's been nice to hear, but why do I feel so detached? A 'hanger-on'? That's not me, not yet.

Watching the evening unfold, I reflect on the fact that I have a great family and a job I love. This isn't my scene any more, not like this. I've loved my time rowing and it would be fantastic to be nineteen again. But I'm not, and if I want to be involved as a thirty-something then I ought to be doing something more 'me' than this . . .

I wake up on the following morning and go for a run to shake off my hangover from the strong beers and a round of cocktails I remember buying a group of rowers. I think it was called a haemorrhage or something. I'm trying not to remember.

I wander into the beautiful centre square in Poznan, where the streets are busy but not full of people dressed in rowing T-shirts and hats. The square is old and has bars with seating and umbrellas all around it. I take it in and feel lucky to have a few hours to myself in such a stunning spot. I walk past last night's bar and realize I need a strong black coffee. I have most of the morning to relax before I go to the airport for an afternoon flight. I need to use this time to get my head back into my normal job, which means preparing for a two-day leadership workshop with Nestlé Cereal Partners. In addition, I have a few hundred emails to plough through – with an intermittent internet connection I hadn't bothered to keep on top of them over the last few days. I must also remember to buy some presents for my kids to go with the official regatta gear I've already purchased.

The coffee does the trick, and as the sun warms my face I feel content, comfortable and in a reflective mood. I have what I'd always hoped for. There is plenty going on and I'm enjoying juggling family, work, sport and me, although I don't feel as though I'm doing it as well as I'd like. Perhaps this is what grown-up life is all about – managing to keep all the balls in the air while never quite succeeding in giving any one of them the full attention they deserve.

The morning passes and I make my way to the airport, which is full of rowers and supporters heading home. I sit in the same small departure lounge as the GB team and chat to one of the guys from the eight, who last night was my best buddy but now, in the cold, sober light of day, I realize I hardly know at all.

I'm on a different flight from the team, heading to London via Warsaw, and I have to wait while their flight is called. As the lounge empties I see some familiar faces and sit down to chat with my old friends and rivals, Jean-Christophe Rolland, who won gold ahead of me in Sydney in the coxless pair; Ramon di Clemente from South Africa, who finished sixth in that race, and Raffaello Leonardo from Italy, who won bronze in Athens. Ramon and Raffaello are still rowing and planning to race in London 2012 while J-C is on the FISA committee.

During the conversation, Ramon turns to me. 'Hey, Greg mon, Jürgen would love to have a great oak like you in the middle of that eight of his.' Jürgen is Jürgen Grobler, head coach of Team GB.

I smile at Ramon. 'Maybe he would,' and there is a moment of silence. My mind is busy.

Ramon and Raffaello's flights leave and I'm left chatting to J-C. Then we hear an announcement.

Warsaw flight delayed.

Warsaw flight cancelled.

We join a queue of people and are eventually told there will be no flight until tomorrow. Deciding to make the best of it we head back into town, where we book into a nice hotel. I haven't ever really connected that well with J-C until now. I'm stuck in Poznan, and although there's loads I ought to be doing, I can't. It's as if someone has hit the pause button on my life and I'm forced to take some time out.

Over dinner we talk about the final of the coxless pair in 2000. It was my last major competitive race and J-C and his team-mate Michel Andrieux blew Ed Coode and me away over the final 750 m. How did that happen? The reasons pour out over the course of the dinner. J-C explains what went right for them on the day, how they used an emotional connection to propel them to glory, while I outline what went wrong for us. During training at the Leander Boat Club with Jürgen, Ed Coode and I had been in the shadow of Steve Redgrave and his four, and I'd had to follow a programme I didn't believe in. I found myself having to act like a child and do what I was told after being a free man in the single scull for three years. I'd been out of place and not true to myself, much like my commentating here. Not really 'me' at my best.

Later that evening, on my own, the same question turns over in my mind, what would I need to do to be 'me' at my best in 2012? The answer came – perhaps it had been coming for a while. I needed to row again. If I'm in rowing then that's who I am. I'm a competitor, a team player, a leader. If I fought my way back into the GB team, if I won a gold medal in front of my kids, my family, my friends and everyone who cares about sport in Britain, then maybe I'd be worthy of being called a legend.

It's a big jump, though, from where I am at the moment. Sure, since 2006 I've been inching myself back into rowing, competing in the Head of the River and at Henley Royal Regatta, that sort of stuff, but in an old-boys boat alongside my brother Jonny and a collection of other guys from my past. We've done OK, but it's a long, long way from there to the Olympics. Too long? I don't think so.

Click, click, click. The tumblers of the combination lock are at last falling in the correct sequence. There have been many chance events that have led to this moment of realization. The safe door is swinging open. Dare I look at what's inside? Determination? Dedication? Ambition? Fear?

The following day, taking a different route home, I fly to Munich with J-C and we talk further about rowing and his plans for 2012. It's all very interesting but I can't wait to be alone for the London leg of the trip. My own plans for 2012 are formulating in my head thick and fast and I want to write them down, worried I am becoming too excited to remember them.

If I'm going to do it then I need to know where I'll be training, who I'll be with and what will be expected of me. I need to be clear on why I'm doing it. Most of all I need to be 'me', doing what I believe in and what I believe to be right.

Finally free of companions on the flight from Munich, I pull out a pad of paper and a pen. I begin to write:

1 September 2009
London 2012, gold, 2 August, 20 years on.
Am I acting like a legend? What could I do? Am I
    practising what I preach?
Jenny, Josie and Adam.
What's the commitment? Are we up for it?
Work. Friendships and relationships. They don't need
    me as a leader right now.
Rowing, training, physiology.
Talk to Jürgen.
Take the tests.
Do the work.
BE A LEGEND.

ONE

PLAY HARD BUT PLAY BY THE RULES

1 August 1992, Barcelona, on the eve of the Olympic final of the coxed pair. My brother Jonny, myself and our cox Garry Herbert are listening to Team GB's sports psychologist Brian Miller and coach Steve Gunn. Tomorrow we will be attempting to achieve what many people believe to be the impossible – overcoming the Italian powerhouse of Carmine and Giuseppe Abbagnale, double Olympic gold medallists and seven times World Champions.

We're in a newly built accommodation block in the Olympic Village, on the banks of Lake Banyoles. Our apartment is on the top floor and we're sitting around the kitchen table. The lounge is shared with other rowers and we want our privacy.

Brian is creating powerful images.

'Picture yourselves sitting around a table with the Abbagnales. Each of you has a candle burning in front of you. Together you lift your right hands from the table and place them three inches above the flame. Which one of you is going to keep their hand there the longest? Don't let it be the Italians.'

Eyeballs bulging and jaws clenched, Jonny and I are totally focused as Brian speaks. A mixture of sweat and tears stings my eyes.

Jonny loves the image being painted. 'Fuck them. They're older than us, they're softer than us, they're uglier than us. We can have them tomorrow.'

Brian turns to me. 'Greg, you've heard of the Russian pole-vaulter Sergey Bubka?'

Of course I have. He won the gold medal in Seoul in 1988 and has broken the world record like a hundred times. Sure I've heard of Bubka.

'Did you know that at the last Olympics he failed his first two vaults at the 5.90-metre height? Both times he clattered the bar a mile short of clearing it. There's only one further attempt left – succeed and he is Olympic champion; fail and he falls back to fourth. As he prepares for the single most important moment in his career, his coach leans over to him and quietly speaks in his ear.'

What? What did he say?

'"Sergey," the coach whispers, "if not now, when? If not you, who?"'

That sums up tomorrow for me.

'Finally, let me leave you with this,' Brian says. 'It concerns a Japanese gymnast called Shun Fujimoto. He was a member of Japan's six-man team at the Montreal Olympics of 1976. During his floor exercise, he lands badly and breaks his kneecap, but instead of withdrawing from the competition he tells no one of the pain he is in and carries on. Somehow he makes it through his pommel horse routine, scoring a vital 9.5, but to give his team-mates a chance of winning gold he has to perform next on the high rings as never before. He's lifted up, runs through his sequence of twists and turns flawlessly, all the time knowing that he has to nail his dismount or his country will lose. Flying off the rings he lands, takes no more than half a step to catch his balance, and raises his arms in completion of his performance. His score is the highest he has ever received and Japan go on to win gold. As Shun limps off the mat his kneecap is virtually hanging off, his leg shattered.

'What are you prepared to do for each other tomorrow?'

Brian knows he's done his job well. We are shaking and shivering with a mixture of anger, excitement and fear. Realizing we might need a little calming down to go with the winding up, he changes his tone and speaks again. 'When you race tomorrow, who is the real opposition? Who is it that stands between you the Olympic gold medal?'

Brian answers his own question. 'It's the face you see in the mirror when you wake up tomorrow morning.'

Lying in bed later there is only one thing on my mind. If that is what Fujimoto was prepared to do for his team, what am I prepared to do for mine?

Our tactics for the forthcoming race have been worked out to the finest detail with Steve Gunn. Until very recently Jonny and I had been rowing in an eight. Tomorrow's Olympic final will only be something like our seventh ever coxed pair race. We have decided this is to our advantage. We are to a large extent an unknown entity and we plan on using that as a strength.

Most people tend to row the coxed pair at about thirty-four strokes per minute. Our plan is to whip along the course at thirty-nine – very, very high for a pair – and then take any changes of pace off that rate. To assist us, Steve sawed a section of the handles off our oars and moved the fulcrum back to where it should be, giving us more in-board leverage and less out-board. As a result, we aren't moving the boat quite as far per stroke, but we can maintain the stroke rate we have set ourselves.

The plan for the race is simple. We know the Abbagnales like to blow the opposition away early, so we will aim to start as well as possible, the first ten strokes at as high a rate as we can manage. For the next ten we'll try to push the boat's speed up as fast as we can, with a view to keeping the pressure on the Italians. We never want them to rest. We aren't going to give anything away for nothing. Then we'll settle into our pace for the remainder of the first 500 m. We'll push hard to maintain our pace during the second 500 m, through halfway, then at the 1250-m mark, when everyone else is hurting, we'll instigate a thirty-stroke surge: ten strokes pushing and pulling as hard as we can, then ten where we lift the rate even further, then a final ten strokes where we reduce the rate slightly and pull with everything we have. At 350 m to go we'll pick it up again for the last push.

Simple.

That night it's hard to sleep. I'm hot, really hot, and I'm incredibly restless. I'm afraid of how much it's going to hurt, afraid I'm going to let Jonny down, that I'm not as tough as Shun Fujimoto, or Jonny. I'm also thinking how cool it would be to win. This time tomorrow I could be Olympic Champion. I have been picturing the race by listening to a tape Brian prepared for us. I know it's not good to focus on the actual winning and I settle for visualizing rowing well. That helps. I know I can do that. I only need 250 great strokes, that's all. If I do that then I get what I deserve, and I think I deserve to win the Olympics.

I have lots of good luck cards, including one from an Australian girl I have had a relationship with at rowing events for the last few years. In it she has written, 'Take what's yours!' I see my gold medal, sitting in a cupboard somewhere waiting for me to collect it tomorrow. I will, and I'll do it by rowing one stroke after another, just like I've done so many times before. Two hundred and fifty great strokes, I can take that on.

I get up and walk into the bathroom, where I look myself in the eye in the mirror. The face I see staring back at me is the only thing standing in the way of a gold medal. I can overcome the challenge it poses, I can do this tomorrow. Safe in that knowledge I am able to sleep.

The weather the following morning is perfect. We go out early and have a good paddle. The race itself is scheduled to begin at 9.30 a.m. We are feeling good; it's as though things are falling into place for us. We had been unable to get hold of any tickets for our parents until the day before, when we bumped into a kid from our old school who was volunteering at the ticket office. Somehow he's managed to get us the two tickets we needed. Mum and Dad will be there to see us, whether we win or lose.

After our paddle, we come in and make our way to the massive tent where the rowers are fed. It's a weird atmosphere. Some of us are racing that day while others, like Steve Redgrave and Matthew Pinsent, raced the previous day – and won. They are keeping out of our way but they are still there, trying to be supportive and invisible at the same time. I want the race to happen but the clock moves so slowly. The three of us sit together and say nothing. Jonny always goes quiet and looks like he's about to kill someone. I do worry that it might be me if I say something ridiculous, which I am prone to, so I keep my mouth shut and focus on rowing well. Two hundred and fifty great strokes. I can do that.

Then it's off to the boat. I feel calm, we all do. Steve talks us through the plan one last time then, as he pushes us off the landing stage, he has this look of hard determination in his eyes. He needs no words. He has been capable of making me terrified and ready to perform ever since I joined the school where he taught. Like my brother, Steve has the ability to project a look of steely determination that's slightly deranged. He has that look today, and as he pushes us off I know we can be as tough as him. We can deliver. Steve looks calm, which means I can *feel* calm. (I later learn that he lit two cigarettes and smoked them simultaneously as soon as we had disappeared from sight.)

The warm-up goes well, with a few technical exercises followed by some powerful bursts of work. The boat seems to be flying. We are full of energy and ready to fight. When Garry calls for race pace we deliver something that's sustainable for 200 m, not the full 2000 m, but we don't care. We are full of adrenalin and desperate to be allowed to smash it out in the race.

During our warm-up the women's eight leave to compete in their final. We have to stop while they line up and then disappear. As we finish our warm-up we can hear the commentary for their race. In what seems like no time, they have gone from here to there, and now one of those crews is Olympic Champion. Four years' work has been completed.

The starter calls our race. It's our turn to manoeuvre the boat into the lane and then to back it into the waiting arms of a small child who holds it straight in her hands. The Romanians are to our left, the Italians to our right.

The starter raises his flag.

'Are you ready . . .'

There are two people above all others who inspired me to take up rowing. My older brother by three years, Jonny, and Martin Cross, the history teacher at our secondary school, Hampton. In 1984 Martin (Mr Cross as I knew him then) disappeared to LA for the summer with a young bloke called Steve Redgrave, along with Andy Holmes, Richard Budgett and cox Adrian Ellison, and came back with a gold medal. I was twelve years old, about to start my second year at Hampton school, and although I had taken almost no interest in rowing up to that point, I thought winning a gold medal was pretty cool – for a teacher.

Up until the age of thirteen I'd played rugby, and even though I'd seen some rowing at school, it wasn't really for me. I thought the guys who did it were all a bit soft and probably only settled for rowing because they weren't much good at anything else.

Prior to attending Hampton, Jonny and I both went to state primary schools in Shepperton (Littleton Infants followed by St Nicholas Primary), where Jonny obviously shone because the teachers at St Nicholas suggested to Mum and Dad that he sit the entrance exams for Hampton, an independent school that offered various bursaries.

The possibility of Jonny winning a bursary was critical. At this stage, when Jonny was eleven, Mum was a teacher and Dad a student. He'd been a policeman, but had recently decided that he wanted to be more involved with his family and that the shift work required in the police force wasn't conducive to how he wanted to live his life. I have very strong memories of coming home from school and having to tiptoe around the house because Dad was asleep upstairs, having been on duty all night. I also remember numerous occasions when he had to wave goodbye to Jonny and me on a Sunday afternoon to go off to work while we played games in the back garden.

So Dad decided to make a change and went back to university to study chartered surveying. On graduating he went into the estate agent business while he completed his professional qualifications, then spent the remainder of his career as a chartered surveyor.

During the three years that Dad was studying, the family income was slashed in half, which would have made Jonny's move to Hampton impossible had his fees not been paid by a bursary. Given Jonny's academic ability the grant was never really in doubt, although he did make it as hard as possible for himself – halfway through the entrance exam he asked to be excused to go to the toilet and promptly got lost, missing a large chunk of exam time. When Dad found out he made sure the school knew what had happened, but he was quickly reassured. 'Mr Searle, I don't think that's going to be a problem.'

While Dad studied, the onus was on Mum to be the main breadwinner, and I can't think of anyone better suited to rise to the challenge. She taught PE, then art, and went on to become head of department; she was one of those teachers who arrived early and went home late. Mum is a tough no-nonsense lady with perhaps the strongest work ethic I have ever come across.

I once managed to convince her that I wasn't well enough to go to school, a rare event in our household. Bubonic plague would just about get you a day in bed, but not much else. Somehow, however, I pulled it off and by lunchtime, amazingly, I was feeling better, so I went down to the town with Dad to get my hair cut. That evening Mum said nothing when she found out, and instead wrote a letter for me to take to school the following day. She didn't beat about the bush: 'Gregory convinced me he wasn't well enough to go to school in the morning, but he obviously was because he went and got his hair cut, so please feel free to give him a Saturday detention or whatever the school feels is appropriate to make up the time he has lost.'

I, of course, was unaware of the contents of the letter and proudly handed it to my form teacher, safe in the knowledge that I had got away with a day off, until I was later summoned and instructed to be at the school gates bright and early on Saturday for extra classes. I didn't try that again.

Mum's attitude came directly from her own mother I believe. She was one of those lived-through-the-war drove-an-ambulance-around-Plymouth kind of grannies. In a word, tough. She was a mother of four children and my grandfather was a very traditional man who wasn't much involved with his kids. My mother learned early on that if you wanted something done you had to do it yourself; Granny was too busy keeping the household running to have time to indulge anyone.

Mum's can-do attitude hasn't changed since retirement. On one of my wife Jenny's first visits to my parents' home, Mum was out in the garden digging with one of those four-pronged garden forks when we arrived. She explained that she wanted to finish off her borders before coming in for a cup of coffee; she'd been out there for an hour and said she had another hour or so left to do. As I stood there chatting I noticed her work rate wasn't as high as usual and that she was hobbling a little. Then I spotted a small trail of blood on the grass. When I asked Mum if everything was OK she said she was fine, but that she'd accidently hit her foot with the fork earlier. I feel bad now but I left her to it and went inside as I didn't fancy waiting an hour for that cup of coffee. When she eventually hobbled in I realized she was more injured than she'd let on. There was a hole in the top of her wellie around the middle of her foot – and a matching hole in the sole! She'd jabbed the fork right through her foot and carried on digging for another couple of hours! It took a fair bit of cajoling for her to allow me and Jenny to drive her to hospital to get it looked at. I guess that must have been when Jenny realized what she'd taken on.

I like to think Dad's determination to achieve his goals and Mum's work ethic both rubbed off on me – point me in the right direction and I'll do it. What I know is that I've inherited their competitive spirit, and Jonny, too, maybe even more so.

Mum had been a good all-round athlete in her youth, and reached county level at netball and track and field, while my dad was very keen on rugby and cricket and had also played at a decent level. He's one of three boys and by nature competitive. He isn't one to talk himself up but he'll always do everything he can to win. His father owned a shop in Plymouth during and after the war, and he used to go along to watch my dad and his brothers play sports – usually from outside the school fence. I think he wanted them to do well, but he never wanted to make a big show of it. Jonny's and my home life was similar to my father's: quietly competitive. This approach seemed to cover most things we did, from cricket in the garden to eating a Chinese takeaway (from the Wing Wah House) on a Saturday night.

Both Jonny and I were brought up with very firm views on how we should conduct ourselves: play hard but play by the rules. If the umpire indicated you were caught out during a cricket match, there would never be a moment's hesitation, regardless of whether you thought you'd nicked the ball or not. You always walked. That's how Dad taught us to play. Same for our Chinese treat.

The rules were clear. We'd have four main dishes and you were definitely only allowed a quarter of each. Get too greedy and you were in trouble! But equally, if you were too slow, then your portion of sweet and sour pork became fair game.

To help with the family finances Dad used to buy and sell all sorts of old rubbish. We'd put adverts in the local paper and end up buying collections of cigarette cards, coins, medals, stamps . . . then at the weekends we'd take a stall at an antique fair and sell whatever we could. If it went well we'd have earned that visit to the Wing Wah House on the way home, and whatever profit was left went towards our holidays.

Holidays tended to involve touring around Europe with a tent in the back of the car. Once pitched at a site, we would check out whatever local attractions we could find. We weren't fussy. On one trip to a lake in southern France I remember Jonny and I becoming involved in an England versus the rest of the world tug of war. It ended badly with me and some French kid fighting in the water.

In the evening the four of us used to sit up and play cards. As far as my parents are concerned there is only one card game worth the time of day, and that's bridge, which our parents taught us to play. In many ways it reflects our family ethos: competitive, intellectually stimulating and all-consuming.

Jonny securing his place at Hampton opened the door to rowing. Up until then we had no knowledge or interest in the sport; the opportunity to give it a go had never arisen and that's probably how it would have stayed had Jonny not passed his entrance exam. Rugby was the thing for me back then, and when I was eight Dad took me along to Staines Rugby Club, where during my first session he saw me running down the middle of the pitch, handing off the opposition and scoring time and again between the posts. He was quietly impressed and wondered what sort of rugby future might lie ahead of me. Twickenham maybe? It was a bit of a letdown, therefore, when the coach came over for a chat at the end. 'Yes, Mr Searle, your son isn't a bad player. Next week he can join in with our "A" team group.'

It hadn't been a bad debut, but it had been against the kids who only turned up once in a while. The following week against the regulars was a bit of a reality check, but at least I was playing alongside the best kids, who knew how to pass, tackle and really make a game of it.

My path to the classrooms of Hampton was not as smooth as my brother's. In fact, I was unsure whether I wanted to go there at all, but my parents decided they ought to give both of us the same opportunity. The fact that Jonny was considerably more academic than me had two consequences. One, my parents had to work very hard with me to help me through the entrance exam (which I passed, just), even organizing additional tuition, and two, because I was neither a high-flyer, nor from an underprivileged background, we had to pay the full fees. Dad was just starting out as an estate agent, and it required a considerable tightening of the family belts, which they were happy to do. I didn't appreciate any of that at the time – like all kids everything just seemed, well, normal – but I realize now that I wouldn't be writing this book had it not been for the personal sacrifices Mum and Dad were willing to make.

Jonny started rowing when he was fourteen years old, under the guidance of a teacher called Mr Creber. Up until then Jonny hadn't been particularly sporty, that adjective was more often associated with me, but Mr Creber saw his potential and encouraged him into a boat, saying, 'I will make an athlete of you one day.' That proved to be a very important quote for my life as much as Jonny's, because if my brother hadn't taken to the water I think it's questionable whether I would have.

Hampton's approach to rowing has been pivotal to my attitude towards the sport, and also in a more general sense. The coaching there followed a very clear path: first, under Mr Creber's guidance we learned the technique, then we learned to enjoy it, then we became hungry for success. That way of thinking is important to me now with my own kids, because I don't get overly excited about my daughter, say, hitting a personal best aged ten. I am pleased that she likes swimming and enjoys it, and I want to be incredibly supportive, but keep her achievements and disappointments in perspective. Let her have fun to start with; if she wants to move things on later, fine, we'll take that when it comes.

How this manifested itself at Hampton was by not putting the best eight boys in a boat together during the first couple of years, even for competitive races. I think that's a very clever way of creating a positive feel for sport in a school environment. The reason they did this was because a rower's long-term potential doesn't necessarily come out at the beginning, and the coaches were looking to avoid two things: first crushing confidence early on, and second giving an over-inflated sense of achievement, only for disappointment to follow. Where is the fun in either of those scenarios?

Adolescent boys grow at very different rates. When you first set foot on one of those awkward, wobbly, unnatural structures called a boat, it can be very off-putting, and it's often the shorter, more co-ordinated boys, those who are likely to be fairly sporty already, who do well straight away. But after a year, do they have the stickability for a sport that's tough, painful, tedious and doesn't offer the immediate results boys like that might be used to, such as scoring a goal or a try? Equally, leverage in rowing is crucial. The taller you are, the longer your reach and the faster you can propel the boat. But someone who is tall for his age at fourteen might not be at sixteen. So rather than creating an environment that produces a man-of-the-match every day – instant gratification if you like – at Hampton they encouraged an attitude that said,

'We are all learning, we are all performing, we are all growing together.'

When it came to the summer, after a year of rowing, the school might have had an inkling about who were the best boys out of the twenty or so they had, but they still mixed everyone up between the various boats – an eight, two fours and a quad scull – which meant other schools would come along and win the races we entered. Those schools would be thrilled at how fast they were progressing, but two years down the line would those kids still be motivated and training hard having experienced success so early?

Come the second season, and with a group of boys who had proved their genuine enthusiasm for rowing, Hampton moved up a gear, putting out a definite first eight comprising a group of lads who were not only taller and stronger but, most importantly, determined. In 1984 Jonny made it into the under-fifteens eight, J-15 in rowing jargon, and his boat won the National Schools' Regatta at Nottingham. This was the first time I really sat up and took notice of rowing. I was still too young to become involved, but I was very happy for my brother. It was amazing to think he'd found a sport where he could be the best in Britain.

The following year, with Jonny having moved up to the school's overall first eight, he swept the board, winning what is known as the Triple – the Schools' Head of the River on the Thames (a time trial over the Boat Race course), the National Schools' (British schools only) and the Princess Elizabeth Challenge Cup at Henley (the big one, involving all-comers).

When he won at Henley, I was seriously impressed. Henley is a great event because you have the best of all rowers racing alongside one another. For instance, on the same afternoon as Jonny's race in the Hampton School first eight, racing on the same course and rowing for Great Britain was our teacher Martin Cross, who had become an Olympic champion less than a year earlier. It was no surprise, therefore, that Jonny and his school buddies, the ones

I had seen punishing themselves at the gym, running around the street by our school or just sitting in our kitchen eating loads of toast, were suddenly big stars. I was delighted for him. When we competed against each other, of course I wanted to win, but no more than when I played against anyone else. For me, beating my brother was not an additional motivation; there wasn't a hint of sibling rivalry between us. We always had similar interests but different strengths, which is why I've always been happy to support him.

In the Henley final Jonny's crew were up against some big, strong American boys from a school called St Paul's, Concord. If you were to compare the average weights of the two crews, the Hampton lads probably came in at around 11 or 12 stone, whereas the Americans were probably nearer 14 stone. Think of it like this, our bowman was smaller than their cox.

What Hampton had, however, was a toughness and technically brilliant coaching, in particular from the biology teacher, Steve Gunn. Looking back from a distance, it's quite incredible the hotbed of talent the school had in that department. First there was the awareness of Mr Creber and other staff members, who had an ability to make young lads understand the fundamentals of the sport, and more importantly took time to nurture their talent. As these boys progressed through the school, with that solid foundation they were well equipped to cope with the far tougher regime that was to follow, where they would be expected to take responsibility for themselves and act like men, pushing everything to the limit. Pupils falling exhausted off the rowing machine and puking in a corner of the gym was a common sight.

Then there was the inspiration that was Martin Cross, a fantastic hero, plus the technical excellence of Steve Gunn who was prepared to put rowing ahead of everything else in order to train his crews to care and be passionate and successful. It's no surprise that after steering Hampton to become the best rowing school in the country for six years, Steve went on to coach the British team over many years and is now head of the talent development programme.

I followed Jonny's race as much as I could. We hadn't been to Henley before and didn't have the badges that provided access to the nice areas near the finish. We parked the car by the river, somewhere near the start, but were unable to tell what was going on, so I legged it along the bank. I was jumping over picnics, trying not to knock over drunken spectators, in an attempt to keep up with the race, but as the crews disappeared towards the finish line I couldn't tell who was winning.

By the time I'd run the whole way behind the Stewards' Enclosure and made it back to the river I could see both crews totally exhausted and collapsed over their oars. It still wasn't clear who'd won, but I later learned that Hampton had come back from more than a length down to win by about a foot in a race run over more than 2000 m. What was clear, however, was that something special happened for Jonny and his crew that day. Those eight guys, plus the cox and Steve Gunn, had done something that had seemed impossible and which they will take to their graves. They remain close to this day. Having seen this up close, I realized what rowing had to offer – and I wanted some of it.

The first casualty of that decision was rugby. I had moved on from Staines and was a solid member of the school team, No. 8 and pack leader. But the commitment necessary to become a rower made it impossible to pursue both activities and rugby lost out. Mr Timbs, the rugby coach, was very disappointed. Not only was I jumping ship, so were half his forwards. He did his best to persuade me otherwise, insisting I had the potential to be the best No. 8 the school had ever produced (I'm pretty sure he was flattering me), but my heart was set on emulating Jonny. I have remained friends with Mr Timbs over the years and whenever I go back to Hampton for a presentation or just to say hello, he admits now that I probably made the correct choice.

My other motivation was girls. Hampton was a boys-only day school, with a girls' school next door, Lady Eleanor Holles, and rowing was one of the few things we jointly participated in. I would be lying if I said this had no effect at all on my decision, but it was a secondary factor, honestly.

The impact of Hampton winning the Triple in 1985 was immediate. Jonny's eight were all either in the fifth form or lower sixth, and their success resulted in the boys below them training even harder as they pushed for a seat in the boat. I was a bit nervous taking up rowing immediately after Jonny had done so well, but he was very supportive. He competed for England in the Anglo-French match, which I thought was great in itself, but he was a bit gutted not to have made the full Great Britain team, and when he returned he gave me his England shirt, which I wore for training pretty much straight away. Kitted out like that I had to make sure I wasn't messing about.

Occasionally at lunchtimes the boys in Jonny's year wheeled the ergo – an indoor rowing machine – from the gym out into the quadrangle in the middle of the school. Me and a bunch of other rowing hopefuls would watch them as they trained, going at it as hard as they possibly could until they collapsed from their seat into a sweating bundle on the grass, legs twitching, arms strained beyond the point of intense pain and vomiting from exertion. That's cool, I would think. I want to do that. That's what it's supposed to be like. With those guys as my role models, from day one, even though I was still a bit of a jester, I tried to push myself at every opportunity, and that attitude, combined with my natural physiology, resulted in me rising through the rowing ranks fairly quickly.

My first ever win was against Kingston Grammar School at the Thames Ditton Regatta in 1986. It's held on the Kingston stretch of the river outside Hampton Court Palace and is a classic, lovely regatta with about eight entries, knockout rounds and a final that pitted Hampton against a Kingston crew that included James Cracknell. It proved to be the first of many occasions over the coming years when James' and my paths would cross. We are the same age and our rowing histories have been very much intertwined.

I'm not sure we were a better boat than Kingston. I've talked to James about it since and he is pretty certain of what happened. The race was close until their cox steered off course and we were able to row through them. Whatever happened, it was great to win a 'pot'. In the case of the Thames Ditton Regatta the 'pot' was a nice glass tankard with the event engraved on it. Jonny had loads of these things and now I had one of my own to drink orange squash from!

I loved the feeling that the win brought and I wanted more of it, but unfortunately the following year at J-15 we were anything but spectacular, failing to match the success of Jonny's eight at the National Schools' Regatta. That was disappointing, and I realized that in order to taste victory again I would have to work hard to make it into the school's first eight, where I could have a go at winning the Triple.

As I joined the fifth form and the top rowing group in the school, Jonny left Hampton for Oxford University, having lifted the Triple again in 1986 with exactly the same eight, but not before he was selected to represent Britain in the coxless four at the Junior World Championships for a second time. The previous year Mum, Dad and I had driven to Roudnice in Czechoslovakia to watch him win silver, and in the summer of 1987 we were off again, this time to Cologne. From a standing start three years earlier, rowing had quickly become a major part of Searle family life.

In Cologne I had a school friend with me and we felt very

grown up, sharing a hotel room and having the freedom to explore without Mum and Dad supervising us. This was a big event, with posters plastered all over the city, and during our attempts to chat up pretty German girls we tried to introduce the topic of 'Rudern' in the hope that some of the star quality of the athletes would rub off on us. It didn't work, so we settled for messing about in the hotel pool instead. This also didn't turn out too well. One day we were kicking a football around, trying to do diving headers into the water, when we ended up knocking a rather impressive plant pot into the water. The contents expanded like a filthy cloud and we were forced to scarper pretty fast. I imagine the hotelier was in no doubt who the culprits were.

For all the fun and games we got up to, however, on the whole we were captivated by the rowing itself. That's what we were there for and that's what we loved: watching it, being involved and soaking up the atmosphere. Suddenly, however vicariously, I was part of big-time sport. It doesn't get much better, I thought, as Jonny's boat lined up for the final. Well maybe it could get a bit better. Come on, Jonny!

Jonny's four was coached by Steve Gunn and consisted of a guy from Nottingham, Toby Hessian, who went to the Olympics; Tim Foster, gold medallist in 2000 with Redgrave, and Rupert Obholzer, known as Obby, who was to row with us at the Atlanta Olympics. No British team had ever won a gold at the Juniors, not even Steve Redgrave, who'd given it a go but had returned with 'just' a silver.

This time we knew where to sit and what to watch out for. Jonny had 'trained' my parents well and they knew he needed to focus. We got there in loads of time and sat with the other British supporters. The events before the men's four went as expected, with the other British crews doing quite well but not winning. Finally it came to Jonny's race. I stood and watched with my folks as the rest of the British supporters chanted, 'GB, GB,' which I've always thought sounds a little ridiculous. And then they delivered. They were the best-drilled crew in the race and I knew there wouldn't be many tougher. Britain had won their first gold and my brother had played an essential part in achieving that. It was a brilliant feeling. The taste of success was sweet, even when it wasn't my own. Just think what I would feel like if I could ever achieve that myself?

Despite the school's relative lack of success at J-15, at the beginning of my fifth year at Hampton, out of the twenty or twenty-five guys who were rowing, I knew I was a strong contender for the first eight. I'd been putting in the hours and consistently performing during the punishing programme we had to fit in around classes. A typical week would consist of a six-mile run to Bushy Park and back on a Monday lunchtime with weights at night; Tuesday was weights in the evening; Wednesday rowing and games; Thursday evening weights; Friday ergo at lunchtime and Saturday rowing twice in the morning, with optional additional rowing on Sunday. With that foundation, and following my results in the trials that autumn and winter, I fought my way into the first eight, becoming one of only two fifth-formers in the boat.

In terms of the rest of the school, that set me apart to some extent. The 'Boaties', as we were known, definitely didn't have the street cred of the rugby boys. We were totally focused – no smoking, drinking or chasing girls. In fact, I think it would be fair to say we were regarded as slightly geeky. That didn't bother me in the slightest; it wasn't as though I felt I was making a sacrifice, on the contrary, I was making a choice. I was well aware of what I was turning my back on, and I knew what I was moving towards. I'd experienced it at Henley and in Cologne.

In my mind it was cooler to be one of the rowers, who would win races and go to World Championships, than to be just one of the rest. In truth, for me it wasn't such a black and white issue anyway. Unlike Jonny, I'd played rugby for the first couple of years at school and was still friends with a lot of that crowd. I just chose not to socialize with them out of school hours because I preferred to train and hang out with the other rowers, who were a really tight, close-knit group.

Despite having lost Jonny and the other guys in his year, Hampton's first eight for the 1988 season was still strong, with some very good guys, including Obby, still basking in the light of his World Junior gold and now in the upper sixth. Obby had been Jonny's partner in the pairs, and when I found myself stepping into a boat with him that year it was fantastic. I'd never really felt I was in Jonny's shadow, but if anyone *had* thought that it must surely have been dispelled when they saw me shoulder to shoulder and holding my own with one of the country's best junior rowers. It certainly gave me added confidence as we set out on our mission to maintain the school's momentum of the past few years and capture the Triple again.

I could go into a lot of detail here of how that season progressed, the various races we competed in and won against schools like Eton and Radley and men's clubs such as Tideway Scullers and Kingston, but I don't think it's necessary. Suffice to say, the more we raced, the better we became. What is important is that we developed a signature way of racing – we'd be tough and find a good pace, then we'd always have a strong finish. It was ingrained in everything we did, from our Bushy Park runs, which always ended in a mile-long mad sprint back to school, during which your sole desire was to catch the bloke in front and stay ahead of the bloke behind (throwing up at the end of those runs was a common occurrence, and then it was time to grab a bite to eat before lessons resumed), to circuit training and the sessions on the ergo, which we would set to, say, 5 km and everyone would bust a gut to beat their personal best time. Basically you pushed yourself until you were exhausted, then you went again. When it came to racing, the bigger, stronger guys might lead for the first half, but they couldn't cope with our blistering finish. Jonny's eight had developed the same style. In 1985 the Americans had taken a substantial lead, but Hampton had reeled them back and rowed through to the line; we were doing the same. It was the Martin Cross way, and when Martin rowed in a coxed four at the Olympics in 1988 in Seoul they seemed to come from nowhere to qualify for the final – the commentator identified it as the 'Cross Factor'! Four years later it was to pay me the biggest dividend of them all.

Having won the first leg of the Triple, the Schools' Head of the River, we came up against Matthew Pinsent's Eton in the finals of the National Schools' and the Princess Elizabeth Cup at Henley. Matthew was already pretty well known in rowing circles, having been the best guy in the GB eight not to make Jonny's four in the World Juniors in 1987. Following that he'd been promoted to partnering Tim Foster in the GB pair, an event they went on to win at the Juniors the following year. To me, though, he was just one of a group of faceless Etonians I wanted to beat.

While neither school could exactly be described as a typical comprehensive, we managed to build up an image of that Eton boat in comparison to our own – privileged posh boys versus tough street fighters; them versus us. We couldn't, wouldn't, let them win. Having developed this mentality, we would then paint ourselves a picture – the Eton boat is half a length up on you, there's 250 m to go, what are we going to do about it?

At the National Schools' we squeezed the start beautifully. It was a classic moment that I still want to teach the GB eight today. As the starter said, 'Attention,' we locked the oars in the water, and the moment he said, 'Go,' we popped the boat right out ahead of them, taking an early lead and then inching away. Every stroke was tough, but we were together and committed. We wouldn't let those soft, posh twats back into the race. (The fact that we were pretty much the same was beside the point!) It might have looked like we jumped the start, but we didn't, we timed it perfectly. Mind you, if he hadn't said, 'Go,' immediately we could have been in trouble with a false start. We could have strained and held on for a split second longer, but only just. As it was, I don't think it really mattered, by the National Schools' we had hit our stride and I don't think Eton could have done anything to stop us, regardless of the start.

If proof were needed, it arrived at Henley with the Princess Elizabeth Cup. We took up residence in the church hall in a little village called Remenham by the river near Henley. We slept on the floor and cooked and ate all our meals together. My best mate was also a sixteen-year-old fifth-former called Doran Tranmer, who fancied himself as a bit of a joker. I'd been sleeping pretty well until the day he decided to get a little too close for comfort, belly flopping on top of me while I lay on my air bed. Doran had a decent-sized stomach on him, causing my bed to pop spectacularly. I didn't sleep as soundly after that, but it didn't detract from our performance.

We went through each round of the competition, winning well and feeling like top dogs, and on the final day we destroyed Matthew Pinsent and his buddies and we loved it. At that age, beating Eton, our arch enemies as we saw them, in such a convincing manner was the best feeling in the world. Any other result would have been a surprise, but we still had to work for it every stroke of the way. We suffered a bout of illness in the final week, but even with the late substitution into our team of a bloke I can only describe as a 'punk rocker nutter' we were still too good.

Winning the Triple felt as fantastic as I had imagined. The deep satisfaction of crossing the line first, knowing you've won, is what drives me still, and Henley that year was the first time the feeling seeped into my soul. It's never left me.

I believe our success that season was based largely on what I now see as one of the most important factors within a team –

trust, which was built on three pillars. We had *credibility* in each other's eyes, we'd all earned our place. We were *reliable* – we proved that individually time and again on the water, on the ergos and in the gym. For instance, in one exercise the cox would blow a whistle every three seconds, and on his signal we all power-pulled weighted bars from the floor on to our shoulders, like a weightlifter about to perform a clean and jerk, without the jerk bit. We'd hold the bar momentarily on our shoulders, drop it and go again on the next whistle. Pull out at ten repetitions and you may as well head straight home. That's not a guy you can rely on. By thirty, everyone would be feeling it, me perhaps more than most. At 6 foot 5" and weighing around 13 stone that bar had a long way to travel, much further than my 5 foot 8", 12½ stone mates! By forty, we all knew we'd been through hell together, until one by one we'd collapse, muscles shaking, sweat dripping, in full view of everyone, finding it physically impossible to continue. Sixty was pretty much anyone's max, and eventually there would be only one man standing. The collective knowledge of the individual effort each member of the crew had put in was an incredibly intense bond.

Finally, we had *intimacy* – we knew each other really well and cared about what each other said and wanted to say, understanding who was tough and who needed more support. The confidence that level of trust instils is immense.

Perhaps most importantly of all, however, we weren't self-interested. We all wanted the same thing: to win together, for ourselves and for each other.

Throughout the year we had become a self-regulating group. If anyone stepped over the line that we'd agreed on, say for instance smoking or turning up for training hungover, we would make their life in the team very hard. That wasn't how the members of our boat acted. For those of us who were driven by the success we were certain the eight could achieve, the thought of the people around you not wanting you there was too much to deal with. So it didn't happen, or very rarely.

After completing the Triple, something extraordinary happened – every member of our eight was selected for the GB Junior squad to go to Milan in the summer of 1988, accounting for more than a quarter of the team. For me it was particularly exciting because I was still only sixteen. If everything went according to plan, that meant I'd have three years as a junior, which was very uncommon; the youngest anyone usually got a shot at the team was seventeen.

Even better was the fact that Doran was coming, too. We were two big, goofy blokes out to have some fun. Dumb and Dumber probably sums us up best. At 15 stone Doran was two stone heavier than me, and over the following two years at school we both increased in weight by a stone each year. By the time we left we were 15 stone and 17 stone respectively – that made us pretty big school boys – and it wasn't all muscle!

Doran and I were put together in the coxed pair, which was the first time I'd ever tried that form of rowing. We had a great time and were the young clowns of the team. The contrast with the other GB coxless pair couldn't have been greater. All the pressure was on Tim Foster and Matthew Pinsent, with Tim going for his second gold and Matthew determined to live up to his growing reputation as the big Etonian who looked like a farmer's son, had amazing physiology and could row a bit. Tim and Pin (as they were known affectionately to some, but not us) were the stars and they weren't afraid to show it.

Then there was Greg and Doran, the reprobates who laughed and joked and mucked around constantly, eating spoonfuls of mustard, bombing each other in the swimming pool while the rest of the team were having cool-down sessions, cutting the sleeves off our kit and wearing silly headbands. Dumb and Dumber as I said, working hard but always with smiles on our faces.

Initially the training camp was in Chester, where we spent about ten days rowing on the river Dee and having a brilliant time. It was not only the longest period I'd been away from home on my own, it was also the first opportunity I'd had to spend a prolonged amount of time with a group of girls who weren't all from Lady Eleanor Holles. I already knew a few of the LEH rowers who'd made the women's team and I was more than happy when they introduced us to their team-mates.

There was one particular girl who rowed at stroke in the women's eight. I thought she was gorgeous. Not only did she look great, but she was lovely and actually seemed impressed by my ability to take an already over-played joke to the next level, or to ask an even more ridiculous question than Doran in a serious meeting about something like drug-testing. It took a while before anything actually happened, but by the time we got to Milan for the World Championships our coach used to tuck us up in bed, then sit in the corridor reading and keeping guard. I'm sure I wouldn't have tried to sneak off to her room – I was far too focused! We lasted through until about Christmas, before we split as a result of me misbehaving.

Mum, Dad and Jonny all came out to Milan to support me – another summer holiday dictated by the rowing calendar. Earlier that year Jonny had won the first of his three Boat Races with Oxford and had been very close to making the British Olympic team for Seoul. To narrowly miss out had been a blow, and I think he viewed the trip to Milan, which he drove to with his mates in our Mini Mayfair – the same car I wrote off later that year, two days after passing my driving test! – as a welcome distraction.

Beyond all expectations, Doran and I finished fourth. That might sound disappointing – people always say that just missing out on a medal is the worst result of all – but we saw it another way: we were two inexperienced British sixteen-year-olds beaten by a couple of Romanians sporting bushy beards! A medal would have been great, of course, but we were pleased just to be there and perform as well as we did.

Part of the reason we did so well in a boat neither of us was familiar with was down to the influential coach we were allocated, a chap called Bruce Grainger, who had been around for a while but had fallen out of favour with British rowing. Presented with two out-of-place youngsters and a coach everyone was unsure what to do with, the management's decision to pair us up was obvious. It worked, Bruce was really good for us. He knew his stuff, and because he was quirky he didn't feel the need to curb our antics and stifle our enthusiasm as other more inexperienced coaches might have. In fact, I think Bruce enjoyed hearing about our escapades and recognized the importance of allowing us to be ourselves and let our personalities show.

Following Hampton's successes in 1988, there was always a risk the following year would be something of a letdown.

At Henley we met Eton in the semi which, given the recent dominance of both boats, in effect amounted to the final. It was hard to imagine either of us losing to the other finalists, a Shiplake crew containing the future Olympic gold medallist and my good friend Ben Hunt-Davis. We were scheduled to race at something like 2 p.m. and we boated at the appropriate time, very much up for the coming battle, until Eton's cox crashed on the way to the start, causing a delay of about an hour while they dealt with repairs. We were left sitting on the river bank the entire time, our frustration growing by the minute, distracted only by Mr Fox, our coach, attempting to tell us jokes to keep our minds off the perceived injustice. It didn't work very well. Comedy wasn't his strong suit.

By the time they were ready we had not only gone off the boil, we weren't even lukewarm. They were up on us from the start and I had a sinking feeling we weren't going to come back. We were going to require something extraordinary to happen, and it did. Their stroke man, Matthew Parish, clipped a wave and lost his oar – it came right out of the gate – and we rowed past them, gaining a couple of lengths before he got himself sorted. They did their best to respond, but even a tepid Hampton boat was never going to give up that advantage and we crossed the line well in front.

Effectively we were lucky to win, I accept that, but I would also contend that had we set off on schedule it would have been a different race. We'd have been with them all the way from the start, and with our surge over the closing stages I feel certain we'd have won. Eton, I suspect, see the race in an entirely different light.

The prediction that Shiplake would not be able to cope with the winner of our semi was well founded, and although we were obviously delighted to win the Princess Elizabeth Cup for the second year running, in reality it was only a consolation prize. Our quest to repeat the Triple had already gone by then. We'd won the first leg, the Schools' Head of the River, with some ease, but had come unstuck at the National Schools', losing out to Eton.

Matthew Parish, or Paz, and I were reacquainted later that summer in Szeged, Hungary, in the Junior GB coxless four, where we teamed up with Adrian Cassidy and Damian Rimmer. Unlike the previous year, the pressure was on this time. Ours was the lead boat and we were expected to do well. In Britain we tend to do much better at rowing as opposed to sculling, one oar rather than two, which only really leaves you the pair, the eight and the four. As a rule we rarely put all our eggs in one basket and go for the eight, so we will generally lead either with a pair or the four. In my brother's year in 1987 it was the four, in 1988 it was Tim Foster and Matthew Pinsent, and in 1989 it was our four.

Once again the family holiday was to another strange part of the world, although by now Mum and Dad were old hands.

They had made some good friends amongst the other parents and together I think they enjoyed the cheap beer and food that Eastern Europe had to offer. This was a very different experience from the fun and games I'd enjoyed with Doran in Milan, and when Jonny lent me his good luck charm – the Hampton School shirt he'd first worn in 1987 and again later when he was warming up for the Boat Race – I accepted it gratefully. I was happy to have all the help I could get.

The weather was not being kind. The wind had picked up to the point that all the day's races were delayed until the final hour. When it was finally 'Go, Go, Go' they set us off at five-minute intervals (as opposed to the planned fifteen) in a desperate bid to make it through the day's events.

We'd already won the heat in convincing fashion and I felt good going into the final. Our coach, Mark Banks, who is now coaching the GB 2012 Olympic quad, spoke to each of us individually, making me feel like I had a load of responsibility but that I was up to it. *Top Gun* was a big film at the time and as we climbed off the team bus at the course one of my crew mates looked at me and quoted Tom Cruise: 'I feel the need, the need for speed!' He was fired up and normally I'd have been right there with him, but at that precise moment the only thing I felt the need for was a pee!

Perhaps I'd worked myself a little too far into the zone and was less aware of those around me than I should have been, but just before we rowed away I leaned over and checked that Paz had done his gate up properly as he'd lost his blade at Henley when he was rowing against us. In hindsight this probably wasn't great for his confidence, but I wasn't too subtle back then!

In the warm-up I wore Jonny's shirt, only removing it at the last moment for the race itself. The Romanians took off fast and we tracked them, with me sitting at two in the boat and giving the calls. After about a minute I made the call for us to 'cruise' at a high speed, and while the Romanians smashed and bashed along we sat comfortably just behind them. Coming through the third 500 m I called the power on and we moved past beautifully, slicing through the water. They had nothing left and in the end we won by about ten seconds. It felt pretty special. Representing my country at seventeen years of age and about to have a gold medal placed around my neck. It doesn't get much better than that . . . unless, of course, you receive the medal half-cut.

Under normal circumstances the procedure at these events is for each race to be immediately followed by the medal ceremony, but because of the wind delay that wasn't possible. They had to get the races off when they could and deal with the ceremonies once the schedule was completed. As we waited, I was called in for my first ever drugs test. To help you pee the usual remedy is a bottle or two of water for rehydration, but this being Hungary they were offering beer. Free beer. And I had time to kill.

I had probably downed three or four before I couldn't hold on any longer and had to fill their bottle. That may not sound like a huge amount of alcohol, but I was young, not much of a drinker and had been in training for months. I was all over the place. From the drug-testing area I went immediately into the medal ceremonies, which they were running back to back, and proceeded to cheer myself and everyone else very loudly all the way through. What a shining example of the cream of British junior sport I must have appeared.

My final year at Hampton was a disappointment in rowing terms. There were two reasons for this: the first was that we had less exposure to Steve Gunn. Although he remained a teacher at the school, and retained a keen interest in the rowing teams, he was no longer involved on a day-to-day basis, as he had been up until 1987. Having first coached the women's four at the Seoul Olympics, Steve then followed Jonny's generation, coaching the

GB men at the Senior World Championships. There is no doubt in my mind that this had a big impact on my group at school. We remained physically strong, but in pretty much all other aspects we let ourselves down. That's the second and main reason for our lack of success that year.

We began messing around too much, we grew complacent and we most certainly didn't create an environment for champions. On one occasion at Henley, Doran and I had walked down to the river to watch the other crews training when a guy in the lower sixth, Mike Reynaud, came rolling around the corner in Doran's Ford Escort.

'What the hell are you doing?' Doran and I yelled as we pulled him out of the car. He was laughing his head off, so we decided to teach him a lesson for a bit of fun. Doran got behind the wheel, I dived into the passenger seat and we chased Mike, driving straight at him so that he had to leap onto the bonnet to escape, grabbing the windscreen wipers to stay on.

The three of us were screeching and laughing manically as we drove in circles around a field, before sweeping back towards the river. Then the wiper snapped and Mike rolled off onto the towpath, right in front of the Eton coach, Paul Wright, who was on his bike watching his eight. They were out training and we were arsing around. It was symptomatic of how things were. And to add injury to insult, Mike broke his wrist in the fall.

We took Mike off to hospital without our coach knowing, he got his arm plastered and promptly proceeded to remove it the following day so he could race, pretty much one-handed. Needless to say we didn't win. A couple of days after the race, Mike told the coach he'd broken his wrist falling down the stairs.

The one positive aspect of this unfortunate tale is that while it illustrates our crew's lack of focus, it also shows that we loved rowing so much that a seventeen-year-old boy was willing to endure that level of discomfort in an attempt to win at Henley.

The principle ingrained in us early at school – to enjoy what we were doing – never left us, and that has to be a good thing.

As a postscript, when Mike went back to have his wrist looked at again the doctor told him that if he didn't get it in plaster immediately he risked permanent damage. With the World Junior trials the following week Mike then asked the team management if he could be permitted to take that risk so that he could try to make the team. They refused.

As a crew at Hampton we might have been mucking around too much and losing focus on the water, but we never let our physical training slip and I was growing stronger. As a result, the disappointments of that final year at school were quickly forgotten in the summer when I made my final visit to the World Juniors. Once again I found myself in the lead boat, a four with James Cracknell, Pete Bridge, who went to the Olympics in 1996, and a guy called Nick Clarry. We won, and won well, blasting to 1000 m in three minutes in flat, calm conditions, taking total control of the race and flying home in 6.06 minutes. That's pretty rapid for a Junior four. I was incredibly proud to win again and become Britain's most successful ever Junior rower. Now I was ready for the next level – and that meant catching up with Jonny and his peers.

In 1989, after I'd won my Junior gold, Jonny competed at the Senior World Championship at Bled, Slovenia, in a young eight with huge talent that raced fantastically well and won bronze. I was aware that I was part of a purple patch in British Junior rowing and I wanted to make my mark. Following the inevitable retirements after the Seoul Games, a vacuum had opened up that was being filled by a mixture of young talent and established stars. Steve Redgrave had the experience of two golds, Matthew Pinsent was beginning to fulfil his early promise, Tim Foster was there, plus Rupert Obholzer and many others, on top of which our golden crop of Juniors were coming of age and already looking strong contenders for the next Olympics.

As I looked on in admiration I realized I had to set my own targets high. Making the Senior Worlds team alongside Jonny, Martin, Tim, Obby and Redgrave within two years was a stretch, but that's the type of goal I thrive off.

Circumstances, and the requirements of a building project, were to turn that aspiration on its head; my goal was closer than I thought.

TWO

ORDINARY PEOPLE, EXTRAORDINARY THINGS

As a forty-year-old looking back on what I've learned through twenty years of sport, I can see the value of having clear, long-term goals and going after them. My 2012 comeback has followed the pre-planned course I set in 2009.

When I was fifteen, however, I didn't spend a lot of time thinking about what might happen in three years' time. In fact, I didn't spend much time planning beyond the next competition. I had witnessed 'ordinary' people like Martin Cross doing 'extraordinary' things, such as winning the Olympics, and I hoped one day to emulate him. In fact, I saw no reason why I shouldn't, so I guess in that respect I did have a far-away picture of me with a gold medal around my neck. In the short term, however, it was all about aiming to win at the Worlds with my mates. The dots between the two ambitions hadn't yet been connected.

During the 1990 season there was a scheduled GB trial taking place on the long stretch of the Thames at Kingston. Jonny was rowing with the rest of the crew from the GB Worlds eight, as were the Leander Club guys, Redgrave, Pinsent, Foster and the rest. The trial was open to all-comers and Jonny came up with a plan. He would row as planned with one of the Americans from Oxford in the morning, which was beneficial to the university squad, but as this bloke wasn't eligible for GB selection Jonny suggested I take the guy's seat for the afternoon session. Why not? There was nothing to lose!

I trained with the school in the morning and then met up with Jonny. It might sound strange but I hadn't been in a boat with my brother very often before then. During the Christmas holidays when he was home from Oxford, but not much more. We'd never really been in the same environment to row together and we certainly hadn't trained for this trial, which at the time just seemed like a good idea. Let's give it a whirl, was my attitude, nothing more momentous than that. From Jonny's perspective, however, I think he was saying something important to me by making the suggestion. He was showing more belief in my ability, more confidence that now was the time for me to step up, than I had in myself. As for me, it wasn't until later that I recognized the significance of that afternoon on how my career progressed.

Granny came to watch us. She was a tough, determined lady and didn't let the fact that she was seventy-five stop her from catching a bus from her home in Teddington, walking three miles along the riverbank and standing around waiting for us to row by. It was rare for Jonny and me to be racing locally, and as she couldn't travel much further afield, she wasn't going to miss this opportunity to support us. She wanted to be there and she made sure she was. That is one of the many things I have learned from my grandmother: that if you want something then you have to put in the hard work to get it.

Her determination that day wasn't wasted. As we rowed past Hampton Court I heard her voice from the riverbank. 'Come on, Jonathan! Come on, Gregory!' Knowing she had made such an effort gave us both a boost just when we needed it.

The race seemed to go well, although I was quite knackered having already done my usual two sessions with the school first.

Jonny and I came fifth overall, behind the likes of Redgrave and Berrisford, Foster and Pinsent, which was a nice surprise for both of us and was later to prove pretty useful to me. The guys we'd taken on were at the top of their game and there I was, an eighteen-year-old, clearly able to swim in the same pond without drowning.

In the run-up to that trial I had been producing big scores on the rowing machine that the Amateur Rowing Association used to transport around to various schools. This was a big orange monster on which I consistently scored around the 5000 mark, equivalent to what Jonny or Tim Foster produced. For a junior, it was an impressive result and acted as another important indicator that I might be ready to take the next step up.

Progressing in rowing was not the only change I was contemplating in the summer of 1990. Following my gold at the World Juniors in France I was set to begin my university education. Sporting ambitions were all very well, but they wouldn't pay the bills. Rowing was still very much an amateur occupation then – significant National Lottery funding for athletes only came later – so alongside my training I had to contemplate a future career. But what?

This is where my dad's experience became important. He had qualified as a chartered surveyor, and the more he spoke of what it entailed, the more it appealed. I was also aware that a lot of the guys I looked up to, club rugby players and rowers, had enlisted in a Land Economy course at Cambridge, and that became my first port of call. I went up for an interview and received a generous offer, a stretch but not beyond me. If I'm honest, I'm not sure it was my academic contributions that interested the college and persuaded them to make the offer. It seems a gold medal in rowing carries a lot of weight up there.

While my rowing had always been very much on an upwards trajectory at Hampton, I couldn't say the same about my studies.

I enjoyed school, and I would categorize it as a great period of my life, but I struggled academically in certain subjects. If it was practical and made sense, like geography and biology, where you put your hand up a lot, talked, asked questions and got involved, I did pretty well. But when it came to anything that required a lot of reading and retention of detail I was on the back foot. History, for instance, was tough despite the fact that I really liked Martin Cross's classes. He adopted an interactive, 'Let's look through my wallet and work out my history on the basis of what we find there,' approach, rather than insisting we recite the names and dates of all the Tudor monarchs, but even so, I found it difficult to engage in the research history required.

It was only once I'd left Hampton that I discovered I'm dyslexic, which explains my ability in some areas and difficulties in others. Quite how it was never diagnosed at school I'm not sure. It may have been partly a consequence of Mum's attitude – work hard and no excuses, you get out of life what you put in – and I also never drew attention to the problem because I wasn't looking for an easy way out.

Somehow I stumbled through a mixture of O levels and GCSEs – I was on the cusp of the system changing – and went on to A levels. I opted for four challenging subjects that I thought I'd enjoy and which I was strong in, but my choices turned out to be a mistake. No one pointed out the wisdom of combining less intense subjects to balance the heavier ones – particularly wise for someone with dyslexia, even though I was undiagnosed at the time – and as a result my work suffered across the board. Out of frustration, I also mucked around too much and ended up finishing Hampton with decent but not fantastic A levels.

I had fancied the idea of Cambridge, no doubt about it, in particular the rowing, although the course itself was also appealing, but just in case I didn't get in I'd also applied to Reading University and Oxford and South Bank polytechnics. When my results came through it was clear I would be swapping punting and debating for a new motorbike and breakfast at the 403 café on the streets of Stockwell in south London, where I began my four-year Estate Management sandwich course at South Bank. Given the path of my rowing over those four years, I have no doubt that this was the best place I could have gone. Luck rather than judgement plays a part in everyone's career at some stage.

I showed up for the beginning of term, was there for a couple of weeks, attended some lectures, met a few people, then announced I was off for six weeks and could someone please take notes for me (I suspect Cambridge wouldn't have embraced such antics). One of my mate's duly obliged and when I reappeared I did my best to catch up. I eventually bumbled my way through the course, coming out the other end with a 2:2. Given the amount of work I put in I was more than happy with that result.

So where did I go after those initial two weeks at South Bank? Tasmania, thanks to Jobsworth.

A certain sequence of events played out to my advantage. I am certain none of it would have happened if I hadn't raised my profile earlier in the year in those GB trials with Jonny. Was I lucky? Well, yes, if you regard, as I do, that 'luck' amounts to 'preparation plus opportunity'. When the opportunity came along, I was ready. I'd shown form in that long-distance trial at Kingston, I was producing good test results and I'd won the Juniors again. So when the opportunity came along, I was prepared.

The Senior World Championships in 1990 were to be held in Tasmania, which meant that rather than being staged in August, as normal, they were pushed back to November to coincide with the southern hemisphere's spring weather.

One of the shoo-ins for the GB eight was Johnny Hulls, also known as Jobsworth, one of the Hampton School eight who'd rowed with my brother at Henley. Jobsworth had trained with the team throughout the summer season, but was becoming increasingly disillusioned with the GB rowing team set-up. He was also under considerable pressure from the firm of builders he worked for to fulfil contracts in September and November, and in the end he quit the squad a week after I'd competed in the Junior Worlds.

The eight were now in desperate need of a new member, but it wasn't going to be an easy position to fill, as the senior rowers who hadn't made the team in the trials earlier that summer would be out of shape. Who was fit, ready and available? I was plucked out of the pack as the best junior, largely because of my trial with Jonny and the ergo results I'd been posting on the orange monster. How do I know the trial made a difference? Because James Cracknell was probably just as good as me, had similar ergo scores, but hadn't shown up at the GB trial, all of which resulted in my being called up ahead of him.

There were two of us up for Jobsworth's seat, myself and a bloke called Guy Campbell, and we were both invited to Twickenham for some training sessions. We each rowed a day with the eight, oddly for me in the bow seat, Jobsworth's position, where I had never previously sat. That tends to be where you place your smallest team-mate, and by then I was already bigger and heavier than most of the others. Apparently it was an open-and-shut case. They rowed with Guy, then they rowed with me, and suddenly, with a bit of a shift-around – me moving from bow to number three, where I was more comfortable, and eventually to number five – I was in.

Barely two weeks after winning the Junior Worlds I was a member of the GB Senior eight. Under normal circumstances this would have been impossible, because the senior and junior regattas are usually more or less simultaneous, or at best no more than a week apart, but because they were being held in Tasmania the Senior Worlds had been pushed back in the calendar, giving me sufficient training time with my new team-mates. It was all a bit of a blur. My promotion to the seniors had happened far quicker than I could ever have anticipated. Added to that, I was replacing Jobsworth, one of the school legends at Hampton. Not that I had much time to ponder this turn of events. My focus was squarely on not screwing up and making sure no one questioned my right to be there.

I didn't care how uncomfortable I was squeezed into the seat at the back of the BA flight to Australia. I was on my way to the World Championships, to row in the Great Britain eight where my brother would be sitting directly behind me in the boat, surrounded on the plane by some of the people I had looked up to most for the past few years. Being part of the GB team was exciting; sitting amongst these guys was something else. However, any danger of my being overawed by the company I was suddenly keeping was tempered by the fact that Tim Foster and Matthew Pinsent were also in the squad. At the Juniors I had thought they were a bit geeky, and as I looked around and assessed my new team-mates I felt that if they were competing in this environment then I should be, too.

When we arrived in Melbourne, we went straight to a training camp in order to acclimatize for a couple of weeks before moving on to Tasmania. In that respect, the campaign was very well organized, with the management recognizing the debilitating effect jet lag can have on an athlete's performance. We were going to a place our Australian coach, Marty Aitken, knew well. Whether that was a coincidence or not, I don't know, but it's certainly true that if Marty wanted something, he tended to get it. He didn't mince his words. His best known catchphrase went something like, 'I'm right, you're wrong, get fucked.' Which might go some way towards explaining Jobsworth's decision to leave.

A bus met us at the airport to transfer us to our camp. There were about fifty in the squad, and as we stumbled off the twenty-four-hour economy flight the majority of us weren't exactly full of the joys of spring, something our over-enthusiastic driver failed to pick up on.

'Welcome to Australia, boys,' he boomed into his microphone. 'If you care to take a look to your left you'll see the prime minister's private jet. That's what he uses to escape when the public learn he's in town!

'And coming up on your right, one of the most-visited sites in Melbourne, the shopping mall! That's where to pick up your souvenir boomerangs! That will keep you coming back again and again!'

This only went on for a few minutes before Peter Haining, one of the real characters in the squad, who was in the lightweight eight and went on to become a world champion single sculler, shouted out from the back, 'For fuck's sake, shut up!'

'Well, I'm guessing you want to get a bit of rest.' The driver turned off the microphone, and we had a couple of hours' quiet shut-eye without this joker giving us a personal commentary on everything he saw.

A few years later, when I decided on a change of course in my rowing career, Peter and I clashed, and I think it's fair to say we always had a bit of a love-hate relationship. He seemed to be shrouded in mystery, even his age was unclear when he was rowing internationally, and he liked to make it seem as though single sculling was some sort of 'dark art'. I was having none of that. Peter was a lively personality, always getting up to something interesting, and during those World Championships I remember arm wrestling with him on a number of occasions, both of us trying to get one up on the other. That sense of competition didn't diminish over the years.

Our camp was in a place called Geelong, just outside of Melbourne, but on the first day of training not all of our boats had arrived. The quad had theirs and had put it together and were preparing for their session, while the rest of us arsed around with a football. Just as they were about to set off, the ball flew into the water, landing next to their boat. One of them reached across, picked it up and they rowed away.

Jonny was furious. When the quad returned he piled into the four guys verbally.

'What the fuck are you playing at! You're lucky to be here in the first place and now you think it's clever to stop us training! Well, I don't think it's fucking clever or funny! Give us our ball back. Now!'

By 'training' I guess Jonny meant our three-and-in kick around.

I stood back, amazed and amused as this was going on, along with the rest of the team. What's he doing? They're the British quad and he's telling them they're lucky to be here. As it turned out, he was right, they weren't that good and didn't do particularly well, but that's beside the point. What I was witnessing was Jonny's ferocious belief that it was the eight that was number one and no one should mess with us or they would have him to answer to. It was an important moment of realization for me. Yes, we were part of a larger group, but all our energies and focus had to be directed towards our own boat, the number one boat as we saw it, the boat I was now a member of. If we wanted to do things one way, that was how we were going to do them. It was a powerful message.

The facilities in Tasmania weren't exactly first class but it didn't matter, from start to finish I found the entire experience hugely enjoyable. We stayed in a backwater, hitchhiker motel called the Edgewater, which looked as though it had been lifted straight out of *Psycho*, and for transport we travelled in the back of the towing vehicle, basically a flatbed truck, the eight of us bumping along the dirt tracks in our Team GB kit. Amateurish? Sure, but we survived. If anything it brought the crew even closer together.

The Opening Ceremony was spectacular. Each participating nation was given their own lane, in which all their boats lined up and proceeded to row the length of the course, the pairs, the fours and the eights all together, with all the rowers proudly wearing their full race kits. It was a very moving spectacle and I was extremely impressed. To me it brought home the fact that I was on the other side of the world representing my country. All around me were people I had admired for years, and suddenly I was part of the gang. I was ready to row and certain I could add value.

Our eight did pretty well, coming in behind West Germany, Canada and East Germany. It was the last time the East German would compete as a separate country, and right up to the line it was touch and go who would take third. Jonny was pretty gutted, having won bronze the previous year behind the two German boats, but from my perspective we'd done OK, and overall I was just happy to be there. I was on a huge learning curve, soaking everything up and confident that I'd be back another day even stronger.

Our fourth-place finish was mirrored by most of the other GB boats. Redgrave and Pinsent picked up a silver in the pair – our best result – but for the rest of the men, the coxless four, the coxed four and our eight, we were all squeezed out of the medals. Overall it wasn't a good result for Britain and it reflected badly on the management, suggesting they didn't recognize who their best rowers were and how to put together the strongest teams. We should have been structured to go for a gold and a bronze, sacrificing the weaker rowers to battle it out for a fifth or a sixth, rather than settling for a disappointingly average fourth across the team.

This reluctance to break up partnerships and find better combinations became a recurring theme over the following few years in British rowing, and it was something the head of GB coaching, Jürgen Grobler, addressed in later years (although he never separated Redgrave and Pinsent and rarely breaks up Andy Hodge and Pete Reed now). In Tasmania Jürgen was the East German women's coach, but his reputation in world rowing went way beyond that, having coached various GDR crews to numerous Olympic successes since 1972. The fall of the Berlin Wall in 1989 opened up new possibilities for Jürgen internationally, and in 1991 he arrived on UK shores to coach at Leander, which quickly led him to Team GB and a string of golds for his adopted country.

It was in 1991 that I first came across Jürgen personally, when I attended a talk he gave about technique to the GB rowers in Nottingham. To me, what he said that day was total gobbledegook, resembling nothing I had ever thought of before in terms of rowing. It was a different approach, methodical and bordering on scientific in the way he prepared his training programmes, and illustrated by an array of graphs that no one could follow. 'What's that bloke on about?' was the general consensus as we filed out of the room at the end. There was one thing he said, however, which has stuck with me to this day. He asked us to imagine two eggs, one under each foot.

'When you roll forward you do not break the eggs,' he explained. 'Then, when the oar goes in the water, bang, you slam your feet down and break both eggs.'

That at least made sense.

Back at our motel the day after the race the athletes held a meeting at which we accepted that as a group we could have done things differently, prepared and performed better, but overall we believed that the responsibility for our disappointing performances lay with the management. It was a weird thing for me to be part of and I didn't contribute much, if anything, to the discussion. I was pretty shocked as I listening, because I felt good about the whole experience. But I also recognized that I hadn't been part of the system until the very last minute and so couldn't comment on the effectiveness or otherwise of the trials leading up to team selection. And so I watched and listened as my team-mates let their obvious passion for rowing success spill out.

In contrast to the professional approach rowing developed in later years, this was in the day when competitors were giving up their holidays from work and spending their own money to race for their country. If they felt rowing was badly run then they were prepared to put their hands up and do something about it.

The result of this uprising was a shake-up in the upper tiers of British rowing. Certain positions in management were rearranged for the 1991 Championships and, more significantly, Jürgen arrived on UK shores. That proved to be the turning point, as over time his powerbase grew and his influence began to be felt.

Such changes do not occur overnight, however, and rowing is a small world at the top. Once you reach a certain position within the British management set-up, you may find yourself shifted out of one position for whatever reason, but it's a dead cert that before long you will reappear in a new role. I've always believed that one bad race doesn't mean an athlete can no longer perform, and the same applies to coaches, or anyone really. What counts are overall results, and if you can contribute to a successful British rowing performance today, then what happened in the past isn't important.

What I think the situation in 1990 illustrates is that there was a relative failure in leadership within the management of British rowing in the early nineties, which hit hardest in the narrowness of the vision presented to the athletes. There didn't seem to be a four-year plan building up through the Olympiad. In fact, we were hamstrung by the trial process, which meant that a rower's performance on a few days over the Easter holidays would set everything for the year ahead. This led to annual changes in boats' line-ups based on how well we'd raced on that weekend.

It was a system that probably helped me and Jonny in 1992, but I don't think it led to sustained high performance, and as a result I believe that for a number of years we let opportunities slip by at the Games. We did pretty well, but we could have dominated.

On our return from Tasmania Jonny and I joined Molesey Boat Club. Why Molesey? Well, to start with we both needed somewhere to train. South Bank offered no rowing facilities and Jonny was back in London, having graduated from Oxford with three consecutive Boat Race wins to his name. Molesey was the natural choice for us both because we knew it well already as the club shared a boat house with Hampton school.

There was another reason. We wanted to assert a degree of independence. Arriving home from the Worlds the British squad proceeded to drift off into their respective enclaves – one group at Leander, others at Oxford, Cambridge and University of London, and we weren't part of any of them. We settled on Molesey and pulled together a great group of lads, waifs and strays with plenty of attitude who enjoyed tough competition on the water and a lot of laughs off it. We made Ye Olde Countrye Kytchen, an up-market café (or down-market restaurant) opposite Hampton Court station, our regular haunt, spending the hour or two between rowing sessions joking around as we tucked into a full English.

Our spiritual leader was an ex-University of London rower called Mark Norton. He was known as Donkey, a nickname he had apparently given himself! He and Jobsworth, who continued rowing with the Molesey group after pulling out of the World Championship team, both worked in the building trade and always had plenty to say. We all had nicknames, which we came to use affectionately in all circumstances. It's something we've never grown out of and sometimes use inappropriately. When Donkey did the honours as best man at Jobsworth's wedding he referred to 'Mrs Jobsworth' more than once in his speech. The grown-ups weren't impressed. This would have been bad enough, but Donkey was actually referring to the girlfriend Jobsworth had split up with a few years earlier, and not his bride! I was known as Terry Fuckwit, after my escapades with Doran in Milan, which isn't hard to explain. When I was assigned that name I was a naïve eighteen-year-old whose ability to play had been well honed, but when my old nickname came up recently during a Team GB session it caused some surprise.

'Why did they call you that?'

'Well, you know me now, but take away twenty years of maturity and imagine what you're left with.' He got the picture. Luckily it was mostly abbreviated to TFW, a godsend in social situations, especially when I met Princess Anne.

So with Squealer (my brother); the Terminator; Herman; Crossy; the Good Doctor; Big Gav; Jobsworth; Singers; Donkey; myself and Spiny Norman, the cox, we had a crew, coached by Paul Wright, the ex-Eton coach. Despite being arch-rivals I had always respected Eton as opponents, so to have their coach was a bonus. Paul had some good insights, although we were a bit concerned on the day he suggested we massage each other because we didn't have a physio. When we looked at him strangely he simply replied that the Eton boys hadn't liked the sound of it either but that they'd taken to it like ducks to water!

Having featured in one World Championships, by the time the GB trials came around again, at Nottingham in April 1991, I definitely felt that the Olympics had moved from an aspiration to a genuine goal. But in what boat? The eight seemed most likely, but would it give me my best chance of a medal?

There had always been a fierce rivalry between the Leander and Molesey clubs, but this had intensified since Jonny and I had decamped to Molesey with the rest of the guys. Jürgen was now coach at Leander, and on arrival at the training camp prior to the Nottingham trials one of the first things we saw was his training schedule pinned to the noticeboard at Holme Pierrepoint. It read something like, '20 k rowing; an hour weights in the gym; 16 k machines.' Ouch. This was low intensity, high endurance. We thought it was fantastic.

'Look at what those half men are doing,' said Donkey, ripping it down from the wall. 'Twenty k steady-state rowing! Why would you do that?'

'I guess they'll be very good at rowing back to the landing stage after they've lost,' I suggested.

Jobsworth took it to the next level. 'Give me your pen, Fuckwit!' I handed it over and he proceeded to write an alternative schedule on the back: '9 a.m. meet in café. Full English. 8 k rowing followed by long talky bit over coffee. Stretching, then 10 x 10 stroke bursts. Back home in time for more tea and an extended talky bit.'

We were taking the piss, but there was some truth in the vast difference between the two approaches. British rowing was on the cusp of a cultural shift driven by Jürgen, with Leander as his guinea pigs, and they were hurting.

What's important to bear in mind is that because Jürgen came from East Germany he was used to coaching full-time athletes who could put that level of work into their training because they then had time to rest and recover. The increase in funding here in recent years has allowed rowers to focus exclusively on their sport, too, after which everyone was able to follow a similar regime, as I do now. There are no half measures and no compromises any more, rowing to me has gone way beyond a mere job; it's my passion and, outside of my family, it's my life. Back in 1991 that couldn't be the case for anyone involved in British rowing except perhaps Redgrave and Pinsent who enjoyed some sponsorship support, allowing them enough freedom to embrace the sport full-time. The rest of us had professional or academic lives off the river, which demanded our attention.

In contrast to Jürgen's programme, the Molesey approach, and that of the London-based clubs in general, was based on shorter, more intense training, where everything felt closer to a six-minute race. We trained for about sixty minutes, with a no-pain, no-gain principle: intense, hard, bursts of work on the machines, focusing on quality and technique. We'd fall off, have a couple of minutes rest, then get back at it flat out for another six minutes or so. We were mimicking race conditions and in the short-term it worked. We were bloody good at winning races and for a while Leander struggled to catch up. The big question we were ignoring, however, was, Where do we go from here? We didn't have the answer.

The key phrase is 'short-term'. What Jürgen was looking to establish was prolonged and lasting success built on a pyramid of fitness achieved through a huge volume of aerobic, long-distance work. In Jürgen's view, the bigger the base of that fitness pyramid, the taller the peak, and I can see now that he might be right. If you have the time and support around you, this approach produces consistently good performances. Leander was able to pioneer Jurgen's methods, but it took years before anyone except Redgrave and Pinsent won anything significant by training that way.

As far as we were concerned, Molesey was on track, and we pitied the poor Leander boys. All right, we revelled in their misfortune.

'How's it going, fellas? When are the 20k World Championships again?'

'Are you training for the Boston Marathon?'

You can imagine the fun we had during that cold, wet November camp as Jürgen sent his troops out before us for an hour and a half, while we were back in forty-five minutes, showered and changed by the time they dragged themselves into the boat house. Even the University of London and GB eight coach Marty Aitken joined in on the act, coining the phrase 'a London 20k' when he actually meant 16 km. That suited us just fine, who needs to do 20 km anyway? Leander, that's who.

At the trials themselves Jonny and I emerged as the third best pair, not far behind Redgrave and Pinsent. We were right up there in contention for whatever the coaches designated would be the lead boat come the World Championships in Vienna later that summer. Or at least I was, because Jürgen regarded me as the sort of person he wanted and his influence within the GB structure was growing. I was the up-and-coming star, tall, physically powerful and young. Unlike Jonny. The opinions voiced regarding my brother tended to be more, 'How does he manage to do it? He's small and not strong on the ergo.' What seemed to turn certain people off was Jonny's style, aggressive and punchy, in contrast to the big, powerful Redgrave and Pinsent mould.

They attempted to split us up by trying out different combinations of guys to see what worked best. I'd be a hypocrite to complain about that now, as it's what I believe is the best approach, but back then I wasn't happy with the manner in which it was done. They decided to use the physiological testing to determine the strongest four, which struck us in Molesey as ridiculous. How could you use such a raw tool ahead of boat-moving ability and how well you raced?

The Physiological Four, as we were known back at my club, consisted of myself and Gavin Stewart from Molesey, and from Leander it was 'Howling' Jim Walker (a quiet bloke, hence the nickname, who later crossed over to Molesey from the dark side after the 1992 Olympics and became a great friend of mine) and John Garrett (the athlete's rep in Tasmania). We were asked to train at Leander, and when I showed up at their beautiful clubhouse in Henley – the Pink Palace as we called it (Leander's club colour is pink) – I parked my car and refused to enter the building. In fact, I wouldn't even set foot on the grounds, choosing instead to walk around the outside wall and meet the others by the landing stage, where the coach had to address us with me dressed head to toe in my own club colours, Molesey black. I even had a black shirt around my head with the sleeves tied tight so the neck created a slit I could see out of.

On the water, still fully kitted out in black and sitting in the stroke seat, I didn't communicate with anyone. By the end of the session my 'hood' was soaked in sweat and saliva. Nevertheless, I'd made the point that I wasn't that happy to be in the crew in that location. After the debrief they went inside to eat while I went to a local café. The next day, and every other day, I did the same thing. I guess it's no surprise I was known as TFW.

The GB selectors would have suggested I go into that four as the system worked along those lines. There were a few appointed head coaches in the Amateur Rowing Association (British rowing in effect), whose job it was to select the team from potential candidates across all the clubs. In addition, there was a group of prominent rowers and coaches attached to certain clubs who wielded considerable influence over the selection process, inevitably pressing the case for their own club members. People within the Molesey ranks would have been as much a part of that process as those in other clubs. From my perspective, I felt I was being pushed in the direction of Leander, as if a decision had been made that I should join that group. Steering me towards the four was all part of that. Fine, I thought, if that's how you want to play it, that's how we'll play it. My nose might be out of joint, but I'm still going to give it my all. I'll show you how good I am, doing things the Molesey way. And when you start throwing the endurance stuff in my direction, no problem, I can do that, but don't expect me to take my hood off.

While this battle of wills unfolded, Jonny was left with what were perceived as the weaker members of the London group. It was as though the selectors had cherry picked the people they rated, hoping the rest would fail; it would make the selection process a lot easier if they did.

There was a classic moment during one meeting when the selectors told Jobsworth, who appeared to be back in contention for the GB team, that he had to prove himself in order to be considered, but when they read out the crews of the day there were three people left over, including Jobsworth, at which point he stood up and laughed.

'What are you on about? How am I going to prove myself in a coxless three?'

I am not sure he really wanted to be up for selection, but it was a matter of principle and it underlined the politics going on behind the scenes.

Despite this general sense of disquiet over the selection process, choices had to be made, and as we approached the start of the 1991 season I was firmly in the four, while Jonny was in what was regarded by the selectors as the lesser eight. I wasn't convinced, however, and put it to the coaches that my preference was for the larger boat. They were having none of it.

During the course of the season we raced in East Berlin, at a place called Grunau, where Jürgen was understandably keen to show his old friends the strength of GB resources. It didn't quite work out as he had hoped. While we did OK, the coxed four struggled badly, losing even to Denmark, who are hardly a rowing powerhouse. Jürgen was seriously unimpressed.

'Dane-mark!' he screeched in anguish during his debrief. 'Who ze fuck is Dane-mark!?'

Jürgen's frustrations during the regatta were matched by my own. Howling Jim and I were out walking by the lake when we were stopped by a rowing enthusiast who wanted our autographs. We were happy to oblige, but when the guy then asked me to note down what crew I was in, I couldn't resist, taking his pen and scribbling, '2++'. There is no such boat, of course, but if there were it would be a pair plus two coxes. Not a great demonstration of crew harmony!

At Henley Jonny and I both raced in our separate boats and won, but against fairly weak opposition, the eight overcoming the Russians and the four defeating the GB Under-23s. If anyone was in danger of being carried away by this supposed success, they were soon brought down to earth in the first big international regatta in Lucerne, where the eight came fourth and we were fifth.

I made my feelings known.

'If our four is meant to be better than the eight, how come they were fourth and we were fifth? This is not right. We're not going anywhere and I no longer want to be part of it. We did all this last year, making the boats the same and all coming outside the medals. It's not good enough.'

I became so disruptive that the team management had little choice but to agree to my demands. My vocal stance was, understandably, causing tension within the boat. In effect I was on the point of killing any chance the others had of a World Championship medal if I remained.

Gavin and John were unhappy with how I was behaving and I can't blame them. They were both Olympians, graduates from Oxford and Cambridge respectively, and very nice blokes, and they had to listen to this young upstart stamping his feet and throwing his toys out of his pram, but at least Howling Jim backed me. He was one of us really and knew he'd be better off with the rest of the London boys. He could tell things weren't moving forward with the four and said as much, but in a far more restrained manner than me, probably because he's a much nicer bloke. While Jim was naturally less pushy, I'd taken a leaf out of Jobsworth's and Jonny's books and knew how to make a scene when I wanted to.

If Jim had made more of a fuss he would probably have been able to get out as well, but as it was they did a straight swap between Cracknell in the eight and me in the four. I don't know what James thought about that, but I'm sure it would have been spun in a very positive manner.

'James, we need you in the four, you are a far better crew-maker than Greg and we need you at stroke.'

I hope that's how it was handled anyway. James certainly never said anything to me to indicate that he was put out by this late change.

The morale within the half of the team not doing Jürgen's programme was pretty good that summer. There was an underlying tension between the groups that made for a difficult atmosphere and not a lot of a 'one-team' feeling. It was particularly evident when Jürgen took us to altitude training in Silvretta, Austria.

My mood had improved dramatically by then. I was much happier training with the eight. It felt like a really good place to be, not just being back with Jonny but also because Martin Cross was in the boat. He was a role model for me in many ways and a man I admired as a tough competitor with limited physical resources but a great racing brain. He should have been a wise head, but he was one of the biggest kids around; he's probably still a role model for me as a senior these days! Our eight was a tight team, there were lots of in-jokes and arsing around, with Garry Herbert as cox. This was the first time I'd properly met Garry. Jonny knew him from the junior squad in 1987 when Garry coxed the eight, following which he had enjoyed a good couple of years with the Under-23 crew before catching up with Jonny again in the senior squad. Having the opportunity to bond with Garry during that training camp was to prove very important in the months to come.

Perhaps the thin air of the Austrian Alps affected us more than we realized, because we decided to make a home movie while we were there called *Escape from Silvretta*, a *Great Escape* send-up inspired by the POW-style huts we were living in. All the guys from the eight were involved, plus anyone else who felt so inclined. It was a good laugh and contributed significantly to the spirit within our group.

It was pretty artless – no Oscar winner here! – but highlights included an escape tunnel, which was started from the roof, a 'camp' commandant with a strong affinity for Lycra, jack (i.e., wellington) boots and whips, a 'London ladder' which proved to be 4 feet too short to climb over the wall and various caricatures of the team coaches, including one of the escape committee, who spoke in such a monotone, boring voice that everyone around the table immediately nodded off.

Quite what Jürgen made of all this I can only imagine, but I do know that there is no way the same thing would happen today. Taking the piss out of the management? No chance. The most subversive thing to happen at a recent team Christmas party was when the coach of the eight, a German guy called Christian, opened his Secret Santa present to reveal a mug bearing a photograph of Jürgen and the message, 'Ich liebe Jürgen.' Crazy.

Back in Austria we even managed to find a drinking establishment on a couple of occasions, staggering back to our huts and waking with crashing hangovers. There was also a trip to a swimming pool where the coxed four flew down a water slide and ended in a tangled heap at the bottom, resulting in a nasty rib injury that ruled one of them out of training for a fortnight.

It was old-school mentality, but twenty-one years ago the situation was very different. As much as we were determined to succeed and were passionate about our sport, this was our summer holiday from work and we wanted to enjoy ourselves. Today rowing *is* our work and everyone is desperate to hang on to their places in the squad. No one would dream of jeopardizing their chances of success with such antics.

To a degree that's a shame, but looking back now, having spanned those two decades, if I could only have one way of doing things – either as we were or in the current era of professionalism

– there is no doubt I would choose the current way. It's the only way to drive sustainable results.

My concerns about the four proved, unfortunately, to be valid. From altitude we went to Chester for a few weeks before moving to the World Championships in Vienna, where our eight picked up a bronze but the four came in seventh. Was James Cracknell pissed off with me? I don't know. Shifting guys around in boats wasn't that unusual, so probably not.

I loved being in Vienna during the build-up to the championships; it's a beautiful city and we had a lot of fun, including a trip to the local palace of Schönborn. As I said earlier, we had a good atmosphere in the eight, we liked to stick together and do our own thing, and this included how we went about our cultural excursions. Visitors were supposed to wait until a guide speaking their language was free, but on arrival we just joined any old group, a German one on this occasion, assuming we'd be able to ditch them once we got inside. It didn't prove easy.

Each room was sealed and the doors were hidden behind curtains, and when we did try to sneak out, one of our fellow sightseers grassed on us to the guide. Eventually we worked out that if we exited our room the moment the door appeared then we might be able to catch the group in front leaving the next room. This meant we had to leg it through every room and miss the talk – which wasn't a problem as we didn't understand a word – until we caught up with an English-speaking group. Our timing was out on a couple of occasions, leaving us to enjoy the delights of two rooms with some Japanese tourists. It was tough for half a dozen British rowers to disappear into the background in that group!

Given that our eight had been regarded as the also-rans of the GB team, we were pleased with our bronze. We felt we'd delivered while the guys around us hadn't produced as expected, which only added fuel to the 'us and them' situation within the squad. We bunkered down in our silo and repelled all invaders, taking no shit from anyone, doing things our way and leaving the rest to do their own thing. And it showed in the banter that came out over that post-Worlds period.

We raced in Paris and one of the blokes from the coxed four, who were supposed to be better than us but had only managed fourth in Vienna, had to substitute for one of our guys. As we were preparing to boat, someone mentioned that this was the most medalled eight Britain had ever put in the water. 'No, no, it's not,' came the response, 'we've got Nick today.'

In October we all met in Nottingham for a GB training session, and during a team meeting one of the coxed four put forward the thought that, 'Next year we ought to put the best people in the eight.' That wasn't going to slip by without comment from one of us.

'I think you'll find we did that last year.'

Was this healthy? I'm not sure. Perhaps we became too isolated, distorting everyone's perspective, ours and the coaches.

It was during the Nottingham meeting that Marty Aitken, the coach, called the eight together for a discussion. He produced a whole load of data that analysed our times over 500 m, 1000 m, our individual ergo scores, all sorts. After presenting it he then said, 'You know what, if we train every day for the next year and do all these things right, I think we have a pretty good chance of Olympic silver.'

Excuse me? Have we given up on gold already?

I was sharing a room with Jonny, and when we got back there I let him know what I thought of Marty's comment: 'He doesn't believe we can win.'

A year out from Barcelona, having been very much in the mix at the World Championships, and we're only shooting for second? If our coach had already thrown in the towel, I couldn't see how he was going to motivate the guys to push on. Jonny and I spoke about the situation long into the night and made a decision: we would make a bid to become the GB pair, although we kept our ambitions to ourselves.

As all the trialling was conducted in pairs, the fact that Jonny and I were rowing together wouldn't raise any eyebrows. Having decided on what we wanted, this was where goal-setting became realistic. We knew our vision and we set our sights clearly on winning gold in Barcelona. We just had to work out how we were going to do it.

The trouble was that the current pair was a certain Redgrave and Pinsent, and we would have to beat them in the trials. Why not? Redgrave, going for his third gold medal, was surely getting on a bit, and I'd already beaten Matthew twice at school. What was there to fear? We convinced ourselves we were good enough and that it didn't matter what anyone else thought.

In November we did a 5 km time trial at Henley in which we came second behind Redgrave and Pinsent. OK, not bad, promising, but not great; we were still eleven seconds off their pace. That could appear an awfully long way back, depending on how you looked at it. It's all about perception. Jonny and I were a little disappointed in our performance, but having set our sights firmly on becoming the British pair, we were not going to allow the result of one trial to destroy our goal. Positive action was required and we decided to share our vision with the best coach we knew, Steve Gunn.

Although Steve was involved with the GB coaching, I hadn't seen much of him since I'd left school. Nothing had changed; he was still the scary biology teacher. Approaching Steve for help was a bigger step for me than I let on because I had always felt jilted by him after he took a back seat in the coaching set-up at Hampton once Jonny's generation had moved on. I'd been disappointed by that at the time, but any schoolboy slights I might have felt were quickly consigned to the dustbin when it became clear that he was buying in big time to what Jonny and I were trying to achieve.

It was Steve and Jonny together who turned the eleven-second problem into something positive, by telling me the story of the American swimmer John Naber. In the 1972 Olympics he was part of the US team, which was primarily there to support Mark Spitz's quest for seven golds. Naber was happy to oblige, swimming in the relay heats and making way for Spitz in the final, but he promised himself that four years later he would be going for gold himself. Following the Munich Games Naber sat down and, based on the general improvements in swimming recorded between 1968 and 1972, he calculated what the likely winning time would be for his preferred event, the 100 m backstroke, at the 1976 Montreal Olympics. Having come up with a time of something like 55 seconds, he compared that to his personal best. He was a good four seconds slower.

So what did he do? He had four years to make up four seconds, that's one second a year, and if you divide the number of training swims he was planning in a twelve-month period, well, it came down to an improvement per session of . . . the time it took to blink. He set to work, and in Montreal John Naber stood on the Olympic podium with a gold medal around his neck.

We took Naber's approach to goal-setting on board and applied it to our own situation. Eleven seconds over 5 km is 2.2 seconds per kilometre, but as an Olympic race is actually 2 km, this meant we were 4.4 seconds behind Redgrave and Pinsent. Suddenly it didn't appear such a daunting task. The British selection trials were set for April, giving us six months to make up 4.4 seconds. Given that they were also going to improve over that period, that boiled down to one second per month. OK, so we train twice a day – that's sixty sessions each month – which means we have to improve by a sixtieth of a second every session.

Now we had focus – and a coach who could identify where improvements could be made.

'You're not steering well.'

'Your boat is pitching end to end.'

'You're falling from side to side.'

'Greg, your blade is going in too slowly.'

'Jonny, you're not squaring early enough.'

These were the type of opportunities we could work on to find that one second a month.

Our training in those critical months was, well, *Rocky*-ish would be the best way to describe it I guess. I was in my second year at South Bank, living in a flat on Gloucester Place with Tim Foster and three girls from University College London. We had a lot of good times there, the usual student fun of parties and making good use of the half-price cocktails at the union on a Wednesday evening. All through that period, however, I thought of myself as a rower who was at college rather than a student who rowed, and I was always careful to ensure I got enough sleep, unlike Tim. Where I would be safely tucked up by midnight or 1 a.m., Tim would often bundle in at four or five in the morning. To my mind he was asking an awful lot of himself if he truly aspired to be an Olympic champion that year.

In the mornings I would ride my bike to Stockwell, where South Bank was located, attend my lectures, then cycle off to the dusty old gym at the Amateur Rowing Association, Hammersmith, for weights, chin-ups done fully clothed – anything I thought would help shave off that sixtieth of a second. I was pushing myself to the limit, with almost disastrous results in one session when I dropped a weight that was so heavy it fell through the floor boards, knocking out a strip light from the ceiling in the room below, which narrowly missed a bloke working away on the rowing machine.

Jonny's regime was much the same. He was at law school at Lancaster Gate and living in a flat nearby, and when he couldn't make it over to the Hammersmith gym he'd have to stay in the City and train at a gym up there. He wouldn't have been hard to spot.

He'd have been the crazy guy on the rowing machine, pounding himself into a near coma while the normal people around him did their regular workout.

On a Tuesday morning, Wednesday night and Thursday morning we'd meet up with the rest of the London eight at Hammersmith and take to the water, incorporating some of Jürgen's endurance programme with our own shorter, sharper approach. On a Saturday we'd always head over to Molesey, where we would train, talk rowing and socialize with the club members. I wasn't yet twenty, and for all my dedication and drive I didn't want to be a slave to rowing, I wanted to enjoy it.

Jonny and I gauged our progress with regular tests, 20 km on the rowing machine in under seventy minutes, looking to see an improvement every week. The first hour we'd go at it strong, then move up a couple of gears for the last ten. It was our signature way of racing – the Hampton finish – and we were determined to build our strength in order to blow the opposition away with our final sprint.

For those long ergo sessions, which Jonny and I had lifted from Jürgen's programme, we would put the machines together, so that for every stroke we pulled we could see how the other compared, reinforcing the bond of total reliability between us. Those 20 km probably came a little easier to me than Jonny – I have a naturally more powerful physique whereas he had to work harder – but that worked to our benefit. I could see how much he wanted it and he could see how strong I was. We were each earning our place; we had credibility. We knew neither of us would ever let the other down, never take a backwards step, and it instilled an incredible sense of belief within us.

As members of the Molesey eight, Jonny and I competed in the Head of the River in March 1992, which provided an important confidence boost. We were setting off from the Amateur Rowing Association, which we shared with Leander that day, just along from the Blue Anchor pub in Hammersmith, and just as we put our boat in the water the Leander eight arrived. We were pretty sure Jürgen was watching, so as we rowed away our cox, Garry Herbert, who we had tempted away from Leander, made a call for us to row deliberately badly. We pushed off as though we were novices, the boat rocking from side to side, leaning away from our riggers, opening our legs wide as though we had big beer bellies to accommodate.

I like to think we left Jürgen shaking his head, wondering how this bunch of clowns could ever achieve anything, but in truth he must have known how we were progressing. Steve Gunn had been allocated to look after Jonny and me for the GB team and he would have been reporting back on our progress. In addition, everyone had to submit their ergo test results to the GB management and Jürgen would have had access to that data. Still, it was fun, and demonstrated to anyone who took notice that we were a tight, happy eight.

We were certainly happy on the morning of the race, when we got to the toilets before Leander and hid all the toilet rolls in a locker. I guess it meant we had a more comfortable pre-race routine than them!

We were even happier by the end of the race – Molesey beat Leander, which was a huge boost for Jonny and me after all the sweat and blood we'd been putting in. The April trials were only weeks away and we saw this victory as an important marker in our quest to become the GB pair. Redgrave and Pinsent were the best two in the Leander boat, while Jonny and I were probably the best in Molesey, and we had defeated them. The speed was coming.

At the Nottingham trials we were very focused. Nervous certainly, but also prepared to be different, prepared to be de-tached, and if that meant seeing everyone else as the opposition, that was fine. Where the others chatted in clusters after the heats,

Jonny and I stuck together a few paces removed. Focus. Focus. Focus.

We made it through to the final, a six-lane race, and it was clear that it would come down to our pair or Redgrave and Pinsent, with them as favourites. They got away well but we hung on, doggedly refusing to allow clear water between the two boats, which was a big boost psychologically. They had gone for it and they hadn't broken us. In the third 500 m we pushed on and pulled up almost level; then in the last quarter, between 1500 m and 1750 m, we surged – those final ten minutes on the 20 km test were paying off – passing them with 250 m to go and, incredibly, pulling away. Twenty strokes from the line, Jonny began shouting with excitement at the top of his lungs – I can't quite remember what he shouted, but it probably wasn't very sporting! We'd done it, that six months spent breaking down our goal had come off. Thank you, Mr Naber. Now our pitch to become the British pair was well and truly in the public domain.

What followed was a few days of confusion amongst the head coaches. Having been confident that the world record holders and world champions in the coxless pair would win the trial, their focus had until then been on what to do with everyone else. Now suddenly there was a Searle-shaped spanner in the works.

To a degree they ended up hedging their bets, and I don't blame them for that. We had made it very clear that we wanted to be the coxless pair for the Olympics, but at the same time Steve and Matthew had their own arguments. I understand that Steve had been struggling with illness and deserved another opportunity to defend his position, so the decision was taken to enter both pairs into the up-coming regatta in Cologne, then sit back and see what happened.

'We'll make our decision after Germany,' we were informed.

Fine. We were ready, we thought.

Both boats qualified for the final and it was there we showed our inexperience. We had never raced internationally in the pair before and, although the starters spoke in English, we discovered to our cost that we shouldn't take their commands too literally.

'Are you ready?' The flag was raised.

It was windy and we had drifted off line. Jonny stuck his hand in the air. 'No!'

The flag came down. 'Go!'

In my ear. 'Don't go! We'll take a false start and get it right next time.'

In a British trial I think they might have called it back, after all, the whole point was to be able to compare the boats, but international races are different. The starting procedure had begun and been completed. That was all that mattered.

The five boats shot off and we sat like a couple of lemons waiting for a bell to be rung, or something, but no, they weren't called back. Had we blown it?

For the second day in Cologne it had been pre-planned that Jonny and I would row the coxed pair with a guy called Spiny Norman (aka Adrian Ellison), and we finished third, which was OK considering it was more or less our first outing in that boat. The difference between coxed and coxless is significant. The best way I can describe it is that the coxless boat feels as though you are riding a bicycle on the flat in third gear, as opposed to the coxed, where suddenly you are on an incline, someone has shifted you up to fifth and you are cycling through treacle. The boat is bigger and heavier with the extra person, an additional 50 kg of dead weight in a combined total of 250 kg, and it moves along slower, with the strokes feeling longer because you spend more time connected to the water. There was a mutual respect between those of us who raced the coxed pair. There was probably also a mutual need to see a physio!

Could we master the coxed boat? Maybe, but it wasn't what we wanted. Once again we spoke to the selectors, and it was agreed that we would have one last race-off in Essen to decide the matter.

We didn't have a great time in the build-up to that race. Jonny was feeling pain in his ribs. They'd been niggling him for a while prior to the Nottingham trials, and all that shouting and yelling he'd done at the end had only aggravated them further. Since then they had been troubling him increasingly badly, to the point that in Essen he was beginning to struggle and we didn't even make the final. After we had dejectedly stowed the boat following our elimination, Jonny sought out Anne Redgrave, the team doctor. Her diagnosis was a stress fracture, which would heal with a two-, maybe three-week stretch away from rowing. He could train on the bike but he couldn't row a stroke.

Having pushed so hard, all of a sudden the decision was not a difficult one to make. Time was against us, we were not going to knock Steve and Matthew off their perch.

'OK, Redgrave and Pinsent do the coxless pair, we'll go coxed.'

It was the correct decision, regardless of Jonny's injury. The truth was, short of our heroics in Nottingham, we hadn't done enough to oust the world champions and world record holders from their chosen discipline.

While Jonny recuperated I took to the water in a single scull, desperately hoping we still had enough time to readjust our focus. The Lucerne regatta would be our only competition before the Olympics, and we had a lot to learn.

THREE

IF NOT NOW, WHEN?

Having been strapped up and unable to set foot in a boat for two weeks after Essen, Jonny being Jonny, declared himself fit and healthy in time for the Lucerne regatta at the end of May. Whether he actually was or not he never revealed and I never asked. I trusted him.

Over the spring and early summer we had been working on Garry Herbert to join us as cox. We knew what he was capable of from our time in the eight and his full-blooded participation in the epic *Escape from Silvretta* reinforced the fact that we were on the same wavelength. During that time in Austria it became clear to me that Garry understood what made me tick, and that level of intimacy would become an all-important building block in the trust that developed between us.

There is a strange chemistry required between the cox and his rowers. He has to know the right psychological buttons to press at the right time to produce the best from his crew. Garry had that intuitively with Jonny and me; he could calm us down, he could gee us up, he communicated clearly and he understood what made us tick as individuals. A cox won't win you a race, but he can lose if for you before you take that first stroke. If you have the slightest hint of doubt that he is misreading a race, if you question any of his calls, even for a split second, you are done for. We'd seen Garry at work and at play and were convinced he was the man for us. A bigger question was whether we were the men for him.

He was being pulled between us and the eight. Within the British team then Garry was very much seen as the number one cox, the guy in demand from the athletes. We wanted him and the eight wanted him, which put Garry in a somewhat unusual situation. In effect he could choose his boat, because the management would listen to his preference. Ultimately his decision came down to sticking with his mates or potentially having the best chance at a gold medal. It was the same call we had made, walking away from Tim Foster and our friend and hero Martin Cross. Clearly Garry saw something in Jonny and me that tipped the balance because by Lucerne he was in our boat.

In Switzerland we also had Steve Gunn and sports psychologist Brian Miller firmly in our camp, with Steve coaching us exclusively and Brian, who was attached to the GB team as a whole, providing a disproportionate amount of psychological support, recognizing, I suspect, that we were enthusiastic buyers for what he was offering. I've always assumed that when I race, everyone we are up against is fit, strong and can row well. The difference is usually down to how well you perform on the day, and the combination of Steve, Garry and Brian got the best out of us when it mattered, which was critical given that we were relatively inexperienced in the coxed boat.

We started the Lucerne race slowly and, at the halfway mark, we were a good six or seven seconds behind the leaders, but from there we began to click, and if we didn't quite manage the full-tilt Hampton finish, we were sufficiently strong to row through the defending Olympic champions, the Abbagnales, and come in fourth. It was a solid step forward and it gave us plenty of hope that with a good six weeks to the Olympics we'd be able to compete with the best in the event. We were happy with the decisions we'd made. With the eight in total disarray – decisions still hadn't been finalized as to who would be in that boat and who would be in the coxless four, which meant the twelve guys were in effect rowing as three fours – jumping into that boat would have been a disaster.

From Lucerne we returned reluctantly to the altitude of Silvretta, worried that the camp there wouldn't lend itself to the quality training with lots of coaching that we were looking for. On arrival our concerns deepened when Steve Gunn produced a custom-made training programme for us, separate from the rest of the guys and focusing on the old no-pain, no-gain mentality. At altitude this was daring. There isn't a lot of oxygen in the air up there to feed your body when it's screaming in pain, and for the first week we suffered and were significantly slower than we ought to have been. With no choice but to trust the process, however, we went with it, and by the second and third week we'd started making real progress.

The rationale behind altitude training is that with the thin air your body has to work harder to achieve the same results as at sea level. To be able to cope you produce additional red blood cells in order to find and carry the oxygen your muscles need. The net result is that when you descend your body is effectively turbo-charged and more efficient for a four-to-twelve-week window.

Not every team sees the benefit of altitude training, but Jürgen was, and still is, a massive fan. It took me some time to be convinced, but now I'm pretty positive about the benefits, although I've needed the perspective of a few years to see how it helped the 1991 eight and me and Jonny in 1992. Jürgen has been taking his teams to the same place for thirty years. It's a home from home for him, but it's very basic. Nowadays the Stalag huts are still there, we eat our meals in a café that serves day-trippers and it's pretty boring, especially given our more professional approach. In 1991 we had the time and freedom to make that home movie and have a bit of fun; on a more recent trip I watched the four DVD box sets of the US drama *Prison Break* on my laptop – that's over fifty hours' worth!

In 1992 we were on the back foot even before we embarked on Steve's brutal training schedule. The building of our boat had only recently been completed because we'd settled on the coxed pair so late, which meant it had to be transported to Silvretta separately. It was on top of a minibus that was towing a trailer, and as it was disembarking from the ferry the trailer kicked up violently, smashing into our boat and breaking 10 inches off the bow section. It was a sorry sight that greeted us when it was delivered to our mountain retreat, and it was only a bodge-job repair that allowed us to train at all. They fixed it up as best as they could, but I'm sure it wasn't straight – we always seemed to be rowing around corners!

Fortunately Steve Gunn had to fly back to the UK mid-camp to man his post at Hampton for the release of the A-level results, and while he was there he approached a boat manufacturer called Aylings to construct a replacement. The boats of choice then and now came from the German maker Empacher, which we had been using up until that point, with the Aylings equivalents deemed less desirable. We had little option but to turn this negative into a positive, regarding our new boat as something that had been made and designed specifically for us, in Britain, for the Olympics. Despite such an upbeat spin, however, we were forced to continue training in our patched-up Empacher until our new boat arrived, just ten days before the Olympics.

For Jonny and me, Silvretta wasn't only about physical preparation, it was also essential that we spend a lot of time with Garry in order to discuss tactics and continue to build the bond between us, and the best way to do this was to lodge together.

The huts in the camp contained a number of two-man rooms – traditional Alpine decor, with lots of pine, two single beds and basic furniture. There was, however, one three-man room, with extra space up in the eves, but this had been allocated to Redgrave and Pinsent. We kicked up a fuss.

'You concentrate on your rowing, we'll sort out the living arrangements,' was the message we received back from the coaches.

If they weren't going to give us a three-man room, we decided to create one ourselves, moving as much furniture as we could out of our room and replacing it with Garry's bed. It mattered to us to get together and do things our way, and we were prepared to make a point even if it meant a bit less comfort. In hindsight it was a master stroke, eliminating one of the major destroyers of trust: self-interest. With the three of us living on top of each other we were making a powerful statement to ourselves that we were firmly in this together.

No matter how well we got on with Garry, no matter how good a bloke he was, there had always been the risk that, given our tight time frame and the fact that Jonny and I were brothers, Garry was going to struggle to carve out his role in the boat. Living in such close proximity for those three weeks changed everything. Lying in bed at night talking, discussing hopes and dreams, revealing self-doubts and weaknesses, we became equal partners, sharing secrets and keeping confidences. In short, we were deepening our levels of intimacy.

It can't have been easy for Garry, having to contend with Jonny and me. I've seen how powerful emotional connection can be in sport, but it can also carry danger. It's just like any relationship. With my brother the emotions I felt were intense and capable of bringing out the very best and worst in me. We didn't need to take the time and effort to be 'nice' to each other. Siblings often don't. We didn't chat and laugh about everyday events and instead tended to jump straight in and say what we felt. Sometimes we landed pretty badly. I'm no psychologist, but I think Jonny understood more than anyone else what made me want to prove myself. I would be driven to try incredibly hard just by a certain look or a few words from him.

Little more than a week before the Opening Ceremony in Barcelona, down from altitude and training in the Italian heat of Varese, I was riding the rollercoaster of sibling emotions. Twenty-four hours earlier our session had gone really well, but that day the opposite was true. I have worked on the same technical points for most of my rowing career – getting my body into a strong position, and not driving too hard or too early – and I am used to being told to correct those faults. That day, for some reason, I didn't want to hear it. As Jonny reminded me to rock over I had bad thoughts going on in my head.

I'd be able to rock over if you'd carry your fucking hands a bit lower!

Then he told me I was rushing back.

I wouldn't be rushing back if you'd actually follow me – that's how it's supposed to work.

Eventually I'd had enough.

'I'm trying, but this is the best I can do!'

'Well it's not working, is it!'

Silence. We carried on with more heated exchanges before the session ended. Afterwards Steve gave us a debrief in which he made everything sound pretty normal. As far as he could see it hadn't been bad at all, which shows the small margins we were seeking.

Then it happened. I was sitting on my own on a bench just along from the rowing club. I was having a total crisis of confidence, convinced that I was screwed. I'd done my best and it wasn't going to get any better. I'd tried and I'd failed. I could feel my lip start to wobble as tears began to roll down my cheeks. Christ, I was having some sort of breakdown.

I'm sure Jonny hadn't wanted me to feel like that, he'd just hit the right buttons – probably subconsciously. Luckily, Garry was around to pull me out of the wreckage.

'You know what Jonny's like – better than anyone,' he said to me. 'He can be a total prick as well. That's what makes him good. Greg, you haven't forgotten how to row overnight. Tomorrow's session will be fine.'

He was right. I have one overriding memory of great rowing, the one I use to visualize when I want to see myself rowing well through my own eyes, and it's from the next day's session. We did ten one-minute-ten-second pieces and we flew. I proved to Jonny, Garry and myself that I hadn't become rubbish overnight, in fact I was still pretty good. I probably managed to rock over a bit as well! Years later, I would make a point of taking my pairs partner Cameron Nichol to that section of the lake to tell him the story. It still carries a powerful punch.

Through instances like that one with my brother I've learned the power of letting my guard down, and that it's OK to show weakness. In fact, I think it requires strength and demonstrates an inner confidence in myself. I'm now more than ready to display my emotions. I'll act happy when I'm happy and pissed off when I'm not, and I think this makes me more credible and more real as a human being. No one is bullet proof, and pretending you are only makes you look arrogant.

From the training camp in Varese it was a short flight to Barcelona. Ben Hunt-Davis and I were now part of the GB Olympic team, but to us it felt like we were back on the junior squad together, and we wanted to have some fun, even though this was a much bigger stage.

At the airport our nose for mischief got the better of us and we managed to upset some team-mates minutes into our arrival on Spanish soil. Ben and I made a point of arriving at baggage reclaim early to get hold of everyone's brand-new matching bright red suitcases. We stood them in a long line like dominoes, and once the rest of the team was there to admire our work we sent them down. Not everyone found it as funny as we did.

Having made such a good impression at the airport we moved on to the Olympic Village. We weren't staying in the village – to get to our digs we needed to head out to Banyoles, a satellite village on the banks of the rowing lake – so I'm not sure why we were there, perhaps just to have a look around and get used to being at the Games. However, by then Ben and I were in full tourist mode and far too excited to act like respectable Olympic athletes. It was pretty warm, and as there wasn't a nice air-conditioned room to hang out in we decided a swim in the village fountain was just about the best idea ever. Once again, not everyone was impressed, and we were met with some disapproving looks as we clambered out, soaking wet. We weren't the least bit bothered and had dried out by the time our bus left for the rowing lake, accompanied by a police escort, which only added to the drama and excitement of the occasion.

This wasn't my first trip to Banyoles lake; I'd been there on a couple of training camps before. They had involved tough work-outs and plenty of fun, but I realized that this visit was going to be different. The Olympics wasn't the time to frequent the bars in the local square or chase girls! That wasn't the only change; the complex had been completed for one thing, and it was very impressive. We were housed in a comfortable three-storey, newly built block, where Jonny, Garry and I shared an apartment with another cox, the spare pair (the guys who weren't going to race unless someone was injured) and a couple of others. We were finally there.

Banyoles is a natural lake, and around the start area, where we turned our boats, there's a public road that comes down almost to the water, where supporters gather and shout encouragement. I was twenty years old and the attention made me feel like a rock star.

The weather was glorious, and so hot I had to take cold showers in my T-shirt before training in a bid to keep cool. Our apartment was on the top floor, which was bad because we had to walk upstairs but good because we had a view, not only of the lake, but of what was going on below us. On the second day, after training, we spotted a few of our mates on their balcony and, given the weather, we decided the only decent thing to do was convert some plastic bottles into water pistols and cool them off a bit. Perhaps unsurprisingly, from there things escalated until they got a little out of hand, resulting in the water supply being turned off in the whole block for the rest of the day. To say we were unpopular with the rest of the team would be an understatement. A lower profile was definitely required after that little stunt.

Training went well. Steve Gunn had set us a comprehensive programme designed to ensure we peaked at exactly the right moment, and we followed it closely – most of the time. Out on the water there were always a number of other crews training, and during one session we were picked up by the Slovenian coxless pair, who ended up with bronze behind Redgrave and Pinsent. Jonny and I were determined racers and as the Slovenians increased their pace to pass us, we responded, both boats blasting the final 250 m to the line as hard as we could in a sprint finish.

We weren't going to give ground and neither were they. As we crossed the line together, the four of us slumped forward in exhaustion, then looked across at each other and grinned. Our coaches might not have been very happy with us, going against their carefully worked-out programmes, but both boats had put down markers of intent, and whilst in the great scheme of things it probably didn't make much of a difference, if it gave us even a sliver more confidence then it was a nudge in the right direction. Confidence is vital when it comes to race day and it can be hard to build from nowhere; a little event like this 'battle paddling' provided another block in our solid wall of self-belief.

When it came to the Opening Ceremony there was a big debate about whether or not we should attend. It was being staged on the Saturday night, from 6 p.m. until near midnight, with the rowing heats set to start the following Monday, racing from around 9 a.m. and the pre-paddle at 6 a.m. Factoring in the two-hour journey back to Banyoles from the stadium, anyone who marched at the ceremony wouldn't get to bed until the early hours of Sunday. That might not sound such a big deal, but the concern was that a late night might affect our body clocks, which should have been tuned to waking early and feeling fresh.

I hadn't intended to go, but at a team meeting the day before it was announced that Steve Redgrave was going to carry the GB flag into the stadium. Despite the fact that we'd competed against Steve that year, his selection changed the way I felt. Steve was one of us and I wanted to be there marching behind him. Jonny chose not to go and Steve Gunn was cool about both decisions.

We were transported to Barcelona in a great convoy of buses full of rowers from each country heading for the stadium. On arrival we were ushered into the gymnastics arena and sat on designated seats while the room filled up all around us as the other nations arrived. By then we had been joined by the rest of the GB team and I started to realize I was part of something pretty big. We were all in high spirits and soon got a bit bored watching the ceremony on the big screens that were suspended from the ceiling, so we filled the time by singing and chanting. The rowers made up one of the biggest groups and we were quite vocal, although I think we were out-done by one team member, who ran onto the mats for a spot of tumbling before attempting some chin-ups on the high bars, followed by what can only be described as 'uncoordinated dangling'.

Following our time in the holding area we lined up in the

stadium tunnel. It was a magical moment. We hadn't seen Steve since he'd left the rowing village earlier in the day, and when he joined us we all chanted his name while the level of anticipation soared. Finally it was time to march out on to the track, with Steve carrying the flag in front of him in one hand – no need for a shoulder harness there! A wall of sound – cheering and screaming – smacked us in the face. I'd never experienced anything close to it before. I switched off from the focus of competing and winning to enjoy this incredible moment.

In sport it's important, I believe, to be able to compartmentalize in this manner. To remain intense the whole time during a competition is impossible, and it's essential you know when to switch on and off if you're to raise your performance to a higher level. It's true that the line between work and play can be very close and sometimes it blurs, and you need to be aware of that danger, but even so, for me, having the chance to step away and enjoy myself is critical when it comes to maintaining my focus when it matters.

Once we had completed our circuit we congregated in the field area in the middle, while the remaining nations enjoyed their turn in the spotlight. This was an opportunity to take photos, say hello to other athletes and soak up the atmosphere. At one point I spotted the swimmer Sharron Davies and decided she must be desperate to meet me, so Ben Hunt-Davis and I made a bee-line for the poor girl. Sharron's first Olympics had been in 1976 and she had seen and done it all before and must have inwardly groaned when she saw a pair of grinning idiots like us approaching, but you would never have known it; she was lovely, pleasant and chatty. And gorgeous, of course.

The finale of the Opening Ceremony was the arrival of the Olympic flame. We all crowded around, straining for a view, as it travelled round the track, then through the middle of the assembled competitors. A chain of famous Spanish athletes and celebrities had been created to pass the flame along on its journey, and when it reached the final link it was used to light the arrow of an archer standing at the top of the stadium, who took aim and launched it into the Spanish night sky. For a moment the flaming arrow seemed to hang in the air before disappearing from view as, simultaneously, whoosh, a cauldron of fire was ignited. It was truly spectacular and brought a lump to my throat – this was special. Now I really was at the Olympic Games.

Attending the ceremony proved much more important than I had anticipated. Up until then I'd been thrilled and excited, but it had felt more like just another race. Not any longer. Suddenly I was a fully-fledged member of the Great Britain team, determined to make my contribution, inspired to perform at my very best.

I experienced no ill effects from our late arrival back at Banyoles. We put back our training session by an hour or so to allow Garry and me a lie-in, and then it was business as usual, although I was slightly preoccupied by a certain swimmer.

Within the village there was a laundrette, a couple of chemists and various shops, one of which contained a bank of computer terminals offering an early version of email. The system was password-protected, and you had to enter the registration number that appeared on your accreditation badge to gain access, but once you were in you could send a private message to any athlete. Everyone seemed to be there sending messages to one another and, full of the joys of youth and the heady confidence of being a young Olympic rower, I decided to send a message to Sharron, saying how lovely it had been to meet her and wishing her good luck in the pool. I wasn't optimistic about receiving a response.

One arrived a day or so later. I logged on and there it was, 'Message received from S Davies'. She wished me luck and said she might make it over to see us race if the swimming was done by then. I thought that was pretty cool, and it's just possible I might have over-egged the significance of her message as I boasted for the rest of the day that Sharron Davis wanted to see what I kept in my Lycra shorts. I probably deserved what happened next.

Logging on the following day I was more than a little surprised to discover I had recently sent Sharron another message while I was out on the water, a message that gave the distinct impression that I was keen to accelerate our non-existent relationship. Clearly the email system was not as secure as one might have hoped.

At that point I bottled it. I wish I hadn't, but I'm afraid I did. I sent her a grovelling note apologizing for the fact that one of my friends had sent a rogue message pretending to be me. (What I should have done was let it ride and see what happened – you never know – but I was too embarrassed.) Sharron replied with a 'don't worry about it' sort of response, containing the clear sub-text, 'You child.' Ah well, my great sporting romance was over before it had begun.

There is a slightly darker side to the story. When my brother eventually got round to logging on to the system he too discovered that someone had masqueraded as him and sent a message to Giuseppe Abbagnale, indicating that we were going to take them down and become the new champions, with a parting shot of, 'Look out for the British!'

Jonny was not the least bit amused by either of these episodes and he and I went on the warpath. We suspected it was one of the guys from the eight and resolved to confront him, crashing our way into their apartment and dragging one of them out of bed, demanding to know what was going on. Jonny had him by the collar of his T-shirt, and the guy was clearly alarmed.

'It, it wasn't me,' he stammered, 'it was Ben!'

Right, no surprise really! Off we went in search of Mr Hunt-Davis, and spotted him a few minutes later strolling around the village. The moment he laid eyes on Ben, Jonny broke into a run and shoved him pretty hard.

'What the fuck do you think you're doing with the email, Ben?'
I was having a flashback to our arrival in Australia when the quad
took our ball.

'Jonny, mate, it's got nothing to do with me!'

'Bullshit! It's just the sort of thing you'd do.'

The two of them went back and forth like that for a while
before ending up tussling on the ground just as one of the US
coaches, Ted Nash, walked by. Ted was not someone you ignored.
Not only was he famous in rowing circles, there were all sorts of
legendary stories about what he'd got up to in Vietnam.

'Guys, save it for the oar handle!' he said as he broke up the
fight. He was right, of course, that's what we should have been
doing with our pent-up emotion.

It all calmed down after that. Ben owned up to the Sharron
Davies email pretty quickly once he'd had the chance to speak,
but not to the one that mattered: the message to Giuseppe
Abbagnale. I really wasn't bothered about the Sharron situation,
it was actually quite funny, but the note to our rivals was a totally
different matter.

The Abbagnales had replied when Jonny next checked. 'In
Italy we say, "The dog that barks too loud never bites."' There
was a sense that the situation might be getting out of hand and
we decided the only course of action was to report what was
going on to the GB team manager and send an official apology,
explaining that we had nothing to do with the original message.
The Abbagnales accepted our explanation and that was that,
although Jonny remained very fired up about it.

Ben sensibly kept out of Jonny's way for a few days, even
though I was pretty sure by then that he wasn't responsible. Ben
would have owned up, so it must have been one of the other guys
in the eight, though who exactly, I wasn't sure.

Fast forward seven years and I am drinking and reminiscing
with a tough Australian rower called Mike McKay when the 1992

Olympics come up. As I am telling the email story I can see in his face that it isn't the first time he's heard it.

'Ah, Greg, about that. Straight up, it wasn't one of you Brits that sent the message. Big Macca was behind it. We thought it was a bit of a giggle. Sorry, mate.' Big Macca was Nick McDonald-Crowley, one half of the Aussie coxless pair, a good bloke but full of mischief. Suddenly it made sense. Mystery solved.

The first heat came down to a straight fight between us and the Romanians for the right to progress direct to the semis. They were a very good pair – with their cox and two other rowers they went on to win gold in the coxed four during the same Games – and we knew that if we could beat them, there weren't many other boats that would worry us. They led from the start, but we tracked them all the way, never losing contact, pulled back in the third 500 m and pushed through on the line. Not only did that win give us a day off, as we avoided the repêchage, an additional heat that allows non-qualifying boats a second bite at the cherry, it also put down a marker for the rest of the field. Up until then we had been an unknown quantity. No longer. Now everyone had to worry about a new set of brothers in a coxed pair. Hopefully doubts would begin to eat away at them, just as we wanted.

We avoided both the Romanians and the Italians in the semi-finals, and instead found ourselves facing the US, the Poles, the French, the Germans and the home favourites Spain. The US boat took it out extremely fast but that didn't worry us, we knew they could smash it along, but probably wouldn't be able to sustain the pace. From halfway we pushed on, knowing we could not only go the distance but also pick up speed if required. From the moment we took the lead we were never in danger of being rowed through. In terms of being in control, that semi-final was probably our best-looking race.

Speed-wise, we were a good four seconds faster than the

Italians' winning time in their semi, but that was deceptive. An analysis of their splits revealed they had been quicker than us to 500 m, quicker again to 1000 m, but we were faster in the third 500 m, while they had clearly paddled in at the end, having been so comfortably in control.

What that told us was that we had everything we needed to mix it with them, and that it would all come down to what we each had up top. From our side we were confident we'd worked hard with Brian Miller and Steve to get our heads in the right place. The rest of it was pretty straightforward. Get our best start; settle into a sustainable pace for the first half; push hard in the third quarter; never, ever even consider winning a silver medal, and when the last 500 m came we'd be on autopilot, knowing we had a well-ingrained pattern to fall back on. Trust the training. Trust each other.

And now we are in our lane, lane three, the Romanians to our left, the Italians to our right.

The starter raises his flag.

'Are you ready . . .'

'Go!'

As expected, the Italians go off fast, taking an early lead. Don't panic, stick to the game plan, keep the Romanians alongside us. Track the Abbagnales.

Long, press, deep, move. Get the boat up to speed fast. We are right in it.

Garry calls the 500 m mark, 'You are so strong. Great rhythm. Heads up.'

I keep looking straight behind, keep my head up. I can tell the Romanians are right there, maybe half a length up. The Italians are further on but Garry sounds so cool.

1000 m. I feel so powerful. It hurts, it hurts like hell, but it's meant to and I know I can deal with it. This is what racing is about. Anyone can get to halfway. It's who wins at the end that counts. Garry calls, 'This is where we are strong. You're harder than anyone. You push, they hurt!'

It hurts so much. But I know our big push is coming. As we reach 1250 m Garry goes quiet, then he says the word, 'Yes.' This is a code that means we're about to do something special. Then he calls, 'Lengthen, harden, go!' I've been preparing to hear this in every race since I was at school.

I press my legs down as hard as I can. I open my back like it's a great drawbridge with an unstoppable force. I claw with my arms like I'm pulling my body weight to save me from falling off a cliff to my death.

Ten strokes later Garry calls, 'Burn, go.'

Now I need to lift the stroke rate. It's already thirty-nine. I move as fast as I can; like a juggler with a dozen balls I move with a speed and timing that looks effortless, but that's because it's so well drilled.

Ten strokes later Garry calls again, 'Push, go.'

The final ten of this thirty-stroke effort requires me to combine the previous twenty strokes. I give it everything physically, moving with the freedom and fluidity of a leopard closing in on its prey.

Our prey is the Italians. I still can't see them. I'm not looking, but I can sense them. I can tell our boat speed has increased and we are not letting it slow now. We have the momentum.

Garry makes the call. 'If not now?' Then he pauses before saying something else. He's forgotten the 'If not you, who?' It doesn't matter. I'm tapping into that emotion we felt the night before. I notice we are rowing past the women's eights. They are shouting for Garry! It's irrelevant. Nothing matters except getting what we deserve. I won't remember the pain at the end of the race.

I can hear from Garry's voice that we have gold in us. He can't know we'll win but I trust him. There are about ten strokes left and I nail every one of them. We lead with the last two strokes of the race; it's what I expected.

For whatever reason I always knew we would win. When I watched the race the next day I couldn't believe how far behind we were in the middle of the race. In my mind we were pressuring them the whole time, and I guess we were.

Reflecting now I think we raced well but they raced badly. They tried to make us give up on gold and race for silver, but that was never going to happen.

I fell back into the boat and laid my head on Jonny's feet. It's my favourite picture. We'd done it – together. It couldn't be any better. This feeling of crossing the line was, and is still, the best thing about sport for me. It's what I do it for.

The 'run off' area at Banyoles is short, so the next thing we had to do was avoid getting stuck in the reeds as the boat drifted on. Then we had a brilliant private few minutes. We went on to the far side of the course to wait for the women's medal ceremony and the next race to come down. We spoke a few words to each other, but we didn't need to say much. I remember looking around and Jonny was collapsed with exhaustion and emotion. His head was down, his shoulders hunched over. The only word to describe how it felt is 'perfect'.

When it was our turn we lined up on the course alongside the other crews. The rowing version of a lap of honour involves the winners paddling down lane one, second place in lane two etc. The Abbagnales were exhausted and could hardly row. I think they were in a less of a hurry to collect their medals than we were! Still, we didn't want to disrespect them by disappearing off, so we matched their snail's pace. When we eventually reached the landing stage we jumped out of the boat and hugged each other.

We were given our medals and turned to face the flags and hear the national anthem. I boomed out the first couple of lines, until I became painfully aware that I couldn't hear another singer except Jonny. The whole lake was developed in a conservation area, which restricted what could be built, so our parents and supporters were miles away in a temporary stand. As for Garry, it took me until the next day to realize he couldn't sing much because he was crying his eyes out. I let my enthusiasm drop off as the anthem went on, but it was still an incredible moment. This was the best rowing experience I could ever have. It was done. It could never be any better. I wonder now, did those thoughts affect the rest of my career?

The first rower to come and congratulate us was Steve Redgrave, who'd won gold the day before with Matthew in the coxless pairs. To me that's a real mark of the man. We'd been head-to-head competitive all year and Jonny and I had tried to oust them from the pair, and yet there was Steve, ready to hug me like the great bear he is.

After that it was party time, especially in the rowing village because we had all finished competing by then. We made the most of it, drinking, swimming in the lake, dancing and singing for a couple of days before we upped sticks and headed to the main village for more of the same.

Rooms in the main village were inevitably at a premium with the Games still having over a week to run, but after a bit of juggling Garry and I found ourselves billeted with the swimmers, in Adrian Moorhouse's apartment. It was one of the best things that ever happened to me. Adrian, a gold medallist from years before, made a very big impression. He was twenty-seven years old, approaching the end of his career and he'd just come in eighth in his event when suddenly he was presented with a young, excited, gold-medal winner, and he was brilliant, a really good bloke.

He shook my hand, congratulated me and we sat down together for breakfast, during which he offered me invaluable advice on which journalists to speak to, who to avoid, how to go about getting an agent and all that. He didn't know me from Adam, he'd just come last in his final, which must have been hard to take, and he still made the time to be friendly and helpful. I have never forgotten that. It's easy to be a great guy when you're a winner, but to act that way when you've lost is something else entirely.

The next few days passed in an idyllic post-winning haze, on a Spanish schedule. I'd get up for lunch in the village, maybe go and see some tennis or hockey, then in the evening I'd head off to the stadium to watch what was happening on the track. The hospitality tents supplied plenty to drink and a few canapés to line the stomach in the evening – the Mercedes-Benz tent was my favourite – and at around midnight we'd grab a taxi into town and lose ourselves in the bright lights of Barcelona. Studio 54 was my preferred haunt as it was where most of the international rowers congregated for a spot of stage diving . . .

The next day I'd do it all again, making sure I was carrying my medal with me the whole time. If I look at it now there are a few dents visible – it took a bit of a battering that week – but I wasn't about to leave it behind in my room. It wasn't that I felt particularly attached to it, rather I'd discovered it acted like a skeleton key, opening a lot of doors. It seemed every club and bar in the city was delighted to welcome a gold medallist. I won't go into detail about all our adventures, but suffice to say, Barcelona had a lot to offer a group of young international rowers who, after months, even years, of training could finally let their hair down.

I spent a lot of time with the Canadians during that week; they were a great bunch, and incredibly upbeat because they'd won gold ahead of the Germans. That result was quite a surprise and it made me think of how Marty Aitken had seemed to write off our chances against the German boat way too early. Clearly they were beatable after all, although unfortunately not by the GB boat.

Our eight finished outside the medals, and I guess they must have had mixed emotions about our victory. I'm certain I would have if the roles had been reversed.

The first time the wider impact of what we had achieved hit me was at my first personal appearance, which I attended that week. It was organized by a company called Sportsworld, who laid on package trips for British fans, including travel, stadium tickets, hospitality and meetings with the athletes. The three of us had been invited and we were more than happy to accept. Nice people, nice party, nice way to start our night out!

We showed up as instructed and thought nothing much of it until we walked into the marquee. The silence that greeted our entrance stopped the three of us dead in our tracks. Were we at the wrong reception? A hundred faces were looking straight at us, and then the clapping began. It was extraordinary; we were completely taken aback, especially when they proceeded to form an orderly welcome queue to shake our hands. We were wearing our medals, of course, and towards the end of the line one of the blokes asked if he could wear it around his neck.

Sure, why not. I handed it to him, had a momentary tinge of 'Why is someone else wearing my medal?' then happily posed for a photo. At which point the orderly queue reformed and we had to go through it all again, so everyone could have a go.

I guess that was the first moment when I felt like Greg Searle, gold medallist, rather than just Greg Searle. Up until then we had been spending most of our time with other sports people who saw me as Greg the rower, but here were members of the public, and their reaction was totally different. It struck me then that not only had I won a race *I* cared about, I'd won a race that *other people* cared about.

The fun and games eventually came to an end and, a week after our victory, the athletes attended the spectacular closing ceremony, which was all fireworks, music, dancing and strange balloons floating up into the night sky. It was fabulous, it really was. The only downside was that the organizers had decided we wouldn't march. From our point of view that was a great shame, we wanted to be part of the proceedings, not bystanders, so in the end we took matters into our own hands.

We'd been sitting in the stands for a couple of hours when we made our move. The Brits were first, quickly supported by the other teams. In the carnival atmosphere we made a break for the centre of the stadium, and as the only security in place were the groups of pleasant but hardly robust volunteers, there was no way of stopping us. With everyone laughing and singing we joined in with the dancers as they twirled their flags and expertly executed the routines they'd been practising for months; whether they felt this was all in the spirit of the occasion I can't say, but I have my suspicions . . .

In the midst of maracas and flamenco-style dancing it didn't take me long to figure out how to stamp my foot, clap my hands and shout, 'Ole!' every now and again to try and blend in. Towards the end of the ceremony, top billing seemed to be given to a bunch of people dressed in pastel shades giving it plenty of this Latin-inspired music. They turned out to be none other than the Gipsy Kings and it was there the organizers decided to draw the line, setting up a defensive cordon in front of the stage. In our exuberant state, we simply saw this as a challenge. I was with Steve Redgrave and persuaded him that we owed it to ourselves to get up there. In full agreement, Steve – all 6 foot 5" of him – made a dash for glory, with me running the line behind. It took at least three of the security staff to drag him down at the final hurdle, and that opened a gap I was more than happy to take advantage of.

So there I was, on stage wearing baggy African trousers, which I'd swapped for my regulation GB pair with a bloke from the Nigerian team, with the band playing and dancers all around me gyrating in time to the music while I threw in the odd 'Ole!' and occasionally stamped my foot. I was having a ball, pleased with myself and sure I was the coolest guy in the stadium, especially when this very pretty girl made eye contact and shimmied over. She's obviously hugely impressed with my adventurous spirit, I thought. A good night just got a whole lot better.

Once up alongside me, the girl took hold of my hands, steered me around so that my back was to the crowd . . . and shoved me in the chest. Off I flew, landing in the waiting arms of the security team, who ushered me off, out of harm's way. Oh well, my youthful dreams of romance may have been shattered once again, but at least I'd been up on the stage in front of millions. Not a bad way to end my first Olympics.

We weren't aware of the impact the race had had back in Britain until we arrived home. Even with Redgrave's exploits in the previous two Olympics, rowing was still very much a minority sport. Our family and friends were excited about our victory, and Molesey threw a fantastic party for us, but did the general public care?

It quickly became clear that they did. Perhaps it was the nature of the win as much as anything that captured the imagination. Two brothers, inexperienced in that particular event, impossibly far behind, then dramatically snatching victory from the reigning champions on the line, plus Garry's tears at the medal ceremony, showing the world what it meant. I guess, when I look back now, that it was quite a story, but at the time I was just amazed and delighted that so many people had been touched by our race. It was an incredible feeling to have total strangers telling us they had woken up early that Sunday morning and ended up jumping around their bedrooms shouting at the TV.

I loved the attention and what it meant. The best way I can describe it is like giving someone a present that they appreciate. It was a great feeling and one I had never expected, but I understood it. When England does well at football or cricket, I love it, I get swept away and I feel the pride and enjoy the excitement of the moment. To have been part of something that generates the same feelings in others is a privilege and it endures to this day. When I talk to a group of people and show them the video of the race, the thrill is still there in their faces as they watch something special unfold in front of them.

The highlight for me in those post-Olympic months was being invited to attend the BBC *Sports Personality of the Year* show in December. This was something we as a family had watched every year since I could remember; it marked the beginning of Christmas for us, and now Jonny, Garry and myself were going to be on the show. Not only that, we were going to participate in the stunt section of the evening's activities, where they persuade some prominent sports people to engage in a moment of stage-managed fun. As thrilled as I was to be there, it terrified me.

In the past we'd had snooker trick shots, Frank Bruno playing golf, Nigel Mansell taking on challengers in a driving game, Scotland versus England table football and hockey shoot-outs; for us the idea was for a Searles versus Redgrave and Pinsent row-off on machines in the studio, with Garry commentating.

We certainly wanted to be involved, but we weren't too keen on the idea as it was originally proposed to us. First, there had been talk of a genuine Searles versus Steve and Matthew race in the spring, and we didn't want to jeopardize that with a simulated version (in fact, that race never happened, but it was very much a possibility in December 1992) and secondly, given the combined strength and size of the two of them they would most likely beat Jonny and me on ergos fairly comfortably. We suggested an individual race instead – the four of us competing against each other – and the BBC went for it.

I suspect this won't be a huge surprise to anyone, but the

outcome of the 'race' was a little pre-arranged. We all realized that as triple gold medallist this was Steve's big night and it was appropriate that he should win, but to even things up Matthew shouldn't come second. Sportingly, he agreed to fall on his sword and make sure I beat him, which I might have done anyway I hasten to add. Jonny was always going to be fourth.

We concocted a plan. Jonny would go out hard and take the lead, then Matthew would overhaul him before fading, and I would come through until the last few strokes, when Steve would overtake me on the line. The outcome really didn't matter, we all realized, but putting on a show did.

On the night, Jonny blasted off for his minute of glory, taking a huge lead and amazing everyone that he had blown Redgrave and Pinsent out of the water. I suspect Jonny had a momentary flash of thinking, I can do this, until Matthew came storming back, before graciously letting me through. If I harboured any naughty thoughts of trying to outlast Steve they were very quickly extinguished as Redgrave went ballistic over the final few metres to win. There was no way in hell he was going to let me hold onto the lead, even if I'd wanted to. The end was exactly as it should have been and made for good television I hope. We enjoyed it anyway, especially once it was over and we could focus on the after-show party!

It was a brilliant end to a brilliant year, but it also marked the moment when the laurels we'd been resting on had to be packed away. We had a prophecy to fulfil, articulated by the BBC commentators as we crossed the line at Banyoles ahead of the Italians.

'We are witnessing the birth of a new era in coxed pairs.'

It was time to get back on the water.

FOUR

TWO PLUS TWO

Birth of a new era? If what we were hearing was true, Barcelona was going to prove to be the exact opposite, the end of one. Early in 1993 rumours began circulating that the coxed pair and coxed four were going to be cut from future Games.

The logic behind this proposed change was an attempt to open up the sport to a broader range of countries. By axing those events the authorities could then introduce a lightweight coxless four and a lightweight double. It boiled down to a matter of demographics. Purely on account of their smaller national physical traits, a number of countries keen to participate in international rowing were unable to compete in the open weight category. Fair enough, we were all keen to extend the appeal of rowing, and it was suggested that reconfiguring the events in this manner would mean that about twenty more countries would enter boats. That had to be a good thing, and we recognized that, but we still felt it wasn't the best way forward.

As arguments bounced back and forth behind the scenes on this contentious issue, Jonny, Garry and myself were determined that if 1993 was to prove the swansong of our event, we were going to go out on a high, proving that Barcelona hadn't been a fluke.

That was going to be easier said than done. In the six months following Barcelona Jonny and I had both settled into post-Olympic life pretty well, and although we still managed to fit in training, the intensity wasn't there.

Not only was I sharing a flat in Wimbledon with my good mate Howling Jim Walker and enjoying being a young guy in London, I was also fitting in the wonderful (and strange) things that come with being an Olympic gold medallist, from receiving my MBE and handing out Duke of Edinburgh awards at Buckingham Palace, to judging a sandwich-making competition at a local school. Jonny and I even switched on the Christmas lights in Molesey High Street. (Disappointingly, however, I never had the chance to open a supermarket with a giant pair of scissors.)

It's not as though I went crazy, living the high life, but I certainly found the intensity of the pre-Barcelona days hard to sustain. From the single-minded focus of shaving off one-sixtieth of a second with every training session, my mindset shifted to, What can I get away with and still win?

In the build-up to 1992 I didn't stop during a session unless I absolutely had to. I would set the machine to 20 km and always row to the end. There's a school of thought that suggests this is a stupid thing to do and that it's best to set the machine for forty-five minutes, complete that, get off, stretch your back, rehydrate, then reset for the final twenty- to thirty-minute portion. Basically, complete the full distance but look after your body. Before the Olympics I wouldn't have dreamed of taking a break – that would have been soft – but once the gold was won my thinking began to alter. I'd stop for a drink, stretch my legs, look out of the window, have a quick chat, then settle back down on the machine. I justified this by convincing myself I was following sound physio advice. Maybe, but it wasn't how I worked and it began to cost me. It may only have been a small change to my routine, but it blunted my edge.

I recognize now that at a fundamental level my motivation

wasn't strong enough to overcome the various hurdles being placed in my path. My first and incredibly powerful motivation had been to win an Olympic gold medal, and having done that, as I set my sights on Atlanta 1996, my focus became softer. It was a case of, 'I want to win again but I also want these other things from my life.' As my economics teacher used to say, 'Once you've eaten one Mars Bar you're not quite so keen to get your hands on the second.'

Compare my attitude to that of Steve Redgrave. He started out exactly the same as me: 'I want to win the Olympics.' From there I imagine he proceeded to, 'I want to be the best-ever British rower,' then, 'I want to be the best-ever rower from any country,' followed by, 'The best-ever athlete from any country,' and finally, 'Man of the Millennium'. At every stage he set himself an attainable but punishingly difficult target. Me, I liked the idea of another gold medal. That hardly stirs the passion deep in your soul.

Today, I adopt a far more Redgrave-esque approach. I am on the comeback trail to earn Olympic legend status. If that doesn't get me going I might as well pack up my Lycra shorts, join a Pilates class and start playing a bit of five-a-side.

Jonny and I were facing similar issues: the distractions our success had brought combined with the everyday necessities of life. He was working for a law firm in the City, while I had started life as a chartered surveyor in London for my sandwich year at South Bank.

About a month before Barcelona I'd gone for an interview with a firm of surveyors called Gerald Eve, where I was interviewed by a really nice guy called David Adams. Towards the end of our discussion David said to me, 'If we were to offer you a position, normally our placements begin on the fourteenth of August, will that work for you?'

Five days after the Closing Ceremony. 'Ah, that might be a little tight. I'm hoping to go to the Olympics.'

'Ah, great. You're going to the Olympics. Have you got tickets for something nice?'

'Well, actually I'm hoping to compete.'

'Oh really. Marvellous. Well, all the best with that.' He appeared suitably underwhelmed. 'If we offer you the job we'll see you on the fourteenth.'

Sure enough, there I was on 14 August 1992, rolling up at Gerald Eve on a salary of £8,000 a year, sitting with the other young trainees as an Olympic gold medallist, every now and then having to use a day's holiday to go off and do some sort of personal appearance, which probably paid more in an hour then I earned in a month. It was an odd way to start my working life, surreal even, and it certainly wasn't conducive to sustaining elite performance.

When I wasn't in the office I could be anywhere in the country – on a factory site, counting bays in a car park or measuring up office space. If these trips happened to be in central London I could still fit in a very early morning training session, but more often than not over that period Jonny and I would only manage one dark evening together in a boat during the week, plus a couple of weekend outings.

As for Garry, short of our newly discovered 'celebrity' we didn't see a whole lot of him because we were rowing at Molesey while he'd returned to Leander. It wouldn't be like that now, a cox would train with his boat far more regularly, but back then we didn't regard it as necessary until the summer months.

Without Garry's calming influence, combined with the fact that we both knew we weren't going as fast as we needed to, Jonny's and my emotions occasionally boiled over.

One such incident occurred during a weekend session that Garry had been scheduled to join, but had to pull out of at the last minute because of work commitments. We were at Molesey, in need of a cox, when we were introduced to a young girl of eighteen years old or so, who offered to help. The next best option was to put the toolbox in the coxing seat and we reasoned she couldn't be worse than that.

Unfortunately she was, and the session did not go well. We were both tired after a week's work and she was inexperienced and unfamiliar with our style of training, unintentionally making wrong calls and adding to our stress levels. Eventually, politely I hope, although I wouldn't count on it given how we were feeling, we asked her to stop talking and concentrate on steering while we made our own calls, as if we were a coxless boat.

The session improved until we reached the section requiring four three-minute pieces at thirty strokes per minute. As we came towards the end of the third of these, with about one minute to go, I looked down at my stroke meter, which told me we were on our target rate, and made the call over my shoulder.

'Thirty.'

Jonny started pulling as hard as he could. About half a minute later I made another call.

'Thirty seconds to go.'

'What?' Jonny panted in my ear. 'Why the fuck did you shout thirty when it was a minute to go?'

'So you'd know what the hell was going on.'

'Well you needn't have bothered. You just confused me.'

'You are fucking hard to row with, you know that!'

'Well if it's that hard why don't you piss off, you little dick-head!'

I'd heard enough. 'All right, I will.'

I slipped my feet out and jumped over the side of the boat. The river wasn't too wide, so it didn't take long to get to dry land, and once there I jogged off in the direction of the boat club without a backwards glance. As I started to cool off I realized I'd swum to the wrong bank, which meant I had to climb back in the water and swim the full width of the river. Having made it across successfully, one of the club veterans spotted me walking along the bank, trailing a stream of water behind me.

'How was your session? Is everything OK?' he asked, looking at me strangely.

'The session wasn't the best, no. Nothing to worry about, though.'

Meanwhile, Jonny and his passenger were stranded in the middle of the river, having been lucky not to fall in the water themselves when I abandoned ship. You need two to row a pair, and as the girl wasn't really up to that Steve Gunn, who had witnessed all this from his motor launch with some bemusement, had to clamber into my seat and help Jonny row back, with our unfortunate cox following in Steve's boat.

By the time they arrived back at the club tempers on both sides had subsided. I was actually pleased they hadn't drowned in the middle of the river and that Jonny was ready to apologize. The incident also taught us something unexpected: it was the first time we'd ever seen Steve row, and he wasn't very good. It was nice to see that you don't need to be great at doing something to be great at coaching it.

As for the girl, she never offered to cox for us again.

Had I been with anyone other than Jonny, the incident wouldn't have played out as it did. I might have engaged in a shouting match with another bloke, I might even have tried to thump him, although that's tricky in a boat, but I would never have gone to the extreme of bailing out. It was foolish and only happened because we were brothers, with an incredibly strong connection that sometimes got the better of us. We care passionately about our rowing, and during that period, although we struggled to admit it, subconsciously we recognized that we were letting ourselves down, and as a result we became defensive. The most inconsequential events would get blown out of proportion and we'd either flare up or, worse, we'd let issues fester and not deal with them.

For a while we couldn't escape the emotional rollercoaster, and although often it brought out the best in each of us, sometimes it drew out the worst.

Given that background, it's no surprise that we failed to perform in our first race of the 1993 season.

The regatta was in Duisburg, Germany, and we were essentially racing the same crews we'd beaten in Barcelona, bar the Italians who were absent. We made a fairly ordinary start, with the other boats pulling away, and at the 1500 m mark we were lying fifth. Garry then called the surge, and as we strained our muscles in response, I became aware of raucous cheering ringing out from the crowds lining the banks.

Here we go, I thought, the Searle brothers do it again, slaying them on the line. The crowds love it. This is brilliant. As the pride began to swell in my chest I glanced right. The boat next to us was upside down. Our supposed 'surge' proved little more than a disappointing sideshow; the real entertainment focused on the young pair who'd fallen in. At the line we moved through to fourth, which considering only five crews finished was hardly what we'd been looking for.

There was a lot of work still to be done, but at least we had a month in which to do it, each of us having saved our annual holiday in order to escape for some focused training with the rest of the squad. Having that dedicated stretch together paid dividends. Free of distractions we made up considerable ground, our confidence returned and we arrived at the Racice World Championships in better shape than we'd been all year. As we lined up for the finals we knew it was probably going to come down to us or the Abbagnales for the gold medal. We also knew that because of the changes to the Olympic programme this was likely to be the last ever seriously classy coxed pairs race in history.

A year on from Cologne you'd think we'd have learned our lesson. Then we'd been an inexperienced boat, now we were Olympic champions. There is no way we could make the same mistake twice, surely.

The rain was pelting down as the starter raised his flag.

'Are you ready?'

Unfortunately not. Jonny was still tapping the boat straight in the lane.

'Go!'

This time we knew we had to respond. I waited for Jonny to be ready. It felt like ages as the other boats pulled away before I heard Jonny scream, 'Now!' We'd given the Italians half a length for nothing.

With 500 m gone we were last, but with Garry's help we remained calm, rowing our way back into our rhythm and starting to move up the field. At halfway we were back in contention with the leaders. I think the Italians were trying different tactics, but I was confident that they wouldn't be able to hold us once we got into the final sprint. I think everyone knew we would push on in the third quarter, and when we did they had no answer.

Into the last 500 m we hit the front, and with 250 m to go I was looking at all the other boats behind us. We were going to win, no question, it was the best we'd ever raced and it felt incredibly satisfying. We'd proved Barcelona hadn't been a freak result, achieved purely by surprising the Italians. Here they knew full well what to expect and they still couldn't cope. As we came into the closing stages I heard Jonny's voice behind me, 'Enjoy this. It could be the last time we ever do it together.'

In terms of a major championship, he was correct. The decision was taken to drop the coxed pair from the Olympic Games. At the same time the authorities also introduced qualifying competitions, with guaranteed places for winners in the regions where they wanted to develop rowing. I still think this measure alone would have been enough to increase Olympic participation and that rowing shouldn't have had to promote events for those who don't have the natural physique for it. It's comparable to having basketball games for people under 6 feet tall. Within racing-based sports, rather than combat or lifting where safety is an issue, rowing is the only one to categorize events in this way. On the down side it meant we wouldn't be able to defend our title, but on the up side it means we're still reigning Olympic champions!

With the coxed pair no longer able to feed our ambitions, Jonny and I had to find another boat in time for Atlanta, and by April 1994 it was clear that wasn't going to be the coxless pair.

At the Nottingham trials we didn't get near Redgrave and Pinsent, so we quickly turned our attention to the coxless four, which I had begun to think was going to be the boat for us. I was certainly ready to gain some crew mates, and I suspect Jonny was, too.

Early on in the selection process it became clear, rightly or wrongly, that Jonny and I were seen as definites for the four, with four others in contention to join us. In effect it came down to either Howling Jim and James Cracknell, or Tim Foster and Obby, as both pairs were set in stone. The selectors would either put in one set, or the other as our trialling was insufficiently flexible to contemplate any other combinations.

As the team management sat down to contemplate who would make up their second boat I don't believe they looked at the options properly. Jonny and I ticked a lot of boxes and were apparently 'safe', but how could anybody know that was the correct decision? We certainly hadn't impressed in the coxless pair for a while. They probably should have mixed us up, racing the boat without me as much as anyone else, in order to judge fairly what four worked best. Instead they played it safe, never even contemplating breaking up the fixed pairings.

Jonny and I raced one regatta with Jim and James, the next

with Tim and Obby, and based on that a view was taken from the bank that the best combination was with Tim and Obby. Understandably, I think, Jim and James were quite bitter about that, although it was far from an open-and-shut case whether they would have made the boat go faster than Tim and Obby. Did James have the necessary maturity and quality? Did Jim have the ability to row at stroke, where Tim was ultimately to sit? It's impossible to say. James and Obby, and Tim and Jim, were in direct competition, yet they were never even assessed in a straight race against each other. It seems incredible now, but that's how it was.

It was a hard situation for Jim and James to deal with. They were there, right on the edge of the four, and I suspect they believed their performances had been enough to earn the opportunity to prove themselves. It must have been very frustrating and I wonder if it influenced either of their subsequent decisions. Jim joined the crew of the eight, but James opted out and went for the double scull with Bobby Thatcher. Ultimately, the choice James made proved irrelevant because luck turned against him. He qualified for Atlanta and travelled with the team, but a nasty bout of tonsillitis kept him off the water for the duration of the Games. As for the eight, they had a tough journey and didn't make the final.

As I suggested earlier, the state of affairs that existed back then stemmed, I believe, from a lack of leadership at the top of British rowing. I can't even remember who was in charge at the time, which speaks volumes in itself. There was no clarity and no structure. The individual clubs were sometimes effective, but more often through luck than judgement. Steve, Matthew and Jürgen came together under the Leander umbrella and delivered, but as an overall team Great Britain seemed dysfunctional and disorganized. For example, in my entire rowing career I only ever rowed with Steve Redgrave once, and that was training in a four.

Steve and Matthew were an incredible partnership, and it made sense not to break that up, but given the opportunity I'm certain I and others could have learned from rowing with them more often in a team.

Rowing today couldn't be more different. Jürgen has made it very clear that he is prepared to mix and match and change things as he sees fit in order to give us the best chance of success. I respect him for having been so openly transparent. No one knows for sure what the eventual make-up of the various boats will be, which means we have to fight for our places until the day the final selection is made. And that's as it should be.

There is no doubt that this creates extra pressure to perform, and everyone feels it as we push ourselves as hard as possible to be the fastest guy in the team. What this has created is healthy competition, whereas in the early and mid-nineties the opposite was often true. We had factions – Molesey, Leander and others – and I believe this lack of a one-team mentality dealt a significant blow to Britain's overall success.

What I have learned over the intervening years is that it's essential to stay competitive on the water, but not to gloat or attempt to sabotage the efforts of my team-mates by playing psychological games. Contributing positively to our overall training and performance is now a benchmark we set ourselves because we recognize that when we improve as individuals, the team grows stronger.

Back in 1994, regardless of the inadequacies of the selection process, I was happy with how the four ended up. I got on well with Tim, and Obby had been around for a while. For me it was a bit of light relief for the pressure not to rest entirely on my brother and myself; in simple terms, it was more fun in a four; more chat about football, more laughs and more camaraderie.

That was all very well, but more important was the fact that we all rated the boat and each other. It was a strong team and I believed in it as we approached the 1994 World Championships in Indianapolis. In the run-up, although we hadn't been winning races, I felt we were growing stronger after each regatta, and building our own identity as the GB coxless four. The purchase of some Union Jack all-in-ones certainly helped with this sense of coming together and working towards a common goal. Was it going to be enough? I thought so. With our training camp having gone well I was convinced that gold was very much a realistic proposition.

We came in third. I was devastated, and as we stored our boat after the race I couldn't hold back the tears. For the first time in my career I felt I'd taken a step backwards; I'd failed to hit my target. From the age of sixteen I had improved year on year, including the ups and downs I had experienced in 1993, because when it came to the crunch, at the World Championships, we had beaten the Italians by an even greater margin than in Barcelona. Now, after Indianapolis, I felt a failure, as though the cloak of invincibility had slipped from my shoulders. Suddenly I was vulnerable.

What happened? Where did we go wrong? I believe a key aspect was that despite our efforts to the contrary, deep down we were operating as two pairs rather than a unified boat. Jonny and I always shared a room together, as did Obby and Tim. In training, when we rowed as pairs, I was always with Jonny, and Tim with Obby. This may not sound particularly critical, but I think it was, and the situation was made worse by the fact that Jonny and I were Olympic champions and may therefore have been treated as the senior pair, even though we didn't necessarily deserve it. Added to this, the boat's coach was our coach, Steve Gunn, and the combination of these things increased the sense of separation. It's not that we didn't get on with each other, we did, very well, but we weren't integrated as a single unit.

Had we been, we would have made different decisions on how we rowed, how we trained and the tactics we employed for races. Jonny and I would suggest one approach, while Tim and Obby would put forward another. This would then result in a stalemate, with only one possible outcome – an uncomfortable and unsatisfactory compromise rather than a full-blown discussion aimed at figuring out the best way forward. Everyone in that boat was strong willed and none of us was prepared to take a backwards step. Ultimately this led to a 'lowest common denominator' approach, rather than finding out what was best.

Another aspect chipping away at the effectiveness of our four was a financial imbalance that we failed to address all the way through to Atlanta. Following our gold medal success, Jonny, Garry and I agreed a sponsorship deal with Andersen Consulting for the coxed pair, and when that boat disappeared the deal was transferred to Jonny and me in the four. As a result, we continued to receive a good whack of cash, and all the attention, while Tim and Obby benefited to the extent of those great Union Jack all-in-ones and a few free T-shirts! In hindsight, we didn't handle the situation very well. I'm not suggesting we should have handed over half the money we received – that came to us from the sponsors in exchange for developing an ongoing relationship – but I'd like to have been more transparent about it. Just talking about it would have let me know how the others felt and had there been any issues of resentment we'd have been able to deal with them openly.

In addition to this financial disparity, I don't think the four of us were honest enough with each other on a deeper level. Because we got on so well we allowed our laddishness to mask our true feelings. We were all guilty of this to some extent. We would talk about what had to be done, but when it came to how we felt about it, why we were doing it and what it might mean for us to do it, well, we didn't really go there. That requires a level of openness and trust that we didn't achieve. If we had managed to, if we had all been honest and open, who knows, things may have been different.

We did manage to pull off one joint sponsorship deal, with a clothing company called No Fear, but even that backfired. They supplied T-shirts bearing an assortment of slogans that weren't totally 'us', but we thought they were quite funny and weren't shy about showing them off during training camps.

'Second place is the first loser.'

'Don't mess with the best, die like the rest.'

'It ain't the size of the dog in the fight, it's the size of the fight in the dog.'

As you can imagine, our popularity skyrocketed whenever we wore them.

At the World Championships in Finland in 1995 we came second, an improvement on the previous year and an indication that we were moving in the right direction, but it was still disappointing. We believed we were better than that. We might have been the only ones who did. During the competition heats all the crews had their photographs taken and they were pinned up at the team hotel. As we trudged back there after the medal ceremony, somewhat despondent at once more failing to hit the heights we had aimed for, I glanced at the photo of our four. Someone had scribbled across it, 'Second place is the first loser.'

Fair enough.

In September 1995 I sat the Assessment of Professional Competence (APC) exam – the professional qualifications for becoming a chartered surveyor – and failed. I was gutted at the time, but it proved to be a significant turning point in my life, because on the back of that disappointment I decided the profession might have to do without me for good. I had enjoyed working at Gerald Eve since graduating, and they agreed that from January 1996 they would grant me what amounted to a sabbatical until I returned from Atlanta, which meant that I could become a full-time athlete, making only rare appearances in the office and surviving on my sponsorship deals while I concentrated on building my physicality ahead of the Olympics.

It worked. By March I had broken the world record on the 2 km ergo, 5.44.1. That was pretty special as, for me, it was a demonstration of the fact that I was now the strongest guy in the British team, and for a short period of time, in the world. Confidence-wise, following the 1994 and 1995 Worlds, it was just what I needed.

Fast forward briefly to October 2010 when I produced an impressive personal best in a thirty-minute test on the rowing machine. Jürgen came up to me and shook my hand. This is a special moment, everyone who has trained with Jürgen knows he only does the handshake when you have set a PB or won something significant.

'Good, Greg.' A half-smile spread across his face. 'But just think how good you could have been.'

I managed that score in 2010 because, for the previous six months, I'd been training with a discipline I had never been able to muster before, save perhaps for those three months in 1996 as a full-time rower when I set the world record. It's an utterly pointless exercise, I know, but I can't help but wonder sometimes, if I'd been in a position to maintain that level of dedication earlier, what might have been . . .

In July 1996 we arrived in Atlanta with hope in our hearts rather than total belief. Winning had continued to elude us throughout the summer, but despite our results the boat felt good and we convinced ourselves we were peaking at exactly the right moment.

This time we were staying in the main village, which was fun, but very noisy and busy. The GB block was next to the water-polo pool, and as I lay in bed trying to get to sleep at around 10 p.m., facing an early start to get to training – I'll get to the transport, that's another issue altogether – I had to endure at least an hour's worth of a loud, grating American poolside commentator desperately trying to explain the rules and whip up some excitement from a clearly baffled crowd. It wasn't the end of the world, but it was a pain and introduced a gnawing sensation that maybe everything wasn't going quite as well as we'd hoped.

The transport situation only added to our concerns. The organizers had commandeered a fleet of classic American yellow school buses – yes *school* buses – as a shuttle service to and from the lake, into which they expected to cram 6-foot-5" rowers. If that wasn't bad enough, for security reasons they instructed the drivers to take a variety of routes. Confusion reigned. I can remember on more than one occasion speeding along the highway watching the exit we should have taken disappear into the distance behind us. The water-polo commentator had been annoying, but these buses were fast becoming a problem.

A few days before the heats a decision was taken to move us out of the village to a city called Gainesville, a ten-minute minibus drive from the lake. Team GB had arranged accommodation there for some non-accredited coaches plus the spare rowers, and by moving them out we were able to free up . . . six beds. These were allotted to the four of us, plus Redgrave and Pinsent.

I was incredibly grateful for the change, but could understand the frustrations it caused within the squad. Had there been any doubt in anyone's mind – and there wasn't – that we were first-class passengers and the rest of the team were in second-class, this confirmed it. Everyone had been complaining about the journey to the lake – the women's eight had even staged a sit-in one day, demanding that a proper bus be dispatched – but a remedy was found only for the six of us. Did any of this matter? Well, the rowing team won only two medals – Steve's boat and ours – which was less than expected. I don't think the two issues were unrelated.

As for the racing, our regatta went almost exactly as we had planned, save for a few hundred metres. We won our heat and then semi, giving us a centre lane in the final. On the day of the race we had just received our final words of encouragement and strategy from Steve Gunn when there was a surreal moment. Just as we were lifting our boat off the rack the British national anthem rang out celebrating Steve and Matthew's victory a few minutes earlier. I remember stopping and feeling a shiver, despite the humid Georgian summer. We turned away from the boat and looked each other in the eye. We all knew we wanted to hear that tune being played for us. I let my mind imagine that I was at Twickenham or Wembley, hearing the anthem before the match. It revved me up with increased confidence and optimism.

The wind had been quite changeable that day and we'd decided there was likely to be a slight tailwind, so we hardened our gearing, meaning we had a little less handle and more outboard oar, which is more difficult to pull through the water, but with the wind pushing us it should have increased our speed.

During the warm-up I had a slight sinking feeling. I could feel that the breeze had switched to a headwind and it was too late to do anything about the gearing. This wasn't a fatal error by any stretch, but it tugged at my focus, causing me to think about something other than rowing well and burying myself for the next six minutes.

'Are you ready?'

'Go!'

We got away OK, despite the gearing, and through halfway I knew I was in another special race. After 1000 m of rowing virtually nothing had changed, all six boats seemed to be more or less level across the course. We pushed on and looked to increase our pace. So did everyone else. With 500 m to go there were still six crews virtually in a line. It would come down to a 500 m sprint race and any one of us could win. I knew I needed to keep my head up, look straight down the boat and dig deeper than anyone else. We were good in the last 500 m – this was our time – the Hampton finish.

Everything seemed frantic. I could hear the calls from behind me. Without a cox there are no eloquent 'If not now's; it's just a series of 'Go's.

I looked across to my right and saw the Australians had a jump on us of about a length. When did that happen?

Twenty-five to go, I glance again. We're neck and neck.

Five to go. Last look. It's not our day.

I think we would have beaten the French if it had been a fight for the top of the podium, but as it was, when the Australians crossed the line and the hooter went, our heads dropped and the French charged, snatching silver on the line.

The Australian boat was the Oarsome Foursome, the defending champions, who had taken a year off in 1993, raced the coxed four in 1994 for a bit of fun, and in 1995 had done just enough to qualify for the Olympics at the World Championships. We hadn't thought they had enough to trouble us . . . until now.

Standing on the medal podium I felt I had lost a gold rather than won a bronze. Everything had been set up for us to win; we should have been quickest in the final 500 m, but we'd failed to deliver.

Why?

All the little things eventually added up. When you are exhausted in a race you switch to autopilot, all the training and muscle memory takes over and you survive on the raw emotion of wanting to win, which is what happened to Jonny and me in 1992. In Atlanta, however, the four of us hadn't clicked into the same programme. We were all doing something similar, but slightly different. When it was just Jonny and me, we sold our souls to each other for a common goal. That connection, that intangible, unbreakable bond, just wasn't there in our four.

Atlanta 1996 laid bare my mortality in the sport. It was a close race and previously I had always come out on the right side of close races. When I'd failed in 1994, I'd been able to justify it as a new event for me. Then I'd improved with the silver, but now, in the biggest race of all, I'd gone backwards again. There could be no easy explanations or justifications and it was tough to take. I needed time to reflect and deal with the changes that were fast coming my way.

With his legal career in the City taking off, Jonny decided to retire after Atlanta.

I wanted to continue rowing, but with a totally new challenge.

I needed a job.

I needed to grow up.

I wanted to get married.

FIVE

EGO, LOYALTY, IDENTITY

Proving I could do the toughest thing in rowing, something even Steve Redgrave hadn't done, and possibly showing my old rival Peter Haining that he was wrong, both played a part in the decision I took to go it alone in 1997.

Single sculling – one small boat, one rower, two oars – wasn't exactly an alien concept to me. It had formed a part of my regular training schedule throughout my rowing career, and while I would say that, for a rower, I was a decent sculler, I hadn't shown any particular aptitude for the discipline. Steady rather than spectacular would pretty much sum it up. In my eyes those hours spent sculling up and down the Thames in the depths of winter were a means to an end, to build fitness, stamina and strength. After the Atlanta Games, however, my focus began to shift. My bruised ego was in need of repair and perhaps, just perhaps, going out and demonstrating what I could do on my own might be the perfect cure.

I wanted to prove to myself, and to others, that I was a better athlete than the bronze medal that had accompanied me home from the US indicated. In saying that, in no way am I seeking to undermine the achievement of those who have come away from the Olympics with a medal other than gold. I recognize the huge honour that comes with being selected to represent your country. To become an Olympian is the dream of thousands of dedicated competitors, let alone to make it through to a final and stand at any level on the podium, but for me, because I'd won gold in Barcelona, anything else felt like losing.

After Atlanta my overriding sense was that I should have done better, that I had let myself down. At twenty-four years of age I was at the peak of my physical abilities and yet I hadn't delivered. I was determined to right that wrong, to set the record straight in my own mind. To satisfy my ego, if you like. The question was, how?

I had options. Immediately after winning his fourth gold in Atlanta with Matthew in the coxless pair, Steve Redgrave had famously granted permission for anyone to shoot him if they caught him back in a boat. Within a short period of time, however, he had changed his mind, and it became clear that British rowing intended to build a four around Steve to go for gold in Sydney in 2000. Matthew was a dead cert for one of the seats, and with Jonny having indicated that he wanted to focus on his career and take a backward step from competitive rowing, I was probably the natural choice for stroke side for Redgrave's boat.

I didn't even try for it. Why? Well, there were a number of reasons, all of which boiled down to three things: ego, loyalty and identity.

This new British boat, whatever the combination of individuals who sat in it, would always be seen as Redgrave's four, and I felt very strongly that I didn't want to be part of that. I wanted to be my own man, not merely another guy sitting next to Steve Redgrave, withering, as I saw it, in his shadow. If I was to prove myself, I had to do it on my own. The more I thought about it, the stronger that belief grew. That's not how I rationalized it at the time, of course. I wasn't willing to admit that ego played any part at all. Instead, I saw my decision as the only logical one to take.

I didn't doubt for a second that throughout the 1997 season Redgrave's four would be a very fast boat. The same would probably apply for 1998 but then, I reasoned, as the big push for Sydney got underway, they would begin to falter. Redgrave would be thirty-eight by the time the Millennium Games arrived; surely there was no way he could sustain a gold-medal level of performance?

While the four would surely be going backwards I, on the other hand, would be powering forwards. With two or three years' sculling experience behind me I was convinced I would arrive in Australia as the fastest single sculler in the world, and leave with a second gold medal around my neck. That would be the big story of the Sydney Games. Why shouldn't it happen? I held the record for 2 km on the rowing machine, a clear indication that I was the strongest physical rower in the world, so why shouldn't I be able to make the single scull go faster than anybody else?

The second consideration that turned me away from staking my claim on the four was that it would require a move to Leander, which I felt certain would upset Jonny. The 'healthy' rivalry between Molesey and Leander had developed a sharper edge over the years, certainly in Jonny's eyes. He had rowed there on a few occasions early in his career and had disliked the experience, returning to Molesey with tales of how he hadn't been treated as he would have hoped. If I had jumped ship, I think it would have been a kick in the teeth to my brother.

It wasn't as if I had any particular issue with Leander myself, even though my experience rowing in a hood with the Physiological Four hadn't been a good one, but it would have felt like I was dropping everything I'd stood for if I'd joined the club. I could have done it, and behaved as Jürgen wanted me to, but I couldn't change my identity. I could change what I did, but I wasn't going to change who I was. They wore pink, I wore black, and I was proud of that fact.

With these thoughts swirling around in my mind, luck once again played its part. In autumn 1996 I attended a function at one of the rowing clubs in Hammersmith. I have to admit I have forgotten everything about the evening except for one conversation, which had a massive impact on the next three and a half years of my life.

I was talking to an ex-Cambridge University rower called Jim Garman, who had tried to make a go of single sculling, but it hadn't quite worked out for him.

'So what's next, Greg? I understand Jonny has decided to take a back seat. Are you trying to find a new partner for the pair? Tim maybe, or has the glamour of Steve's four seduced you?'

'That all sounds good, but I fancy a go at the single. I reckon I can win the Diamonds at Henley and get a medal at the Worlds. That would be a pretty good start.' Winning a World Championship medal was something Steve Redgrave had failed to do during his time as a single sculler, a fact that I confess gave me an additional incentive.

At that point Jim looked me straight in the eye, as if he was assessing me. 'That's going to be tough, but if anyone can do it then you have everything you need. And I'll tell you what, if you win the Diamonds and even make the final of the Worlds, then you can look forward to celebrating with a bottle of champagne from me.'

Jim's words made a difference, even though I don't even really drink champagne. I liked him as a bloke and respected his opinion. He had experienced the pressures of being out on the water with no one but himself to rely on, and while he hadn't quite made it, he seemed to believe I could. I would probably have made the decision anyway, but there is no question that the following morning, after that conversation, my mind was made up.

Jim had one more scene to play in this unfolding drama. It was offstage and involved a telephone call to a New Zealand world champion rower called Tony Brook.

It would be a number of weeks before the consequences of that phone call hit home, and in the meantime I set about making it clear that Greg Searle was now all about single sculling. I didn't actually say anything to anyone, not in an official capacity anyway, deciding instead that actions, and sometimes the lack of them, speak louder than words. If I had swallowed my pride, packed away my loyalty and headed for Leander, I reckon I'd have had a good chance of sitting directly behind Steve Redgrave in his boat, the seat that James Cracknell ended up occupying so well. Instead, it felt right not to compete with James. I'd spent enough years getting in the way of someone I very much liked and respected, so I kept my head down and made a point of turning up at every GB session with my single strapped to the roof of my car and a determined look on my face.

Saturday morning, and I am enjoying a bowl of Shreddies after training when the telephone rings.

'Greg, Tony Brook here. You might not know me but I coach at KCS Wimbledon. I hope you don't mind me calling you like this, but I was given your number by Jim Garman. Jim and I were having a chat and he mentioned that you were thinking of going for the single. Is that correct?'

'Yeah, it is. I kind of think that if I don't do it now I never will, but Jim wasn't kidding. It's really tough.'

'Well, I think I might be able to help there. There's a guy you should speak to, take down his number. I've spoken to him already and he's expecting your call. You won't regret it, I promise. I've worked with him before in the New Zealand eight when we won the World Championship. He's a genius. Give him a call, Greg, see what happens. His name is Harry, Harry Mahon.'

Right there, my life got better.

I called Harry and we agreed to meet the next day at Molesey Boat Club, ostensibly for a light workout but really to size each other up. At the time Harry was undertaking an eclectic range of roles. At weekends he could often be found in Ely with the Cambridge University boat crew, during the week he might turn up at any one of the number of clubs and crews who wanted his services, or he would be at King's College School, Wimbledon, whose boat house he lived above, helping his friend Tony Brook by coaching the pupils.

I had never actually met Harry before, but I'd certainly heard of him. His skills were fast becoming legendary. While he would never have admitted this himself, claiming always only to be one of a team, many people regarded Harry as the primary reason Cambridge had dramatically turned their fortunes around in the Boat Race. He first showed up there in 1992, at which point Cambridge had lost sixteen out of the last seventeen confrontations with Oxford. In 1993 Cambridge came home victorious and from there they went on to maintain a winning streak that lasted right up until 2000. They regained their supremacy in 2001, after which Harry was no longer involved (Oxford won in 2002 and 2003).

My first encounter with him, on a misty winter's morning in late 1996, opened my eyes to a whole new world. Up until then, with my brother and under the guidance of Steve Gunn, I had adopted a very simple approach to rowing. I was a very strong, physical unit who mostly focused on what I could do to make the boat go faster, rarely thinking about what I did to slow it down or whether I was truly efficient. I didn't spend much time thinking about why I rowed like I did, I just got on with it. That was unacceptable to Harry. In his opinion rowing was as much about your state of mind and your approach to change as it was about having power in your arms and legs, and never is that more true than in a single scull.

This challenged some of what I believed in. In fact, it's true to say that my fourth motivation to go solo was to prove that there was no 'dark art' to single sculling. This is where Peter Haining crops up again. I mentioned earlier that Peter and I had a love-hate relationship. I found him good company and very entertaining, and he was probably this country's fastest sculler at the time, but it used to really wind me up when he went on about how sculling was an art form rather than a physical activity. Big, clumsy rowers could never master it, he would intimate. I guess in Peter's eyes I was one of those guys, and if so, I wanted to prove that sculling was well within my capabilities. I didn't believe there was anything special about it that wasn't present in any other form of rowing. If I am good in bigger boats, I reasoned, I will be good in a single. And I will enjoy proving it to Peter.

After a session or two with Harry, however, I began to suspect there was something in what Peter had said. What Harry made me realize, even on that very first morning, was that if I applied myself I could produce the same speed as I had previously but with a lot less effort. Simply put, up until I met Harry I'd achieved what I had by fitting into a mould of how rowing 'should' be done, all strength and power. Under his guidance I learned there was more to it than that, I just needed to free myself up and I could be so much better.

I can't over-state what a revelation this was, and it all started at that initial session together.

My first vision of Harry was of him clambering out of a little borrowed car. He was small, with rounded shoulders and wrapped up against the cold, as if he was about to trek across the Antarctic. He seemed reluctant to make eye contact, and when he introduced himself I could barely discern his New Zealand accent because he spoke into his beard.

'Greg,' he said after we had completed the minimal amount of pleasantries, 'I'll watch you for a bit, then let's see what we might do together.'

It took a while to realize that water was clearly his element. He spent a full ten minutes watching me make my way up the river without saying a word. I wondered what he thought as he gave nothing away. And then it started! Although he was still speaking softly there was total confidence in his voice, and I began to see the strong-willed visionary who knew how to get the best out of anyone who sat in a boat.

'Greg,' he mumbled into his megaphone, 'pretend you don't have those big strong arms. Pretend they're weedy little twigs like mine. Right, now don't bend them so early. Watch and then bend them when I bend mine.'

I looked across and he was imitating a rowing motion, which I began to follow, keeping in time with this odd little man chugging along behind me. After twenty strokes or so I looked down at my SpeedCoach (speedometer) and then at my heart rate monitor. Velocity up, beats per minute constant. With no extra effort the boat was going faster. Welcome to rowing Nirvana.

Harry brought so much more to my rowing than a shift in my arm movements. He created images that helped me make the changes he knew I was capable of. A favourite day of mine, which took me back to Jürgen's talk in 1991 involving eggs, came when we had watched an All Blacks game with Tony Brook. In the session that followed he used what was freshest in his mind.

'When you are looking to pick up the boat as the oar goes in the water, instead of banging it in as hard as you can, imagine you are holding a rugby ball and dropping it out of your hands and kicking it with your foot. Just relax and drop the oar into the water, like a ball, then drive with your feet, just as you want to kick it. Time it as though you're attempting a drop goal.'

This was soon followed by, 'Now leave your arms straight, but relaxed, like you're handing someone off in a match.'

Instead of hammering the boat along with the oars missing, splashing or banging into the water and then slamming my feet down in unison, Harry wanted me to concentrate on timing, feeling the boat move through the water rather than forcing it. As the mist cleared from my brain and I began to 'get' Harry, he pushed for continual assessment and reassessment to drive progress, calling out comments on each of my strokes as I sought to follow his lead. He used to ask me to score myself out of ten as I rowed along.

'What did you think of that stroke?'

'Six.'

'What did you think of that stroke?'

'Six.'

'How well did your legs connect there?'

'Seven.'

'And there?'

'Nine.'

'Good, good, good. Let's talk about that last one. What went right?'

This was revolutionary, and to an extent it still is. The traditional approach to coaching is to set the boats off over a distance, starting the stopwatch when they leave and stopping it when they come back again, with instructions bellowed from a bike or boat via a megaphone, or if that's not practical we use a walkie-talkie. However it's done, coaching tends to be instructional, whereas with Harry you were engaged in a dialogue.

Over the following months I soaked up as much as I possibly could. Previously I had been set in my ways, convinced I knew what was best for me because it had worked in the past. Almost overnight that changed. When I saw how Harry had helped me increase my speed without expending extra energy, lights went on in my brain. I began to properly understand what rowing was all about and how power was not the only available instrument to increase speed.

He also made me realize that winning is largely about taking responsibility. In both my 1992 and 1996 Olympic campaigns we had agreed a plan as to how we were going to race. It was set in stone, and regardless of what might happen, we were sticking to it. In comparison, Harry's race strategy would go something like this.

'Well, you can vary your stroke rate, you can surge, you can keep pace, you can change your technique, and we could try and agree when you are going to do all that, but in truth they are all just sitting in a bag at your feet. You have all these tricks, Greg, what you have to do is take out whatever one you need from the bag, whenever you need it, to beat the other guys. And once you have them beaten, stop taking the tricks out and row through to the finish.'

Understand what you've got, and use it to win. Simple and mind-blowing at the same time.

The whole secret of Harry was that he coached for the joy of coaching. There would be times when he and I would have been out on the water for an hour, both of us focusing intently, and suddenly he would say, 'Greg, keep at it. I'll pick you up in a bit.' And he would be off, chasing after some novice who had just passed us, someone who Harry might not have coached before, just so he could help them get more out of the sport. I remember him once pointing out a little kid who looked like he'd only just started rowing, but Harry could see something good in what he was doing.

'You see the way he slides forward, in time with the boat. You watch that and maybe you could do that as well as him.'

Harry provided me with more than merely a rowing education. Early in 1997 he received a call from the South African Rowing Association asking him to come over and help coach their team. He agreed, on the proviso that I join him.

'Greg,' he said to me when he suggested the trip, 'it will help with your rowing. Absorb everything you can while we are out there. From the South African team, but also from whatever is around you. The broader your range of experiences, the better an athlete you will become. Perhaps more confident, perhaps more open to new ideas, perhaps more inquisitive. Who knows what it will be, but it will be something.'

We stayed in a house on someone's property, surrounded by high fences and barbed wire. That in itself was an eye-opener to a boy from Chertsey in Surrey, but it was Harry's attitude that left the most lasting impression. The Association had provided us with a small run-around car and Harry loved to set off on expeditions, stopping in areas of Johannesburg where we had been advised not to go. Harry took no notice. It wasn't that he was reckless, he understood there were dangerous neighbourhoods in the city and we steered clear of them but, according to Harry, just because certain sections of the populace might feel uncomfortable venturing too far afield was no reason for us not to explore.

So we drove around, stopping to buy biltong along the way, striking up conversations, learning how people lived and generally experiencing a new country. He was introducing me to a sense of adventure, showing me a glimpse of what was possible if you chose to make it happen. It was a growing-up experience, and one that I welcomed, along with all the others I'd been embracing since my return from Atlanta.

After the Barcelona Games I had been building my career as a chartered surveyor, but when I failed the APC exam my desire to pursue that occupation started to fade. Since January 1996, thanks to Gerald Eve's flexibility, I had committed myself to full-time training as much as possible while living off sponsorship money, but that was never going to be a realistic option in non-Olympic years. The bald facts were that I needed to find a job. One option was to take the APC again, and although I returned to Gerald Eve after Atlanta, I sensed it wouldn't be long term. Soon afterwards I shared a taxi home with Adrian Moorhouse and my head was turned.

I had stayed in irregular contact with Adrian when we came across each other from time to time at charity sporting functions, and it was on the way home from one such occasion that he explained about Lane4, a business he had started with a couple of other guys, Graham Jones and Adrian Hutchinson. Demand for their business, which takes lessons from sport and applies them to a business situation, was growing fast, and they were looking to expand out of his living room and into office space. Adrian thought I might be a good fit because I understood performance at the highest level and I also knew what it meant to have a full-time job.

I continued working at Gerald Eve until the end of 1996, but once I'd met Adrian and Hutch (as the other Adrian was known) I knew Lane4 was where my heart lay. Their mission statement, taken from the swimming pool at University of California, Berkeley, where Adrian Moorhouse used to train, had struck a chord with me. 'The aim of this establishment is to create an environment where champions are inevitable.' That phrase took me back to Hampton school, and what Steve Gunn and his colleagues had created there: the possibility of turning seemingly average boys into winners. It was an approach that resonated strongly with me from those early days, and here was a company applying the same mentality in the commercial world.

I was also delighted with a culture change that required me to get to the office on 19 December 1996 to sign my contract before the two Adrians headed off skiing in Canada, not to return until my first day on 1 January 1997. Adrian was brilliant. As an Olympic athlete himself he understood my needs and was willing to accommodate them as much as was practically possible. I had explained my ambition to represent Britain as a single sculler in Sydney, outlining what that would entail in terms of time commitments, and he had agreed to take me on part-time. Not only was I being paid as much as I had been at Gerald Eve, I was working for a company that I believed would help with my rowing. It was like Harry said, 'If you open yourself to new experiences you're bound to find something that will make you stronger.' At Lane4 that proved to be true in abundance.

I joined as a performance consultant and learned on the job from the people I worked with. They taught me how to wear a second hat whenever I was participating in a client workshop: 'Don't view yourself as just an athlete, see yourself as a coach, too. As an athlete you will appear to be very heroic, but it won't be very useful. It's great to tell your story, maybe even entertain the people who are sitting in front of you, but there has to be meaning behind what you say and it has to relate to other people. Ultimately, we make sure what we are doing is all about them, not you! We want to be sure that if they work with you on a Friday afternoon then they will want to do something different when they show up at the office on Monday morning.'

It was exciting to hear, and even more exhilarating to put into practice. I placed myself in the position of a coach, which entailed getting over my own ego and focusing on other people. I quickly learned to do more listening and less talking.

Initially I was worried that our clients knew a lot more about 'business' than I did, but I soon came to realize this was irrelevant. Just as Jürgen or Steve Gunn aren't great rowers and Adrian's coach couldn't swim, they weren't employing me to tell them how to do what they already did. They were interested in my ability to help them interact with people, challenge effectively, set goals, give feedback, believe in themselves and their people and do all the other things that came more naturally to me.

I wanted to help encourage the clients I worked with to engage in the honest conversations you have in a sports team. Over the years I've seen the positive power of that honesty with Jonny and Garry, and the flipside with the four that took bronze in Atlanta. If I could use my experiences to demonstrate how important it is to open up, then I felt I could make a significant contribution. In a crew, for instance, we look to uncover what drives each person to train hard when the only thing they have to look forward to is a punishing and repetitive training session. In rowing, like many sports, the reason is often very clear: a love of the activity and a passion to succeed.

It's what is known as intrinsic motivation and every one of us has it for something – family, church, a hobby – and within that chosen environment we stretch ourselves. When it comes to work, however, intrinsic motivation is often absent, leaving us to operate at a totally different level. We turn up every day purely to receive a wage, not because we love what we are doing. In my role as a performance coach at Lane4, what I set out to do was release the enthusiasm people have for those things outside of the office and replicate it in the workplace.

Having been a bit rudderless in my career for some time, suddenly I was in an environment where I could make a difference, and where I felt I belonged. To me it was concrete evidence that I could take control of my life in a positive manner, and I carried that knowledge with me into my single-seater boat every morning before work.

I had to because, despite the wonders that Harry was showing me, he wasn't there by my side at every session when the hard yards had to be made. He might be able to cast a spell over a boat, but it would be wasted if the person he was coaching didn't have the stamina and strength to deliver when it mattered.

During the week my training took place very early, before work, either at Molesey or in Hammersmith, both of which were convenient to Wimbledon, where I was living at the time. Lane4, however, was situated out of town, towards Marlow and, ironically, close to Leander. Logistically life would have been a lot easier had I waved my hands in the air when I'd had the chance and jumped in alongside Steve and Matthew, but I hadn't, and in a strange way the hassle of all that toing and froing along the M4 acted as additional motivation: this is hard, it's tiring and I'm going to make it pay off.

Training in the single provided me with one major plus – the opportunity to be out there with whoever I liked. I became close friends with two very good guys who helped me enormously on mornings when the cold, rain, sleet and snow would make even a saint climb back into bed and hit the snooze button. Will Castle and Bob Tucker were their names and we were first introduced through an Australian friend of mine called Dodge, who had failed to make the Australian team for Atlanta and had decided to stay on in the UK.

Dodge knew Will and Bob through rowing; they were keen amateurs with big jobs in the City, and when he heard that I was slogging it out on my own he suggested the three of us get together for early morning sessions. For the times when Harry wasn't around, having Will and Bob there was a godsend, because it not only added a level of camaraderie, it also introduced a degree of competitiveness. We would race each other, pair versus single, and it was a good challenge to try and keep up, undoubtedly better than I would have maintained had I been entirely on my own. I like having people around me, which begs the question: what on earth was I doing in a single scull?

There was one final element that added to the overriding sense of independence from the GB team that I enjoyed post-Atlanta. One of the more senior Molesey club members called Jonathan Steel helped me out by speaking to some of the more commercially successful members of the club. Consequently Neil Richardson agreed to buy me a brand-new Empacher sculling boat, which meant I had the best equipment going, and then Rob

Garnsworthy came forward with an even better proposition: 'Greg, my company would like to sponsor you.'

They had cooked up a clever concept and, needless to say, I jumped at the chance. Rob was managing director of an Australian financial services firm called Colonial, and their idea was that on the road to Sydney an Australian company was going to back some Poms, even if the Poms didn't back themselves. From their point of view it was also a happy coincidence that I had been beaten by the Oarsome Foursome in Atlanta, because it made for even more of an interesting story.

Colonial's vision went beyond just me; they were keen to sponsor a team of four aspiring British talents, and once I was on board Rob asked me for suggestions. I put forward sailor Ben Ainslie, athlete Denise Lewis and swimmer Paul Palmer. I didn't know any of them personally, but with the connections I was making at Lane4 I was able to track each of them down and make a call. It felt pretty good to contact a fellow athlete and put them in the way of some money, and if I say so myself, I'm not a bad judge of potential. Out of the four of us, two won gold and only one failed to win a medal.

The Colonial sponsorship was critically important because, combined with my Lane4 salary, I now had a degree of financial security that would allow me to do the things I felt necessary to improve my performance. Money worries, as everybody knows, can be incredibly distracting and overwhelming, especially if you know that significant expenditure is looming on the horizon.

That was certainly the case for me in 1997, as I had a wedding planned for October.

I met Jenny through her work at SportsAid, or the SportsAid Foundation (SAF) as it was then called. This was in 1992 when the foundation offered to support Jonny and me with a grant of £5,000, which was the only funding we received in the run-up to Barcelona. I suspect we may have been regarded by many as a couple of no-hopers, so the money from the SAF was very gratefully received and contributed significantly, I believe, to our success at the Olympics.

On our return, of course, the world had changed and we were invited to all sorts of interesting events. Jonny and I were happy to attend many of these functions, but we also made it clear that we were very much attached to the SAF and prioritized events in which they were involved.

Prior to Barcelona I had run into Jenny through the SAF and we had got on very well. She was gorgeous, funny, intelligent, had a keen interest in sport, and, I hoped, an equally keen interest in this particular sportsman. On my return from Barcelona I found a range of somewhat flimsy pretexts to call her at the SAF as often as I thought I could get away with without appearing like a besotted fool. You would have to ask Jenny whether I got away with that or not. In time, the phone calls nudged towards flirty banter, until eventually the key moment came at a black-tie dinner the SAF had organized in early 1993, to which Jonny, Garry, Adrian Moorhouse and myself, amongst a host of other sports people, had been invited.

While we were chatting over drinks prior to the event kicking off, we studied the table plan. Jonny was at a table full of accountants who supported the charity, Adrian was with the IT firm that provided technical backup for the SAF and I was sitting next to one Jenny Hickman and her friend Mick Skinner, the rugby player, who was married to one of Jenny's best friends. Basically, it was a table full of Jenny's mates. It was her do and she could arrange the seating as she saw fit. Needless to say I admired her organizational skills. Jonny and Adrian were less impressed, I suspect.

Emboldened by Mick the Munch's words of encouragement – when he leans over and drapes his massive arms around your shoulders and swings his mullet dangerously close to your face he's a hard man to ignore – plus a gallon or two of red wine, I asked Jenny out on a date. Much to my delight, she agreed.

Soon after that I had to disappear off to Germany for a regatta, and I told Jenny I would call her after the event, which I duly did on the Sunday.

'Oh hi, Greg. When did you get back?' She was surprised by my answer. I think she must have been expecting me to play it cool and say I'd been home at least a few hours, or maybe even that I'd arrived back the previous day.

'About twenty minutes ago.'

Normally I think Jenny would have been put off by this level of keenness, but fortunately when it came to me she wasn't. Perhaps it had something to do with her mum. They'd been watching telly one evening after the Barcelona Games and when *A Question of Sport* came on, with me as one of the guests, her mum commented, 'You ought to meet a nice rower like that boy there.' Jenny must have been paying attention because she agreed to a second date with me, and we've been together ever since.

Our timing could not have been better. That summer Jenny watched on television as I took World Championship gold in the coxed pair. I love the fact that she witnessed that achievement. Hopefully next time I stand tall on a podium it will be when she's there in person.

Jenny and I rented a flat in Fulham for a couple of years near my friends Dodge, Will, Bob and lots of other rowing and non-rowing friends. Then, in 1996, we bought a two-up two-down terraced house in Wimbledon, and after the Olympics I popped the question. I had intended doing so on numerous occasions throughout the year, but with everything that was going on at the time I never quite managed to find the perfect moment. With Atlanta behind me, however, I resolved to create my own future rather than allow circumstances to dictate how my life played out. Asking Jenny to marry me, finding Lane4, securing sponsorship and setting my sights on becoming the world's fastest rower was all part of growing up, and it felt really good.

Before the wedding, however, there was the small matter of establishing my credentials as a single sculler. I had a long way to go if I was going to emerge from Sydney on top of the world.

In May I flew out to Piediluco in Italy for my first real test as a single. Throughout the year, under Harry's tutelage, I had been steadily improving, winning GB sculling trials and establishing myself as a genuine contender in the discipline. But only a contender. Emerging as the front-runner in the British team was all well and good, but I was yet to test myself at international level. Piediluco changed all that.

I was extremely relaxed throughout the regatta. None of the GB team was there, but Jenny and Harry were with me, plus Will, Bob and Bob's wife, all of whom came out on the Friday after they'd finished work. We were all travelling under our own steam, and for us the weekend was an opportunity to have fun. Such a group would be unthinkable nowadays. Perhaps somewhat paradoxically I am well regarded in Italy because of the 1992 victory over Carmine and Giuseppe Abbagnale. The Italians love their rowing and rather than adopting a narrow-minded, if-we-don't-win-then-we're-not-interested approach, they appreciate the effort and commitment *all* competitors put into the sport. The fact that Jonny, Garry and myself overcame the great Abbagnales in dramatic fashion is something that's applauded by rowing enthusiasts in Italy, which became very clear to Will and Bob on the day they arrived.

They were having difficulties explaining who they were at our hotel reception, and after much good-natured miscommunication Bob eventually mentioned my name. At that, the receptionist's arms were flung wide open and Will and Bob were welcomed with broad smiles as 'Amici Searle'. I can tell you, I got a lot of mileage out of that over the two days we were there, demanding to be waited on hand and foot by *Amici* Searle!

There's no doubt that it's easier to perform when I'm comfortable in myself and when I feel I have my own identity. This was something else Harry really believed in, and which was so different to what I'd experienced before. I was making my debut on the world stage in an event in which I had never competed, and on the Saturday I came in third behind two of the world's top scullers, Ali Ibrahim from Egypt and Iztok Cop from Slovenia, who was one of the pair in Barcelona that Jonny and I had 'raced' during our training session. On the Sunday I went one better, second behind Ali and ahead of Italy's Giovanni Calabrese, who went on to win bronze in the double scull in Sydney. This was a world-class field and I was not out of my depth. I was upbeat, feeling as though I was taking positive steps forward.

The feeling didn't last. On the banks of the Thames early one morning after my return from Italy harsh reality gate-crashed my buoyant mood in devastating fashion. Harry and I were about to set off for a session when he gently touched my arm just as I was about to climb into my boat.

'Greg, I've had a bit of bad news. I think you'd better know that I've been diagnosed with cancer. It's been playing havoc with my guts for a bit, but now it's in my liver too. They say it's not too good long term, but best not listen to that too much. We've started something good here and I'm sure I'll be there in Sydney. Now let's get going – we'll work on your leg drive today, I think.'

That was Harry through and through, incredibly matter-of-fact about a situation that would have floored anybody else. I couldn't quite believe we were going to go out and have a normal session after this news. The tears were welling in my eyes as we spoke, but he wouldn't entertain the notion of cancelling. In Harry's world, if a problem arose the only possible response was to deal with it and move on. That's how he was in his coaching and his life. It wasn't that he was ignoring the cancer, instead he chose to accept its existence and focus on defeating it through a combination of diet, exercise, alternative therapies and traditional medical care. Whatever was available he would investigate and make use of it.

The World Championships that year were due to take place in France at the beginning of September, and in the run-up Harry and I had targeted Henley, and what is known as the Diamond Sculls, as my next big race.

Harry not only changed my rowing technique, he also changed my whole attitude to racing. From the age of sixteen or seventeen I had been immersed in the Steve Gunn tradition of pre-race preparation. Just before we went out Steve would address his crew, revving us up about how tough it was going to be, how we would have to put ourselves on the line if we were to succeed, how we would have to overcome pain and exhaustion to defeat the other boats and how guts and courage led to victory, so that by the time we stepped into our boat our hearts were thumping and our eyes were popping, brimming with tears.

That became my way to race, that was *the* way to race to ensure I was always up for the challenge. It was the same with Jonny. Throughout our career together, on race days we would be very insular, staring at walls, letting 'the rage' fill our veins, building ourselves up to a crescendo. I didn't think there was any other way to behave . . . until Harry came along.

At Henley, Harry had spoken to the stewards and made a special request that my heats would be around ten o'clock in the morning, because he was undergoing chemotherapy and had to be able to make his hospital appointments later in the day. This was a major advantage to me because the temperature would be cooler and the river less busy, which suits a single sculler. The wash from other boats has a far greater impact on the single, for obvious weight reasons, than it does on a larger boat. Under these conditions I knew I should have a fairly safe passage into the semi-final.

On the morning of my first heat, I was looking forward to

Harry's pep talk. How was he going to motivate me? How was he going to start my blood pumping and get my juices flowing? Not as I had expected.

'So Greg, on a scale of one to ten, how "up" are you for this race?'

I was ready for that question, I knew the correct answer. 'Probably about seven, Harry, but I reckon I can get up to nine by the time I reach the start.'

'Right. Well I reckon you're going to beat this guy fairly easily. Why don't you try getting to about three before the start. That should do it.'

Once again Harry was spot on. He knew that ninety-nine times out of a hundred I was going to win this race, so I should go into it relaxed and prepared, reserving my energy for the stiffer challenges ahead. Usain Bolt over Linford Christie if you like.

'The more relaxed you are,' Harry told me, 'the better you will row. Enjoy the atmosphere, feed off the spectators, be aware of the conditions and how the water feels, that way your mind will be open to pulling the tricks out of your bag when you need them.'

What can I say? I have rarely been given better advice, and of course it worked. Henley was a triumph. In the semi-final I defeated the American Jamie Koven, who was one of his country's most accomplished oarsmen, World Championship gold medallist in the eight in 1994 and favourite on the day. He was also a friend of Will's, which made things a little weird, as Will was torn about who to support. It was a close race and I required pretty much all of Harry's tricks to see me over the line, with Jamie upping his stroke rate considerably in the second half in order to fight back after I had taken an early lead. With both of us pushing so hard, I eventually won by just over a length, and it was no surprise to learn later that I had been twenty seconds faster than the winner of the other semi, Peter Haining.

When I had first contemplated single sculling this was one of the moments I had imagined, warrior versus magician. Now, however, it was more akin to sorcerer versus sorcerer, with Harry having opened up his spell book and allowed me a peek inside.

The winner was never really in doubt after the first minute as we reached the top of the island. To be fair to Peter he was perhaps past his best and hadn't trained with the same desire as me; he had probably done well to make the final at all. By around halfway I was five lengths clear, eventually winning, as they say at Henley, by a verdict of 'easily'. It was a sweet moment.

I chose not to go to altitude training in Silvretta that year with the British squad because I didn't have to and I was following my own path. I still had a huge amount of ground to make up if I was going to make an impression in the World Championships, and I wanted lots of coaching from Harry in his boat alongside me. So instead we drove to Lucerne in Switzerland, where we joined the Swiss team, which Harry had previously coached.

The camp there went well, my boat was moving fast, and I benefited enormously from having Harry's undivided attention. Well, almost undivided. From time to time he would disappear into his room to engage in very personal telephone conversations with a faith healer in Nottingham. Harry had visited this person on a number of occasions and was suitably convinced that the laying on of hands was helping his cancer, so they devised a method whereby the same effect could be produced over the phone. I realize this sounds crazy, and under other circumstances I would probably have dismissed it out of hand, but I saw the benefit that Harry derived from those calls, and in my opinion that's all that matters.

From Switzerland, Harry and I drove over to Varese in Italy to meet up with the rest of the GB team. Jenny then flew out and I took a few days off, during which we went to Verona. Once again this would never happen nowadays. I enjoyed the final warm-weather camp with everyone else before moving on to Lac d'Aiguebelette in France for the Worlds where, on 7 September, I sat on the lake in lane two, happy in the knowledge that I had a bottle of champagne waiting for me on my return home. I had made my target for the year: I was in the final of the World Championships. Now I wanted more.

It will come as no surprise by now to learn that a big start was not one of the tricks in my bag, and as I got into my race pace I was comfortably at the back of the field. But I knew what to do: keep it moving and stay loose. At 1000 m I was four and a half seconds behind Ali Ibrahim. Ali had a reputation for going off strong, but fading in the second half of races, and his cause wasn't helped by the fact that he struggled to steer his boat, so I wasn't surprised that he was the first one I clawed back at around the 1500 m mark. I couldn't see it, but I was almost five seconds behind new-leader Jamie Koven, which was a surprise as I'd beaten him at Henley and didn't expect him to be so strong. With 500 m to go Jamie made a decisive strike for home, stealing a stretch of clear water from the 1994 world champion André Willms of Germany and the multiple silver medalist Václav Chalupa of the Czech Republic, while ahead of me was the 1995 champion Iztok Cop. This was a class field. If I was going to come away with anything, I had to do something special.

It was time to pull one of my oldest tricks out of the bag, the Hampton finish.

With twenty strokes to go I glance right. Koven's next to me in lane three but I can see from the dying waves that he's too far out to be caught. Chalupa is fading fast. Risk another glance – two lanes over Cop is surging, a length ahead, but there's panic in his eyes. Drop kick that ball Greg and you might have him. Feel the boat surge under you.

Ten to go. Cop's only half a length up. Pull the back through, Greg, like Harry taught you. Accelerate, strong, long. Drive.

Eight. I'm level with Cop, as we had been during our training dual in Barcelona. On the far side Willms has three-quarters of a length.

Five. I have Cop. Willms has half a length and he's going crazy.

Three. Willms a quarter.

Two. A few feet.

One. Eyeballs.

Line. Willms by not much more than the bow ball at the end of his boat.

Disappointing, but honestly I didn't care. Bronze in my first World Championships as a sculler. Pretty amazing. Thank you, Harry. This is just the beginning.

If only.

It is 18 October 1997 and everyone is gathered in a room at the Trafalgar Tavern in Greenwich. Garry, most of the guys from the 1991 eight, Harry, Martin Cross, Will, Bob, Gavin Stewart, a crowd from Molesey, Obby, James Cracknell, they are all inside. I'm standing outside with my best man, Jonny.

'It's time, Greg,' he tells me. 'Time to get married. Let's go.'

In the function room the seats have been lined up to create an aisle. As I walk down to take my place at the front, I laugh, joke and shake hands with the people who mean most to me in life. This truly is the happiest day.

I sit down to await Jenny's entrance. The pianist turns in his seat, looks at me and nods. He's a family friend, giving me last-minute encouragement. That's good of him. I wink in response. He turns back, flexes his fingers and begins to play the bridal chorus.

Wait, did he think my wink . . .

Oh shit, I can't stop him now.

He plays it through once and starts again. The hush that had originally fallen over the congregation is lifting. Murmurs begin. This is unusual.

Clatter.

The door. Here she comes, the woman I am going to spend the rest of my life with. Along with everybody else in the room, except our pianist, I turn to catch my first glimpse of her dress and to bask in the radiance of her dazzling smile.

My mate Donkey is standing there in a pale blue suit I know he bought in Thailand; it's about as far from Savile Row as you can get.

'Sorry, everyone. Am I late?'

The room erupts into laughter.

When the door opens for real, Jenny is standing there looking stunningly beautiful. She receives a rapturous round of applause. It's perfect, just as we had wanted, a joyous occasion, fun and laughter, with friends and family to share it.

We honeymooned on one of the tiny Gili islands off the north-west tip of Lombok, near Bali. It was idyllic and wonderful, but if Jenny had any doubts about my bloody-mindedness and insistence on doing things my way (she didn't) they would have been washed away on those picture-postcard beaches.

'Greg, I really don't think you should drink the tap water here. There are bottles in the fridge.'

'Jenny, for goodness' sake. I've drunk water all over the world and I've never had a problem.'

I downed two pints and spent the second and third days of our holiday no further than a quick sprint away from a toilet.

Having recovered fully, I discovered I could run all the way round the island in about an hour, which I did every morning while Jenny relaxed reading her book. Towards the end of the honeymoon, however, this was no longer sufficient to feed my need to achieve something.

'Come on, Jenny, let's learn to scuba dive. It will be fun.'

'But I was just about to order a cocktail . . .'

We spent the next two days in an airless room being taught the basics. I loved every minute of it, seeing it as a new challenge to be overcome. Jenny was petrified.

Once she got past that initial reluctance to trust her equipment, however, she took to the sport like, well, like a duck to water. Along with horse riding, scuba diving is one of the activities that Jenny and I enjoy together, and which she is much better at than me. Part of the reason for that is that I am unable to stay under-water for as long as she does. My oxygen tank seems to empty significantly faster than anybody else's. I guess that's one of the downsides of having a pair of sportsmen's lungs.

On our return from honeymoon I went out on the river for the first time in almost a month. It was an easy session, allowing time to reflect on the year I had just experienced. Save for Harry's devastating news about his illness, things had gone well. I was making my way in the world with Jenny by my side, and a World Championship medal to add to my collection.

'This is just the beginning,' I had thought as I crossed the line in France. I was right. It was the beginning of the end.

Harry's illness began to take a stronger grip in 1998 and that, plus the fact that he was coaching more rowers, meant he was unable to focus as much attention on me as before. I encouraged him to do what he had to do to beat the cancer, and I admired his determination to continue helping as many people as he was able to, but from a personal point of view there is no doubt that my sculling suffered as a result. With so much going on in Harry's life, it was impossible for him to be out following me in his motorboat, offering immediate feedback and engaging in dialogue, as often as he used to. Instead he would sometimes send me out on my own and we'd discuss the session on my return. In those circumstances

I found it hard to motivate myself. I am by nature a gregarious man, and the loneliness of the 2 km rower was beginning to have an impact.

The intensity of my gym sessions began to slip as I convinced myself that, with Harry's magic dust having been sprinkled on me, I no longer required the power I'd once had. I would do a little bit of this and a little bit of that, with no real focus or target in mind, and certainly not many weights and few long, tough ergo sessions. It even got to the point that on occasion, after a morning on the water, I'd go home, dig out Jenny's Elle Macpherson *The Body Workout* video and convince myself that an hour spent following that in the living room amounted to a full training session.

The result was I became less strong, and without Harry to guide me, coupled with the distractions of building a career and married life, my results suffered. At Henley I lost in the final of the Diamond Sculls to Jamie Koven and in the World Championships in Cologne I crossed the line in fifth place.

Rolling into 1999 I was still the fastest sculler in Britain, but my lack of focus in the gym throughout the previous year was beginning to take its toll. For the first time in my life, and brought on by the fact that I was simply less robust, I suffered from back problems, to the extent that I was in so much pain I struggled to put my shoes on.

A number of guys in the British squad recommended that I visit a particular physiotherapist in whom they put great faith. She was very authoritarian in style, insisting that if I followed her regime to the letter she would cure my problem. She had identified that my body was out of balance – a strong back with limited stomach muscles, powerful quads but no hamstrings – and recommended I concentrate on building up the areas where I was weakest. I bought into it entirely – you had to if you were going to work with her!

Imagine Jenny and I are at a friend's house for dinner and I still have a round of exercises to complete. I unbuckle my belt, unbutton my trousers, pull them down to my ankles to give myself freedom of movement, lie on the floor and complete my stomach crunches. It's not everyone's perfect start to an evening out, but I was determined to do whatever was necessary to fix my back, which was precisely what the course of exercises I had been prescribed were designed to achieve. Unfortunately, what they were not good for was maintaining the physique of an elite rower.

I was losing strength daily in my arms and legs as I diligently pursued my new regime. This is not a criticism of the physiotherapist who was helping me; I'm pretty sure I wouldn't be contemplating the London 2012 Olympics as anything other than a spectator without her, but in the short term, coupled with the fact that Harry and I were now engaged in very little hands-on coaching, throughout 1999 the impact on my career was disastrous.

It was Jürgen who rescued me. I've always been grateful for that, particularly after I turned my back on him and Redgrave's four by choosing to go solo in 1996. With Harry's personal focus on his treatment and with his professional attention pulled in other directions by the Great Britain set-up, Jürgen stepped in and invited me to join the squad at altitude, where he made me one of his group and prepared me for the World Championships in Canada.

By then, however, I was a lost cause. I was as low as I have ever been, both physically and mentally, which was all too obvious from my fourteenth-place finish in the Worlds, a result that meant I failed to qualify for the following year's Olympic Games.

Given that I had set myself a vision after the World Championship in 1997 to move from bronze to silver and gold by 1999, with gold again in 2000, as Redgrave and his crew undoubtedly slid in the other direction, I found the reality hard to cope with.

How could I find a way back in time for Sydney?

SIX

THE EMPTY PLACE

'Here they come, the gold medallists.'

The comment came from the Australian pair James Tompkins and Matthew Long as Ed Coode and I walked past, our rowing vests still wet after slapping the water moments earlier in celebration at having beaten our rivals.

Unfortunately, this was only the first heat of the Sydney Olympics and Tompkins and Long weren't the same pair who had dominated the 1999 World Championships. In the course of the preceding year Drew Ginn, who had partnered Tompkins in that majestic boat, had suffered a serious back injury and been replaced by Matthew, throwing the race for Olympic supremacy in 2000 wide open. The gold medal was still a long way off, not that you would have known it from my over-exuberance out on the water. Over-anxious and insecure? You didn't need to be a trained psychiatrist to read the signs.

A few days later in the semi-final we seemed to be controlling the race comfortably up until the 1500 m mark, a length ahead of the French. With both boats in strong positions to qualify that was surely the most likely finishing positions. Until the French decided they had something to prove.

We responded to their burst of speed and held them for the

following 250 m, at which point they cranked it up again, drawing level. 'Let them have it,' I called to Ed. 'It doesn't matter.' Conserving energy was more important.

We allowed them through to qualify as winners, with us safe in second place. It didn't seem to be a particularly momentous moment in my life. We knew we had the ability to surge past them if circumstances later demanded. And if we had lulled them into a false sense of superiority, so much the better.

In the final, lining up in lane two, with the Americans on our right and the Australian, French, Yugoslavian and South African boats to our left, Ed and I were both confident. We had been rowing well together, keeping something in reserve, with a game plan that we felt was strong enough, given our results in the heats and semi-final, to take the gold medal.

We got away well and at the halfway point we were awesome. For the amount of effort being expended we were going incredibly fast and I began to feel invincible. We are not just going to win, I thought, we are going to destroy the field. The best the world had to offer was strewn behind us in clear view; we were a full length up on the Yugoslavians, with the French and Americans a further half length behind. In the knowledge that we possessed a devastating finish, I almost smiled through the pain of racing. Against all the odds, I was on the verge of winning Olympic gold again. It had been a difficult year, with neither Ed nor I really wanting to be in the pair, but it was about to end in spectacular style.

We hold our position for a further 250 m, and then it all falls apart. The French come past us at an extraordinary pace, which we are unable to match. In perhaps three blinks of an eye, it is clear we are no longer set for victory by a country mile and instead are in a battle. Keep your nerve, Greg, we can respond. In the final quarter we are too strong. Let them make their move. They've panicked and gone too early. Stick to the plan and we'll haul them back.

With 500 m to go we look to pick up speed as prearranged, to move the boat through the water at blistering pace. But we have run out of gears. What the fuck is happening?

We are struggling to make any impression on the race. What had once been the glistening water of the Sydney International Regatta Centre has been transformed into treacle, grabbing at our oars and sapping our strength.

The French are pulling away as the remainder of the field begins to swallow us up with the line approaching. Barely five strokes to go and it's clear we are in a three-way bust-up with the Australians and Americans for silver and bronze. Crossing the line, it's impossible to tell where we have come. In agony, we sit waiting for the results of the photo finish. When they eventually make the announcement it is as I feared. Fourth, the empty place. There is no slapping of the water this time. Less than a second separates the three boats. We've missed silver by a foot, bronze by a couple of inches and the podium by a million miles.

At the halfway point I could feel the weight of the gold medal around my neck; three minutes later I was slumped forward in my boat in despair.

'Here they come, the gold medallists.' Had there been a hint of mockery in that statement six days earlier? Had the Australians sensed that my over-the-top celebration at winning the heat betrayed relief rather than displayed confidence? Had they seen through the veneer of our performance to the soft underbelly that lay beneath? Or were they merely enjoying a gentle moment of gamesmanship, winding us up just for the hell of it? It doesn't matter now because the result speaks for itself.

'Here they come, the gold medallists.' There they go, the losers.

Immediately after the race Ed and I are interviewed by the BBC's man-on-the-spot, Steve Rider. It's hideous. I am extremely upset at the result and I suspect it's a very awkward moment for

Steve Rider too. I'm sure when the BBC were planning this they had anticipated grabbing Ed and me for a celebratory few words before we disappeared off to receive a medal of some sort, followed by a montage of Steve Redgrave's greatest hits, then cutting to the build-up to Steve's quest for a fifth gold. Now, however, instead of basking in a wonderful few minutes of the glory of British rowing they are suddenly faced with time to fill and Ed and I are the only available option.

I am not proud of the race that day as a piece of rowing, but I am quite proud of how I handled myself in that interview. My overwhelming sensation was one of numbness, as if all the vitality and energy that had been sparking from my fingertips as we sat at the start line had been left to shrivel in the Australian sun. I was crushed, and frankly the last place in the world I wanted to be was in front of that BBC camera, and yet there I was, being asked to explain how I felt the gold medal had been won and lost. Very politely and professionally, Steve Rider was basically asking whether we'd screwed up our race strategy. I replied with complete frankness.

'We tried to do our race and we did it as well as we could. They were just quicker. I'm devastated really. I thought we were quick enough to win this race and I've never imagined any situation of us not winning. It's a shock more than anything else.

'As much as we could have done it felt like we were doing everything right. Yeah, [sigh], it felt like we were doing everything right, but then they came through didn't they? But we rowed our best race and we couldn't do more than that.

'There's nothing more I can say than that, really. That's racing, isn't it? There's one big day that matters, one six-minute race that matters. We might have won it on another day, but we didn't. We haven't blown it, because that makes it sound like we threw it away. We just didn't win it.'

Everything I said in the interview is absolutely true. During the race I don't think there was one single moment when we didn't act as planned, and I don't believe we could have raced any differently. If I look at our splits they were pretty much what we said we were going to do, fast, a bit slower, pretty similar, nearly as fast as at the start. That was our aim, and that is what we achieved.

If I look at the French splits however, they went slow, slow, ridiculously quick, pretty quick. Where did that come from? As for the Australians and the Americans, we led them for most of the race until the final burst when, inexplicably, they were just quicker than us.

On reflection, I can see that we had underestimated the quality of the French boat. In the semi-final we had experienced first hand their ability to close a race and we hadn't tested ourselves adequately against them, allowing them to row through when we should have proved we could hold our position. For the final, we *believed* we had the power to overcome them in a sprint for the line, but crucially we didn't *know* this. All the way through our Olympic campaign we had stuck to plan A, for the simple reason that we didn't have a plan B.

In all honesty the danger that the French posed should not have come as a surprise. In the World Championships the previous year they had come in second behind the awesome Australian pair, well clear of the field. In Sydney, with the Australian boat weakened through the loss of Drew Ginn, it should have been obvious to everyone that it was now the French who were most likely to be the strongest boat in the field. We ignored that glaring reality, however, focusing instead on our misplaced belief that in the final run-up to the Games we had been able to overcome the various obstacles that had been placed – or more accurately which I had placed – in our way. From a technical point of view that was probably true; in an emotional context we ended up where I deserved, as hard as that is to admit now.

Ed and I could undoubtedly *row* well together, but when the pressure was on we failed to *perform* well together. The fault for that lies at my door.

In late 1999, following my poor showing in the single scull at the World Championships in Canada, Jürgen called me into his office at Leander.

'Greg,' he told me, 'I don't think you should scull any longer. You have to come into the pair. Who will join you, I do not know yet. But that is the only way I see you having a chance of a medal in Sydney.'

The chance of *a* medal, not a *gold* medal. Disappointing. What he was telling me was that in his estimation the realistic aspirations of the GB team were for the four to go for gold, while the pair and the eight could hope for a medal. Let's just see what happens, I thought. I'm going to prove you wrong, Jürgen.

There was no suggestion of a seat in Redgrave's four, which was understandable. I was in no position to attempt to force my way into that boat at James Cracknell's expense.

I wasn't complaining. I was in this situation because of my own bloody-mindedness and I was happy to grasp the lifeline being offered. Following my disappointing result at the World Championships, sticking on my own would have been madness. Having failed in Canada, the next opportunity to qualify for the Olympics was not until June, and with my sculling performances seemingly in rapid reverse there was no guarantee I could engineer a dramatic change in fortunes. As such I recognized the wisdom of Jürgen's words. With my experience of rowing in a pair I had a far better chance of enjoying Australian hospitality in September 2000 in that boat; otherwise the likelihood was I would be watching from my sofa at home.

This was not the first occasion on which the idea of me dropping out of the single and joining a pair had been raised. A month or so prior to the 1999 World Championships the suggestion had been floated that I team up with Tim Foster, but I had shied away. I was way too low to open myself up to new possibilities at that stage, stuck in a blind alley trying to survive rather than allowing myself to prosper, desperately trying to convince myself that I could fulfil my own prophecy of becoming king of the Sydney lake. In hindsight, that may have been a mistake.

Tim and I had a strong connection, we got on well, we had shared a flat together and we were both undergoing rehabilitation on our backs at the time. Tim's greatest asset within any crew was his technical ability; he instinctively knew how to ensure a boat cut through the water with maximum efficiency, allowing stronger team-mates to concentrate on supplying the power. My physicality, coupled with everything I had learned from Harry and combined with Tim's rowing savvy could have created a potent mix. Could have. I'll never know, having chosen to step away from the possibility when it was raised.

Tim's fightback from injury was the reason Jürgen was unable to name my partner when we spoke in his office. In 1998 Tim had injured his hand, recklessly smashing it through a window at a party; he had then undergone unrelated back surgery towards the end of the year. While Tim's comeback had been impressive, it hadn't been sufficient in Jürgen's eyes to oust his replacement in the four – Ed Coode. Whether Tim knew of the suggestion to join up with me in the pair I don't know; what is beyond doubt is that Jürgen kept Ed in the four and moved Tim into the eight for the Worlds, where he helped steer the boat to a silver medal. The four won gold.

Following those championships, with Tim's fitness and focus clearly fully restored, Jürgen was left with a difficult choice to make. Five into four doesn't go, so someone had to be dropped and that someone would join me – either Tim, Ed or, incredible as it now seems, Steve Redgrave himself. Unknown to many people at the time, Steve was not a certainty for his 'own' boat. He was battling age, fitness and a worsening colitis condition brought on, most crucially of all, by diabetes. He had been struggling during training camps, but being the man he is he'd vowed to return to optimum condition in time for Sydney. Understandably, Jürgen wanted to give him time to overcome those problems and prove he was worthy of his place. As a result, Jürgen held off his final decision for as long as possible – until April 2000. Barely five months before the Olympics.

Having made his plan clear at our meeting, Jürgen went on to explain that he wanted me to train at Leander with Steve, Matthew, James, Ed and Tim as the sixth member of a very successful group of rowers. It felt really good to know that I was still regarded as part of the elite, but unfortunately I didn't make the most of the opportunity that was handed to me. I still had baggage regarding Leander, which I struggled to cast aside. I doubt I even tried, which I know was stupid, but there is a belligerent, stubborn streak in me that has on occasion been a strength, but can also, I admit, be a massive hindrance.

Part of the problem was Steve and Matthew, and to some extent Jürgen himself. I had been invited into the fold, which was both generous and a confidence boost, but I was clearly playing second fiddle – there was no other way to look at it – and it was a role I hadn't played since almost the first day I laid my schoolboy hands on an oar. It didn't sit comfortably with me. Had I been mature enough to have turned this situation on its head, events in Australia could potentially have turned out very differently.

Instead of viewing Steve and Matthew as the guys I'd always wanted to be, the top guys, the guys I had failed to overtake, I should have embraced the alternative reality. At the very least I was being recognized as the fifth or sixth best athlete in the Great Britain rowing team. Second fiddle? Yeah, perhaps. But shit, it wasn't a bad position to be in considering I had recently come fourteenth in the world. I should have got a grip on my-self, kept my head down and worked as hard as Jürgen asked me to.

What did I actually do? I set about challenging everything under the sun, using Leander as an excuse. I was hurting and I wanted to prove to myself as much as to anyone else that my way was still the best way. I didn't want to admit that my lack of form over the previous eighteen months could possibly have been down to *my* training methods. It had worked for Barcelona, so why wouldn't it work now? My back problems, the lack of a dedicated coach, the distractions of my personal life, these were the reasons for my relative lack of success, nothing else.

Having had my eyes opened to new ideas by Harry, once he was forced to step away I'd unconsciously put my blinkers back on and shunned change. I refused to embrace Jürgen's philosophy of building a pyramid of fitness with as wide a base as possible to ensure sustained performance and success. Today I have bought wholeheartedly into the idea that these training methods are the way forward, but back in 2000 I thought it was all bollocks.

Initially my attitude was less of a problem as I was often left to my own devices in terms of supervision during training sessions while Jürgen worked with the four. I could interpret his instructions as I saw fit. However, when in early April Jürgen announced that Steve's position was safe and Tim would be taking the final seat in the boat, thrusting Ed and I together, the consequences of my ambivalence became more of an issue. With so little time before the Olympics I should have been looking to establish a strong foundation with Ed, from which we could launch our assault on the gold medal. Instead, I chipped away at our confidence, which ran the risk of disintegrating under the intense glare of the competition we would inevitably face in Sydney.

There were no grand gestures of defiance, no deliberate attempts to undermine Jürgen's authority and management. I genuinely thought I was doing the best for the two of us, supporting Ed with the benefit of my experience. In many ways that was the worst scenario of all because I wasn't aware of the impact I was having. Inadvertently I was weakening our already brittle confidence with a maze of tiny fault lines, which had the potential to shatter at any moment.

If Jürgen laid out a training session I would nod as though I had been taking it all in, but after we had placed our boat in the water and were preparing to climb on board I would take Ed to one side.

'I know Jürgen has told us to do twenty k solid and steady at eighteen strokes a minute, but I'm not sure that's what we need to focus on right now. Let's look to work on how we are rowing technically and do a few exercises at the top end. Then we can get our breath back before putting the hammer down a bit on the way back. It's how I've approached this sort of session before and it really worked for me then.'

This had a twofold effect. Not only was I pulling us a step away from Jürgen's carefully prepared programme, I was also confusing Ed. Ed is an extremely nice guy who just wanted to do what was right, and he found himself torn between me as his friend and Jürgen as his coach. With no clear strategy, doubt was probably the only emotion left to fill the void.

The issue that arose over who was going to coach us casts further light on how I felt. Jürgen held overall responsibility for the programme's implementation, or lack of in our case, overseen by a separate coach on a day-to-day basis. In my mind there was only one legitimate contender for guiding us towards Olympic success: Harry. By then, however, Harry had been taken under the wing of Martin McIlroy, who coached the eight, as his technical sidekick. Given Harry's health, Martin undertook most of the time-consuming responsibilities, overseeing gym sessions, logistics and making sure the training schedule was written and distributed, while Harry was free to show up, climb in the motor boat and coach what he saw.

I would have loved Harry to undertake that role with us, but Jürgen decided against it, which was entirely within his prerogative. He wanted Harry to stick with the eight, and instead suggested a series of candidates to work alongside Ed and me. I would give each of them a few weeks, but all the time I kept finding holes in their approach, which I then raised with Jürgen and Ed.

I even became entrenched in my views about which boat we should use. In 1992 Jonny and I had made a virtue out of the necessity of rowing the blue and white Aylings, and by 2000 that was the manufacturer-of-choice for the British team. However, my bronze medal in 1997 had been achieved in a yellow Empacher single, and I got it into my head that Ed and I should have the opportunity to try out that version of the pair. I kept on at Jürgen, but each time his response was crystal clear, and he was probably right, although I refused to acknowledge it.

'Greg, this is enough. Forget the boat, it's not important. Focus on what you do in it. The rower makes the difference, not the boat.'

'Yeah, but we haven't even tried it. And I have my own money, I'll buy one.'

'If you want to row in an Empacher then you can row in your single.'

And I guess that was the end of that.

Jürgen's approach was probably correct for the team as a whole. If we'd got an Empacher pair then suddenly the four would have wanted one, causing a big distraction that he didn't need. Once again I was being difficult because it was in my nature and I had some history with Jürgen. I wanted to turn over that rock because I was still searching for solutions. My attitude was that it might make a difference, it might not, but let's give it a go. Jürgen, however, wouldn't hear of it and eventually I had to let the matter drop. Incidentally, we race in Empacher boats now.

Against this background it's hardly surprising that Ed and I found ourselves misfiring throughout the summer season. On paper, given what we had achieved individually, we should have emerged as one of the lead contenders, and occasionally we lived up to our billing. We headed for Sydney with third-place finishes in the first two June World Cup races, Munich and Vienna, and followed that with a good win in the Silver Goblets race at Henley at the end of the month, where we beat the South African boat of Ramon di Clemente and Don Cech in the final. However, the belief those results helped build was given a severe knock-back when we achieved a disappointing seventh in the final World Cup regatta of the season in Lucerne.

Transforming negatives into positives has been a recurrent theme throughout my rowing career, and the wake-up call this time was our failure to make the final in Switzerland, which in turn offered us another opportunity to turn things around. Despite my reservations, Jürgen's fitness-based programme – which we were following – was delivering. We were strong enough, we knew that, but we lacked the ability to move the boat efficiently enough not to run out of steam. The appointment of John West as our coach was the catalyst for change.

I trusted John and his arrival mostly put an end to my constantly questioning and badgering Jürgen. He knew how to handle me, allowing me to have my say and feel I had a significant amount of responsibility, while at the same time making sure I was doing what needed to be done to keep Jürgen happy. Almost overnight I could feel the pieces of the jigsaw slotting into place and I zeroed all my focus and attention on the target – Sydney and the gold medal.

With Ed having most recently rowed in a four his style had developed into a slightly shorter, more upright motion, whilst my years in the single scull had produced longer strokes that came mostly from my terrible back position, known to my colleagues as the 'Searle Curl'. Under John's expert guidance we tweaked aspects of our technique and began to mesh into a single, efficient unit. Identifying the problems was half the battle, and as we worked them through the smoothness of our boat improved significantly.

Changing the technical aspects was critical, but it was symptomatic of a more important shift. With John on board the distractions of the previous three months disappeared, the quality of our training sessions improved and the intensity of our gym work increased as our mutual belief in each other grew. Ed and I had always got on well, that had never been a problem, but in the month between Lucerne and flying out to Australia, which included altitude training in the Austrian Alps, our friendship deepened into something more fundamental: trust.

On arrival at our holding camp on the Gold Coast, my confidence was high. Reflecting on my history, I knew I had always been a slow starter with a big finish. That had applied not merely to race days but also to my training schedule. During the periods when I was either working or studying, the long hours pushing myself to the limits on the Thames, or the countless times collapsing in an exhausted heap from a rowing machine, would maintain a certain level of fitness. But it was only when I embarked on the intense summer training camps that the quality of my performances began to take off. This felt the same. In 1992 Jonny and I had surprised everybody with our win after a faltering build-up in an unfamiliar boat. Why should 2000 be any different?

The omens were favourable. On the Gold Coast we rowed on a lake called the Hinze Dam which, similar to the Olympic venue in Penrith, Sydney, was often windy and rough, and we were handling it well. In one session, a series of short 250 m bursts, we flew, reaching speeds greater than Redgrave and Pinsent had ever produced, despite the waves breaking over our riggers. We were on fire, peaking at just the right time.

The feeling of well-being continued on our arrival in the village, which was a truly fabulous experience. Sydney had embraced the Games, and there was an upbeat mood across the entire city, which made all the athletes feel very welcome. Compared to Atlanta, this was a much happier Olympics.

Matthew Pinsent had been chosen to carry the GB flag at the Opening Ceremony. The decision had been taken while we were still on the Gold Coast and Matthew, obviously delighted and extremely proud, wanted to look his best.

Not long after the news was announced, Matthew was seen visiting the tailor in the camp who had issued us all with our, what shall I call them, 'sailor outfits', the official team uniform – baggy white trousers and blue zip-up jackets for the men, with the opposite colour combination for the women. When he was spotted, Matthew had his outfit in a suit carrier draped over his arm.

'Something wrong with your gear, Matt?'

'No, no, erm, nothing really.' He was looking a bit shifty at this point.

'So why are you here? What are you up to?'

'Oh, all right, bloody hell. If you must know I'm having the trousers taken in! I refuse to carry the flag of my country wearing a pair of flares.'

On the day of the ceremony there was the usual discussion concerning who would attend. Ed and I were sharing an apartment with the guys from the eight and they had decided not to go, or at least I think their coach had decided for them, but as this was Ed's first Olympics he was keen to experience everything, and I was more than happy to join him, along with Steve, Tim and James.

You can never match the magic of your first Opening Ceremony, and while Barcelona will always hold a special place in my heart, Sydney came a close second. The atmosphere in the stadium was electric and the reaction of the crowd to every nation was a thing to behold. They were proud Australians, honoured that so many world-class athletes from across the globe had come to enjoy the sights, sounds and smells of their wonderful city and country, and they were going to make sure no one left disappointed.

Having marched around the track with the team we were then funnelled off into the centre of the pitch as the remaining countries trooped past.

'Ed,' I said, nudging him to attract his attention above the incredible noise, 'I'm just about done here. What do you reckon? Fancy doing a runner? We could be back in our apartment before they get round to lighting the flame. You up for it?'

'Let's go.'

We legged it, performing a rarely seen reverse pitch invasion. It could have been the last thing we ever did. Having failed to choose our escape route with due care, we made a mad dash across the running track for the nearest exit just as the Israeli team was marching past. We could feel the tension rising within the massed ranks of security surrounding the athletes as we made an inadvertent beeline towards them, veering off at the last minute to disappear into the crowd and out of the stadium. We were probably lucky not to have been cut down in our prime by rooftop snipers.

Ed and I walked to the village, and on arrival back at the apartment we discovered that the eight were still up, watching the ceremony on television. The whole point of them staying home had been to get plenty of sleep, and suddenly in walked Ed and I, having just experienced the incredible occasion first hand and still managing to beat them to bed. They must have been really pissed off. Not only were we supposedly ranked above them in the team, here we were in front of them, seemingly having our cake and eating it, able to go out and have fun while not screwing up our medal prospects. I suspect I came across as a bit of a smug bastard that evening. It proved to be my last laugh of the Games.

In his interview with us directly after the final, Steve Rider had asked what went wrong. It was a good question. On the surface, Ed and I were in a better position than we could possibly have hoped after the disappointment of Lucerne. John West had helped correct our technical failings, we trusted each other, physically we were in excellent condition, mentally we were positive and we had moved well through the water in the heat and semi-final. Surely there was enough left in the tank to crank it up when required.

So what did go wrong?

It was on the flight from Poznan to Munich in 2009 that I finally found out for sure. I had heard rumours, but I didn't know if they were true until they were confirmed by Jean-Christophe Rolland, the French stroke on that day in Sydney, who was sitting next to me on the plane.

Imagine if you can that microphones had been fitted to ours and the French boat. This is what you would have heard at 1250 m, with us a length and a half up on France and going well, one hand each on the gold medal.

On the mark, Ed calls our set plan. Plan A. Our only plan.

'750. Lengthen. Hard. Push.' I respond as I have programmed myself to.

A second or two later, the French hit the same mark.

'*Pour nos enfants!*' Michel Andrieux then reels off the names of both his and J-C's children. There is no other call.

That's what went wrong. They had been working towards that one moment for years. They understood what it meant to each other, to their families, the sacrifices those closest to them had made to allow this chance at Olympic glory. At their core, Michel and J-C were connected in a way Ed and I could only dream of, and together they surged and continued to surge as a single entity.

Ed and I, for all the trust, hard work and technical fine-tuning, were not linked in the same way. We responded with our brains, not our hearts. Those fault lines created by my constant chipping away had caused too much damage, and somewhere deep down our self-belief was flawed and there had been insufficient time to heal the wounds.

Having concluded our awkward interview we managed to find a degree of anonymity in the bustle of rowers stowing their boats, changing their kit and refuelling. Slipping into the background behind the throngs of British supporters, we then quietly watched history being made as Redgrave's four won gold. How did I feel standing there, detached from the wild celebrations that erupted around us? 'Cold' is probably the best description. I was pleased for Tim as a friend, and I respected the achievement of the others, but my overriding feeling was emptiness. Not negative – I hadn't wished them to fail – but blank. I didn't hang around for the medal ceremony. I couldn't have lifted myself sufficiently to belt out the national anthem, and I was better off out of there. It was their moment and my brooding presence wouldn't have added to it.

If I could have disappeared in a puff of smoke there and then I would have, reappearing in the quiet isolation of my home back in England, but instead I had to make my way back to the village to pick up some clothes before meeting up with Jenny. The guys from the eight were in the apartment, preparing for their final the following day. We were all part of the GB team, and yet there was a sense of them-and-us. The eight had trained at Hammersmith, largely separate from Jürgen's four and our pair at Leander, and over the summer I had mischievously challenged their methods and approach, possibly because I would rather have been doing what they were doing, but wasn't allowed. While it hadn't quite reached the point of fully-fledged conflict, I think it's fair to say I wasn't their favourite bloke.

As a result, they were probably keen to out-do Ed and me, but they wouldn't have wanted us to arrive back empty-handed. They were shell-shocked when we walked in, as unsure what to say to us as we were to them. Mumbled 'hard lucks' were offered while eye contact was avoided. Our Opening Ceremony 'victory' seemed a lifetime ago. Given the circumstances, I think they handled a horrible situation as well as anyone could. I showered and changed as quickly as possible, packed a bag and wished them luck as I made as swift an exit as dignity would allow.

The only person I could bear to see was Jenny, but as I made my way out of the village to meet her I bumped into Tim and James, whose relative lack of media commitments compared to Steve and Matthew had allowed them to escape. I must admit, I was pleased it was just the two of them. Had Redgrave and Pinsent been there my lofty ambitions of 1997 would have rebounded to the surface, increasing the pain and sense of futility I was already experiencing.

I hugged them both. 'Well done, guys.'

'That was fucking tough, Greg. Sorry.' Nothing more was necessary.

I left them to begin no-doubt wild celebrations and took a taxi to John Boultbee's flat – one of the FISA committee and a great bloke – where Jenny was staying. She was on her own when I arrived, which was perfect, but it wasn't going to last. There was no way to avoid the inevitable as Jenny was sharing the apartment with a girl called Dee, Matthew Pinsent's girlfriend. At some point they were going to return and it wasn't an encounter I was look-ing forward to.

I needed some air, so Jenny and I wandered down to the water at Milsons Point near John's apartment. We didn't say much; we didn't need to. I was just happy to be with her and have her support. Then her phone rang. It was Austin Swain, a Lane4 colleague, former sports psychologist to the England rugby team during the 1995 World Cup and now a great friend. He didn't expect Jenny to answer, or me to be with her, he had just intended on leaving a message. Jenny handed me the phone when she found out who was on the line. Austin is a very positive guy to be around, always seeing the best in individuals and possessing a natural understanding of how to lift people.

'Greg, you were awesome in that interview. That must have been really tough and you handled it with dignity. You might have lost the race, but in those few minutes in front of the cameras you proved you're a winner.'

That meant a lot to me.

I had promised Ed we would attend a party that evening which his Newcastle University mates had decided to throw for him. I'm sure they had intended it as a great celebration – banners with Ed and me plastered all over them were everywhere – and the fact that circumstances had dictated otherwise didn't put them off. I was impressed by that. Ed had rowed in an Olympic final, and as far as his friends were concerned, that was something to shout about, regardless of whether he got a medal or not. They were right, of course, but it wasn't how I felt at the time.

While Ed eventually managed to get into the swing of things, thanks to plenty of cocktails, I found it hard, and after a couple of hours Jenny and I made our excuses and left. I suspect I wasn't much missed.

We hadn't been back in the apartment long before Dee and Matthew arrived. This was the moment I had been dreading and I'm afraid it lived up to expectations. I thought Matthew's sensitivity radar was poorly tuned that night as I struggled to deal with what felt like a tactlessness that I'm sure he wasn't aware of.

He may not have realized I was there when he arrived back in the apartment, and no doubt he had been celebrating with a drink or two. He walked in with his gold medal dangling around his neck (no problem) and sat down on a chair across the table from me. After a moment or two of awkward silence, with a dramatic sigh he announced, 'Ah well, the day is coming to an end. I guess it's time for the ceremonial removal of the gold medal.' (Give me a break.) Following which, he elaborately removed the medal with a flourish and made a point of placing it on the table between us. (I could really have done without that).

A memory flashed through my mind of Adrian Moorhouse in Barcelona 1992, last in his final and suddenly confronted with a young gold-medallist in his apartment. He shakes my hand, congratulates me, invites me to share breakfast with him and offers sound advice.

That was an example of losing well. Here, across the table from me, was what felt like an example – completely unintended – of winning badly. It struck a chord and I knew which side of the fence I wanted to be on. I resolved there and then, as a senior member of the British team, to lose well over the coming days, and should I ever have the opportunity again, I was determined I would win well, too.

After a short trip away with Jenny and a friend of ours, Rick Dunn, who had been the spare in the team, I returned to the village with a mission: to start being a good bloke around the rest of the team and essentially live up to Adrian's example. It was time for me to complete my growing-up experience.

The first thing I did was seek out the men's eight. I hadn't been at the course when they'd won their gold, and I wanted to shake each one of them by the hand and congratulate them on what had been an incredible achievement.

I wasn't jealous of them, or of the four. I wanted the British team to do well and their success didn't make me feel any better or worse, I was just sad not to be sharing the experience. I had missed a rare opportunity in life, to succeed again at the very highest level in my sport, and I was painfully aware of the likelihood that it wouldn't come my way again. During our couple of days away, Jenny and I had spoken at length about everything we'd been through together over the past four years since Atlanta, and the decisions we'd made that had brought us to Australia. She'd been with me every step of the way, supporting, encouraging, enjoying the ups and pulling me through the downs. We were a team, and having been so closely involved with everything Jenny felt the disappointment of returning home without a medal as acutely as I did. Perhaps even more so.

'What was the point, Greg? In the end it feels as though it was all just a waste of time.'

I understood how she felt, but as the initial pain subsided, I wasn't sure I agreed. All the hard work, and yes the things I'd chosen to miss, had allowed us to be part of an incredible adventure. We were together, on the other side of the world, that didn't amount to nothing.

I wasn't prepared to view the previous four years as time wasted. There had been some incredible experiences on my own, with Harry, Will, Bob, Dodge, Ed and John, and I had learned so much. This was an experience that would make me stronger for the rest of my life. That's time well spent. As we talked it through, Jenny began to understand that I had the ability to see the best even in the darkest of situations.

Having spoken to the guys in the eight, I then tracked down as many of the British gold medallists as I could, such as Denise Lewis, Audley Harrison, Steph Cook and Jason Queally. Although I didn't get to speak to each of them in person, I made a point of writing to them all when I returned home. I remembered in 1992 how impressed I had been to receive a letter from Steve Ovett, congratulating me on my achievement. If I could, I wanted to pass on the same feeling to others.

Perhaps the most fun I had in that second week in Sydney was hanging out with the sailing crowd. I knew Ben Ainslie a little from the Colonial sponsorship deal, and he proved to be a great introduction to the rest of the team. They had done particularly well, with Ben winning gold, along with Iain Percy and Shirley Robertson, plus silvers for Ian Barker, Simon Hiscocks, Mark Covell and Ian Walker. They were a good bunch to be around and they helped me realize what a privilege it was to be there, regardless of the result. There is more to being a member of a team than winning medals, and I hope my actions over those days showed that I understood that.

Mark Covell and I hit it off particularly well, and we spent a large part of the day of the Closing Ceremony drinking together and talking about our hopes for the future. This resonated particularly strongly with me because Jenny and I were due to become parents in five months' time. Quite what that was going to mean in terms of my rowing, I had no idea, but it was definitely going to mean my life would change.

The flight home sapped a lot of my new-found positivity. Pretty much the entire GB squad travelled on the same plane, but not together. Medallists please turn left for business class, the rest of you down the back. Our arrival at Heathrow compounded my reignited sense of sadness. Walking through Arrivals we were greeted by the sight and sound of hordes of well-wishers clapping and cheering, but not for me. For all that I felt I had made a contribution, and hopefully set an example to others as it had been set to me by Adrian, it was impossible not to escape the feeling of failure. The crowds were there to applaud success, and those who had achieved it were feted by the press. The rest of us were all but ignored. I understand that is the way it must be – ultimately sport is about winning and losing – but it wasn't much fun.

I slipped away as quickly and quietly as possible. All I wanted was to be home, lying low and discussing with Jenny what was going to be next for us and our baby. Big decisions had to be made.

It's January 2001 and the house telephone is ringing.

'Hello, Greg speaking.'

'Greg, it's me, Mark. How are you?' I recognized the voice instantly, Mark Covell.

'Good thanks, and you?'

'Yeah, fine. Listen, I've got a question for you. Do you know what a grinder is?'

SEVEN

A WORLD AWAY

The flight home from Australia and our arrival at Heathrow confirmed something I suppose I already knew – that an Olympic gold medal forever changes the manner in which people react to you. In my case it had also altered the way I felt inside. I have a belief in myself now because of a six-minute race I once won. Despite the fact that I was returning to the UK empty-handed, I nevertheless understood that our exploits in Barcelona in 1992 had forever marked me, Jonny and Garry as Olympic champions and the events of 2000 had not diminished that fact.

I believe the business arena, and life in general, operates in the same way. If you have achieved something truly special then it will raise your self-esteem and affect you positively for the rest of your life. It might be innovating and bringing something to the market or setting up and managing your own company, or in a personal sense it could be running a successful stage production or engaging in amazing charity work. Whatever it is, because you've proved to the wider world, and to yourself, that you have what it takes to succeed, opportunities are more likely to come your way and you're granted greater leeway if further success isn't instant. Winning is important, it shifts you onto a different plane for the rest of your life.

That's not to say that those who miss out on the big prizes are necessarily less talented or do not have the same degree of ability or worth within an organization or team, but the harsh truth is that they are not celebrated in the same way. There were a lot of people with whom I'd rowed over the previous ten years who, one-on-one, were just as talented as the Olympic heroes I've known. The difference is that those other rowers were not fortunate enough to come together at the right time and in the right way.

It can be a cruel business at times, but in the world of elite sport there is a demarcation – gold medallist from non-gold medallist – and however high my opinion is of those other guys, there is no doubt they will never be revered in the same way.

Do they regret putting in all the hours of hard work? I hope not. They gave themselves a chance and I hope they look back on those years with pride and affection. That's what's important. If they hadn't put themselves on the line they might be living their lives now thinking, What if I had given more? That would be far worse I think.

You have to do what it takes to give yourself the opportunity of landing the big one. But as those guys know, it's no guarantee of success. There are also other factors that can be beyond your control, timing for instance, but if you aren't out there, ready to take the chances that might come your way, you may as well accept you are nowhere.

Winning a gold medal brings with it a degree of respect. After Sydney I began to view the guys in the eight in a different light. I could no longer question what they were doing or how they were doing it, because they had been proved right. I had occasionally challenged the intensity with which they trained, I'd raised an eyebrow when they'd attached an extra fin to their boat and I'd been doubtful about the need to spend quite so long lying on the floor in a birthing position doing physio exercises, but now I had to eat my words, because they had won. The challenges I'd made may have been perfectly valid, but that was academic now. Crossing the line first is the most important thing when you are in a race.

The same applies to me. When I tell the story of 1992, with all the selfish things I did and all my pigheaded ways, I tell it looking back on events through the most ridiculously rose-tinted spectacles. I understand that. I also understand that not everything we did was 100 per cent correct in terms of a blueprint; it wasn't necessarily cause and effect, no matter how I paint the picture, but that doesn't invalidate my tale. What we did was right for us in 1992, the end result proves that, and to this day our victory has given me a sense of confidence and self-esteem.

However, that confidence can be a double-edged sword. It can afflict you with tunnel vision – over-confidence if you like – and I believe that's what happened to me in 1996 and 2000. I ignored the changing environment around me, believing that because I'd won before, I knew best. It's easy in retrospect to see that was crazy. Everything had moved on, it was a different event, with two new people, and a lot of new opposition, competitors who might well have learned the lessons of our previous success and improved on them. New and better ideas had emerged and, specifically in my case, Jürgen had taken control, but I hadn't embraced the opportunities as I should have. 'I know best' proved to be a fatal mindset in my quest for a second gold medal.

'Good, Greg, but just think how good you could have been.'

I see now what Jürgen was saying to me in October 2010, after I had produced my personal best on the rowing machine. Perhaps it has taken me until now to grasp fully the mistakes I made, but at least I have learned – hopefully in time to produce my best on Dorney Lake in August 2012.

If over-confidence is the downside, there is also an upside to being able to fall back on previous success. The fact that I know I have it in me gives me strength and helps me view the negative events as positive experiences that can shape my life. With 1992 as my rock, I have the ability to see setbacks as opportunities to learn rather than sucker punches that will knock me out cold. I can do something about them because I have an inner belief in myself. I try to find a purpose in everything that happens and use it to help me grow, whether it's something small or a big life-changing event.

No one is successful all the time. Everybody has a dip in their career when things aren't going as well as they once were and obstacles are placed in their path. Just look at Steve Redgrave. To me he is a brilliant role model because he didn't have it easy all the time. He had to battle through some extremely challenging periods in his life to achieve what he did. Steve pushed himself to the maximum, and often looked as if he was right on the edge, at times forcing himself beyond what I'm sure he felt were his own limits in order to overcome adversity.

Recognizing the strength that can be derived from failure is one of the most important lessons I have learned since Barcelona. In every race I enter I set out to win, but I know that is an impossible ambition. Sometimes you will lose, and, when that happens, you've got to front up and take what you can from the defeat in order to be better prepared for the next challenge. It's important to win, but it's also important to lose. Understanding the reason why you are doing what you are doing is, I believe, the critical point.

Recently I was driving my daughter Josie to her dance class. Halfway there she asked a question.

'Dad, what's the point of life?'

Right. How the hell do I answer that without sounding like a prat?

'That's an interesting question, Josie,' I replied, buying time. 'I think the point of life is what you make of it. Look at us now, we're driving to dance at seven o'clock on Thursday evening and you don't have to go there, you're not even rehearsing for a show.

But here we are, and it's because you want to learn to dance and learn to dance well. That's what's giving you a point to your Thursday nights, which in part is giving a point to your whole life. We choose to do things for a reason, because we feel good about it. You're going to dance because it's fun and because you enjoy it. At the end of this evening you will be a little bit better at dancing, which in turn will make your life better. So I guess that's the point of life, to make improvements every day, big or small, and to feel good about yourself when you do it. From there, who knows what might happen?'

I think she got what I was trying to say, but I didn't dare look in my rear-view mirror. She might have been playing her Nintendo the whole time I was speaking.

From my perspective, I don't have to be training as a full-time athlete. I don't *have* to, but I *want* to, because it's one of the things that has given a point to the last three years of my life. It's not the only one, I'm not even saying it's the most important one, but every morning when I wake up at 6.30 a.m., having the goal of going for gold gives me a positive reason to get up and out.

I thought about this a lot when I was talking to Jenny in Sydney. In her disappointment she worried that I would view the previous four years as a waste of time. But I didn't. Each day, trying to succeed in the single scull and then working with Ed, had value. Each day had purpose and that was worthwhile in itself. All I have to do is look where it has taken me today.

On my arrival home from Australia my purpose over the following months was clear: I wanted to prove I hadn't become rubbish overnight. To achieve that I decided to carry on rowing, and to row with the guys from the Sydney eight. Given some of the things I have just said, that might appear an odd choice, but there was a method to my madness. Partly it was because they were based in London, at Queen's Tower, the alumni club for Imperial College

London, which was relatively convenient to where I was living, and more importantly because it wasn't Leander. The other reason was that they all had a newly minted gold medal and I didn't. Had they cast a magic spell that I knew nothing about? Were their business-class seats home merely down to outside factors rather than greater talent? Training with them was my way of finding out, and the fact that a couple of the guys had retired after the Games gave me the opportunity to join the boat. As it was, circumstances dictated that I was never able fully to answer my own questions.

I took the training seriously. I knew I had some big decisions to make over the coming months and I wanted to leave all the options on the table. If international rowing was going to be my future, I had to stay in shape, and almost nothing was going to get in the way of that. Almost nothing.

It was 28 February and Jenny and I were having a quiet night in with some friends, enjoying a Chinese takeaway. Midway through the evening Jenny pulled me to one side.

'Greg, I think it's started.'

'Eh?'

'The baby. It's on its way. But calm down, don't panic, this is just the very early stages. There's a long way to go.'

'Right. Wow, erm, do we need to go to the hospital right now?'

'No, no. Not until the contractions start. That won't be for a bit yet. We can finish our meal.'

'Right, you guys do that, I'm off upstairs to get in an hour on the ergo. I'm not going to get much training done tomorrow.'

I was right. Jenny and I eventually headed off to the hospital in the early hours of the morning and our daughter Josie was born that day. It didn't take me long to integrate her into my training schedule to give Jenny a break. I would take her down to Queen's Tower and prop her up in her car seat to observe me and the other guys in the eight during our ergo sessions. She never seemed particularly impressed.

I was still rowing with those guys at the beginning of the 2001 season, which resulted in a first for me – I had never previously raced for any club other than Molesey at the Head of the River. We won the race and it was around then that Ed and I agreed to team up again and enter the GB pairs trial in April.

To the casual observer it might have looked like I was staking a claim for a place in the British World Championship squad, but in truth I was undecided where my future lay. By then events had moved on apace and I was approaching crunch time in terms of where my life was going. I'd also received that call from Mark Covell, which had made me question whether I was going to make another play for further Olympic glory or pursue something else entirely – on the other side of the world.

Mark's initial question about the grinder was his way of intro-ducing me to the possibility of jumping ship to a totally new sport – sailing. Specifically, he was referring to the GBR Challenge team, which was being put together to launch the country's first attempt in fifteen years to win the America's Cup in New Zealand. It's the sport's most prestigious contest and a trophy Britain had never won. Mark was already involved and had decided to call me based on the time we'd spent together in Sydney.

'Greg, mate, listen, I've watched you row, I know what shape you're in and I spent enough time with you in Australia to get a feel for the sort of bloke you are. Grinding on a boat is tough, don't think this is going to be plain sailing – sorry about that – but I think you've got what it takes and I think you'll love it.'

'Sure, Mark, I'm interested. Just one thing, what exactly is a grinder?'

Actually I had a fair idea because Steve Redgrave had done a bit of it in 1987 with a very big mate of his, known to all sailors as 'Jabba'. I knew it meant working the winches, but it was good to get Mark's take on the role. Grinders – and there were to be three of them on the GBR Challenge boat – manually operate the winches that move the sails in and out and up and down. There's a bit more to it than that, sometimes the grinders also winch up a crew member to sort out rigging, for instance, but in simple terms it's fair to say they are the muscles of the boat. Perhaps the easiest way to describe the role is that of infantrymen following the orders of the trimmers, who are the sergeants responsible for controlling the positioning of the sails under the command of the officers who steer the boat.

Physically, grinding requires a great deal of upper-body strength and all-round fitness, first to help carry the massive, heavy sails to the boat and then to be able to operate the winch at high speed for short or long bursts of activity, often with minimal periods of rest.

The British challenge, Mark explained, was being put together by technology entrepreneur and sailing fanatic Peter Harrison, who was pumping huge amounts of his own money into his quest to make history in the event. He was looking to recruit a staff of between sixty and seventy people to go with him to Auckland in the summer to train and compete in the Louis Vuitton Cup, a contest to determine who would take on the current holders of the America's Cup in the January 2003 final.

Shortly after the Head of the River I was invited down to the south coast by the GBR Challenge team to try out a bit of sailing, I guess to gauge the sturdiness of my sea legs and to undertake a series of physical tests. These were not the most sophisticated I had ever encountered. Imagine an exercise bike that's been mounted on a table, with the pedals replaced with handles and the seat removed so you can shove your face where it would have been. This was their simulation of a grinder's winch, and I seemed to do OK cranking away at it; I must have scored well enough on the other exercises I was asked to perform, too, because they offered me a contract. The deal would run from May 2001 until we either won or were knocked out of the Cup, a period of around eighteen months.

Financially it made sense. The pay was good, enough to cover the shortfall of Jenny not going back to work after having given birth to Josie at the beginning of March, and with accommodation laid on we could make some money by renting out our house in Wimbledon. The considerations really boiled down to two elements. One, was I prepared to step away from competitive rowing? And two, did Jenny and I want to uproot our lives, and Josie, and move just about as far away as possible from family and friends?

In the end it wasn't a difficult decision to make. The time felt right for me, as I saw it then, to bring down the curtain on my international rowing career. I had been to three Olympics, won gold and bronze, competed in numerous World Championships, with a gold, silver and three bronzes to show for it, and broken the world record on the 2 km rowing machine. With Josie heralding a new chapter in my life, there would never be a better time to move on to new challenges.

For any sportsman, knowing when to bow out is perhaps the hardest decision you have to make – yes, I know I haven't exactly done that yet, but we're talking then not now – and the America's Cup offered me the ideal escape route. Physically I would be off the rowing scene completely; mentally I would still be performing at an incredibly high level in sport; training-wise I would be required to push myself if I was going to succeed, and the whole thing was going to be conducted outdoors. Decision? What decision? This was a no-brainer, a great adventure for the family, like a gap year before we settled down to normal life back in the UK.

I trained hard with Ed up until the April trials, where we came in third, and then announced I didn't want to continue. Ed understood completely. His performance had indicated to the team coaches that he was in great shape and subsequently he was selected for the four, which won gold in the 2001 World Championships and went on to repeat the feat in Athens in 2004.

That was important to me. I had wanted to leave Ed in a decent place before disappearing off and I like to think I achieved that through the work we put in over the spring, helping provide him with the opportunity to progress after what happened in Sydney.

Before the journey to New Zealand, however, I had a very sad event to attend: Harry Mahon's funeral at Radley College. Harry died on 19 May 2001. Over the final couple of years of his life he had continued to be tough and fight the cancer right up until the end. Whenever I saw him during that period he was always more interested in talking about other people and their news rather than dwelling on himself. That is the sort of man he was, self-pity wasn't in his nature. One thing I am glad of is that I had the opportunity to tell him I was opening a new chapter in my life and would soon be heading for his homeland, New Zealand. I think he liked the idea that maybe through his influence I was open to the idea of adventure. Well, that was true. He taught me a lot, much more than just how to row.

If I had thought that sailing was going to offer a relatively gentle slide away from the rigorous demands of rowing, I was set straight within a few days of arriving in Auckland.

First, I was to have two roles – grinding and a secondary position of taking responsibility for the team's gym training. Fair enough, I can do that, but it also turned out that sailing is a really hard job.

Our day began at 6.15 a.m. with a gym session, followed by breakfast at eight, a weather briefing at eight thirty and the loading of the boat, which involved most of the crew lugging the sails down to the dockside, between nine and ten. Then, once the boat had been lifted into the water, it was towed out of Auckland Harbour and into the open space of the Hauraki Gulf. By about eleven we'd be hoisting the sails for five hours of sailing, usually testing and evaluating the equipment. This tended to be quite boring as we had to put one sail up and then try it out for about an hour before changing it for another and seeing how it compared in a controlled test against the first one. On a good day we'd run through some starts and enact a selection of the multitude of scenarios we might face on race days. This boat handling element was fun and the best bit of the job for me. We'd be back on the tow at about four (usually the first opportunity to grab some lunch) and in dock at around five, where we unloaded and washed the boat when it was back on dry land, and hung the sails up to dry. Finally my day would end with servicing my winch. I needed to learn to love that winch like a soldier loves his rifle, only my Lewmar 105 was a lot more complex, with many more fiddly little bits. As long as nothing needed further attention I'd leave the yard at about six thirty. These twelve-hour shifts were undertaken alternately five and six days a week.

For many of the crew this was quite a light workload. A number of the guys had been involved in round-the-world races, and all I can say is that the respect I have for them, and people like Ellen MacArthur, is immense. Out at sea, where you work in cramped, wet conditions and repeat the same monotonous job over and over again in order to cope with the ever-changing weather conditions, if it were possible to stay awake for twenty-four hours you would be busy for every one of them. Nature has no respect for tired limbs or man-made boats, and even with my relatively brief exposure to this world I could see that there would never be a moment when everything on board was working exactly as it should. To this day, it astounds me that people are brave or foolhardy enough to take on such hardship. In comparison, what I was doing was a doss.

It was a world away from what I was used to and it took me some time to adjust. Rowing and sailing are two very different disciplines. Even as a rower who competed at the top level my training day involved no more than four and a half hours of actual activity. It wasn't physically possible to do any more than that which, when you think about it, left nineteen and a half hours to put my feet up.

Even today I still only engage in three one-and-a-half hour sessions a day. That's it. Yes I can follow up with some stretching or perhaps servicing my boat, but to do any more weights or rowing would be crazy. Overdoing intensive training only leads in one direction, towards long-term injury. Rest and recuperation is essential. If you don't allow your body to recover you will not be in a position to go hard at it again the following day.

Given that our mere twelve-hour working days were pretty straightforward to a lot of the guys I was with, it was commonplace for some of them to head off to the pub after everything was stored away, get trashed and then be back in the gym at six fifteen the following morning to start all over again. In rowing that's not possible. We might only be working in blocks of extreme pain that last six minutes, but if you're not mentally sharp and physically at your peak each day you have no chance of making it through. As I said, rowing and sailing are very different disciplines.

Tick . . . tick . . . tick.

I am powering up the hill from the boat yard on the second-hand bike I bought not long after arriving in Auckland. It's a ten-minute ride back to the Duxton hotel, where Jenny, Josie and I are living, and as we do most days, I am racing my best mate out here, Ian Weighell, known as Wheelie, a fellow rower and grinder. He's the guy I have most in common with in the team.

Tick . . . tick . . . tick.

Shit, I am flat out and Wheelie is catching me. What the hell is that noise? The gears? Better change down, I've got to hold him off.

Tick . . . tick . . .

I flip the switch on my handlebar, ready for the last push.

Nothing. No resistance.

Whap!

The road? The pavement? The sky? What the . . .

'Greg! Greg! Are you OK?'

It's Wheelie, I can just about make that out. He's running towards me from the rise of the hill. He's leaping over my bike. It's further up the road, ten yards in front of me. I can feel the rough tarmac of the pavement on my back. Weird.

I sit up. My knee, hip, arm and head all hurt like mad! My face is wet. I touch it and look at my hand. Blood. Shit, I've come off the bike. Obviously. Tick, tick, tick. A time bomb. When I changed gears the chain must have come off the rail. I have a vague sense that my foot slipped off the pedal and hit the road. Bollocks.

Wheelie helps me over to a shop front and sits me down, my back leaning against the window. He's looking at my face. I'm finding it difficult to focus.

'What . . . what happened?'

'I don't know. You suddenly went flying. How are you feeling? You've cut your head. Bad I think. I'm not taking your helmet off just in case. I'm calling an ambulance.'

Ambulance . . . head . . . helmet. Oh no, Jenny.

'Wheelie, call Jenny, please. Ask her to come. She's only a couple of minutes away. Tell her what's happened, but please, please make sure she knows I am OK. It's important.'

Jenny and the ambulance arrive at the same time. My head is clearing and I can see my wife is in a terrible state. White, shaking, but being brave. I know why.

'Jenny, I'm all right I promise. Cuts and bruises, that's all. Hold my hand. It's not—' I can't finish. I can see she's crying. I know how awful this must be for her. Her older brother Keith, a really good guy, a school teacher, forty years old with a wife and son, was in a bike accident seven years ago. It was summer, end of term, hot and he wasn't wearing a helmet. He hit his head but seemed to be OK. He took himself to hospital to be checked over.

179

That's where he collapsed and, despite emergency brain surgery, died two days later.

'Jenny, I'm OK. See, I'm squeezing your hand. I am going to be fine. Promise.'

I am in the ambulance with Jenny next to me as the paramedics check the extent of my injuries.

'Greg, hold this above your left eye, until we reach the hospital.' He hands me some padding and I take it in my left hand.

Ah! Shit!

That's not good. I can't move my arm.

The casualty room in the hospital is busy. I've been registered and I'm waiting. A guy covered in cuts and bruises, nasty as they are, isn't going to get priority. Not that I'm thinking much about that. I'm looking at my elbow, watching as a lump the size of an egg grows in front of my eyes.

The cut on my head wasn't too bad, it just required a few stitches from the nurse, with Jenny helping her out by passing cotton wool and instruments – I guess they must have been short-staffed that day – but the X-ray on my elbow revealed a far more serious problem. Three major breaks in the olecranon bone, which required an immediate operation in which two pins were inserted and twisted together to help the bone mesh.

'The operation went well, Mr Searle,' the surgeon told me once I'd come round from the general anaesthetic and my arm was in plaster, 'but we can't guarantee you will ever be able to straighten your arm fully again. Time will tell.'

Just what a grinder in the America's Cup wants to hear.

I was determined this wasn't going to be the end of our New Zealand adventure. After a few days under observation I was released from hospital with strict instructions not to go near the boat yard for three or four weeks. OK, if that's the case I'm going to view this as an opportunity to spend proper time with Jenny and Josie before going back to work. I was careful not to overdo anything, but within reason the three of us went sightseeing and enjoyed being a family. Thinking about what this could mean financially if my contract was cancelled was a pointless exercise. We wouldn't know anything until the plaster was off, and in the meantime why not seek out the positives from the situation.

Back amongst the team, but still incapacitated, I made a conscious decision to use the downtime to learn more about sailing. I was convinced I would make a full recovery, and in the interim I refused to drop my head. While I would obviously need time to build up my strength again, I figured that once I'd done that, if I was able to rejoin the boat with a deeper understanding of everything going on around me I would surely be a better crew mate. At the same time I would be demonstrating a willingness to participate and be a team player. I had identified my purpose.

I attended the extended weather briefings, I shadowed the trimmers to understand precisely what signs they were looking for, I spoke at length to the helmsman and navigator, and stood with the skipper at the back of the boat as he explained his tactics. While I might not have turned into Sir Francis Chichester overnight, I knew a lot more about sailing by the time the plaster came off than I had before my bike chain did the same thing.

I was fortunate with the timing of the accident in two respects. It happened around mid-January 2002, and as the challenger series of races wasn't scheduled to begin until October that gave me plenty of time to work on my rehabilitation. In addition, over March and April the entire crew was due back in the UK because of some technical rule, which insisted that if we were the British team then our boat had to be built, named and launched in the UK. Up until then we'd be using a couple of boats that Peter Harrison had purchased from the previous Japanese challenge, but then we had to go back to the UK and collect our half-constructed race boat and go through the official ceremonies before it could be sent across the planet in pieces, ready to be reassembled. There didn't seem much logic behind all of this, but that's how it was and it gave us all a much-needed break. From my perspective, with the other guys out of action, it meant I wouldn't be falling too far behind.

In the early morning of 14 April I was crossing a line in Blackheath wearing a pair of shorts and a vest with a number pinned to it, alongside approximately 33,000 other runners, one of whom was dressed as a deep-sea diver. With my plaster having been removed three weeks earlier I was about to tackle the London Marathon. I had run a half marathon in New Zealand before my accident but this was the first time I had taken on the full 26 miles 385 yards and I had set myself a target of breaking three and a half hours. A decent, fit-bloke time I reckoned. I wanted to be sure that on my return to Auckland, even if my arm wasn't yet back up to full power, I would be capable of keeping up the moment I was back in the boat.

Exactly 3 hours, 29 minutes and 7 seconds later I was in Pall Mall having completed the course, a mere 4,704 people ahead of me. Job done. I had proved to myself I was in decent shape, now I had to prove it to my crew mates.

Before our trip back to the UK I had been asked in my capacity as the gym coordinator to devise some physical test aimed specifically at the grinders, something that would simulate as best I could what actually happens on the boat. Until then we had been relying on the good old exercise-bike contraption.

With my arm still in a sling I set about my task, reasoning that the most effective method of recreating what we did was to do it *in situ*. With the boat out of the water and Wheelie and a couple of the other guys doing the heavy labour as I barked instructions, we rigged a spinnaker sail, still in its bag, to the front of the boat and attached a winch. The idea was that the grinders had to raise the spinnaker once a minute eight times. It was a good, tough, realistic test and it was the first challenge I had to face on my return to New Zealand.

I was nervous. Although I'd done my best to remain visible throughout my rehabilitation, inevitably I was somewhat out of the loop, and I knew that if I screwed up my own invention it was going to be hard to win back the crew's respect. Excuses were irrelevant. Quite rightly, I was either in or out. The Louis Vuitton Cup series was looming and there was no room for passengers. I surprised even myself. I might not have been the quickest, but I wasn't far off. I had earned my place back in the boat.

Our campaign began on 1 October with a loss to the American boat *Stars & Stripes* by a margin of twenty seconds. Given that each race lasts approximately two hours, this at least demonstrated that we were legitimate challengers. There were nine boats competing in the series in a round-robin format, with one-on-one contests against each other. As the races tended to be held on consecutive days, except when weather conditions forced an abandonment, the grinders were rotated, which resulted in me being involved in about two thirds of the races.

In the first round we won four and lost four, placing us mid-table, ahead of Stars & Stripes but behind the big guns OneWorld (USA), who we actually beat by thirty-six seconds, Alinghi (Swiss) and Oracle (USA). Taking Formula 1 as an analogy, we were not showing ourselves to be one of the top teams, such as Red Bull or McLaren, but we were in the mix, more like Renault, a team that would occasionally manage a podium finish but was unlikely to win the championship.

In the second round-robin we won three and lost five, this time beating Stars & Stripes, as well as the French and Italian teams. That placed us sixth in the table, earning us a quarter-final encounter with the team one place below us, Stars & Stripes. The knockout stage was to be decided over the best of seven races, and we got off to a flying start on 13 November when we beat the Americans by a full minute. Unfortunately, it was downhill from there. We lost the next four races and were dumped out of the competition.

Realistically, the quarter-final was probably about right for us. Perhaps we could have beaten the American boat and made it through to the semis, but that would almost certainly have been as far as we could have progressed. As it was, Alinghi and Oracle fought their way through to the best-of-nine final showdown, with the Swiss romping home 5–1, and eventually going on to beat Team New Zealand and capture the America's Cup for the first time. By then, of course, Jenny, Josie and I were back in England.

If I look at the GBR Challenge project as a whole I would say we made one fatal mistake. We were a two-boat campaign, which I believe overstretched our resources, even though Peter Harrison invested something like £25 million of his own money into the campaign. Competitive sailing is an expensive business, even at entry level, and to mount a challenge on the America's Cup takes it right off the scale. I know Peter had hoped to find another major sponsor to join him, and although we received contributions in kind – kit, vehicles etc. – he was unable to secure a significant additional injection of cash. As improbable as it might sound, £25 million just wasn't enough to sustain two boats.

What we should have done is channelled all the available money into producing one exceptional vessel. The quest to design a second wonder boat with an innovative keel proved to be a major distraction, and we didn't make the most of our number-one boat because the designers and a significant number of our team were focusing their energy elsewhere. If we could have saved some money by not having that second boat, Team GBR Challenge could potentially have returned for the next series having learned an enormous amount from the first campaign. Under those circumstances we might have been in with a realistic shot. Instead, the team fell apart and didn't participate when the event was next staged in Valencia four and a half years later.

Our family enjoyed a good life in New Zealand and I know Jenny is glad we made the decision to go, but I also know she wasn't too disappointed when the time came to return to the UK. Although she made good friends with some of the partners she found the sailing world rather cliquey. With no shared history or experiences in common she was always something of an outsider and what with coping with a small baby and me working twelve-hour days, she missed her family and friends back home.

The biggest disappointment for me was that I didn't find myself becoming enthralled by sailing. I enjoyed it and it was a tremendous experience, but equally I think it's fair to say that it didn't change my life. Part of that was because in my role as grinder I had very little influence on how well we did in the races. Competition is in my blood, from playing games with Jonny and bridge with my parents, rugby, and of course throughout my rowing career. Crossing the line first, winning, being number one and taking responsibility for my own future are the things that drive me forward. Crouching down and occasionally winding like crazy when required just didn't do it for me. I didn't feel particularly happy when we won or sad when we lost, because whatever happened wasn't really down to me. I found myself regarding the practice sessions and drills as work, whereas I have never seen rowing in that way, no matter how hard and painful the hours of training. There was always a purpose to the grind – to put myself in a position where I could defeat opponents – and there just wasn't enough of that in New Zealand.

A far greater issue for me was the lack of personal responsibility, which I found hard to come to terms with. As a grinder I was a tiny cog in a large machine. In rowing, the smallest fraction of contribution you can make is one eighth, but in sailing, if you are the bloke who grinds the handles you are responsible for no more than 1 per cent of the team's overall performance. I would undertake my tasks as well as I possibly could, but the fact that winning or losing had very little to do with how I performed ultimately left me cold. I am happy to take the accolades when I do well, and I am equally prepared to accept my share of the blame if I screw things up, but that didn't really apply on GBR Challenge. The truth is it didn't matter if it was me or the next guy who worked the handle, and this made the competition for places on the boat less transparent than I was used to.

In rowing you earn your seat based on clear and easily defined results, on a rowing machine or simply by the fact that your presence makes the boat go faster. In sailing it didn't feel like there was the same healthy competition. All the grinders were desperate to prove they were better than the next guy. Each of us wanted to demonstrate we deserved to be in one of the key positions, but given the fact that none of us could make that big a difference on our own, selection was often based on subjective criteria. A number of the guys I was working with had sailed long, arduous voyages together, using the same toothbrush and bed, so the fact that I might be able to hoist a sail slightly quicker than someone else didn't count for much. I understood that, but it was another element of the sport with which I felt less than comfortable.

None of that changes the fact, however, that I am extremely proud and pleased to have been involved in the America's Cup. It was a brilliant experience and a fabulous adventure for Jenny and me, giving us the opportunity to explore a new and fascinating country and spend time together with our daughter, away from the distractions of home.

Sailing may not have changed my life, but the news that Jenny was expecting our second child at the end of April 2003 definitely did. Having grown up over the past few years, it was now time to settle down into proper family life.

EIGHT

CLICK, CLICK, CLICK

Can I really live here?

I'm standing with an estate agent in Marlow looking at a set of particulars for a house that's available to rent. Jenny and I had been desperate to buy a place before the new baby came along, but the house we offered on fell through. We needed somewhere and we needed it fast. We had a buyer lined up for our house in Wimbledon and the last thing we needed was for that sale to be messed up as well. A short-term lease while we looked for somewhere to buy seemed like the best option, but did it really need to be this house? Could I swallow my pride?

I looked again at the piece of paper. 'Is there nothing else?'

'I'm afraid not, Mr Searle, not that's available right now. The rental market is booming in this neck of the woods and nothing stays on the market for very long.'

Don't be so stupid, Greg, of course you can do this. In fact, it's probably a good thing. It's time to move on with your life and this will be a cathartic experience.

'OK, let's go and take a look.'

Inevitably the house was ideally suited to what we needed – the right location, the right size, modern, clean, easy to maintain, and we could move in immediately. So in March 2003, Jenny, Josie, the bump and I moved into our rented accommodation.

My new lifestyle as a happily married family man, working full time in a job I enjoyed, looking to buy a nice, safe, sensible, grown-up house out of town, was well underway and I was loving every moment of it. Strangely, though, rowing never let me escape entirely.

Our new temporary address? Redgrave Place, Marlow, named after the great man himself.

Five weeks on and Jenny and I were once again proud parents of a new-born. Our son Adam arrived at the end of April, just in time. Had he arrived a few days later I would have been on my way to Spain and missed his birth. I would have hated it if that had happened, but having made a commitment to go there, as far as I was concerned, that was it, I was going. Bloody-minded? Me? As it was, his timely arrival meant Jenny and Adam had a few days to recover before they, together with Jenny's sister, Sue, jetted off with me to La Manga, while Josie stayed home with my parents. The reason for our trip was for my status to be briefly elevated from 'retired sportsman' to 'current superstar'. After a gap of almost two decades, the BBC had decided to breathe life back into *Superstars*, the classic sports-blokes-competing-against-each-other-in-different-disciplines format, and while I wasn't entirely convinced I wouldn't be nobbled by the Trading Standards authorities for misrepresentation, I was very happy to be involved.

Someone at the BBC had come up with a neat twist for this new series, which partly accounted for my presence in Spain. They had decided they wanted a set of brothers to compete in each of the four heats, and although it didn't quite work out – Scott Hastings wasn't there alongside his brother Gavin – they did manage to lure Jonny and me, Rory and Tony Underwood and Graham and Martin Bell to La Manga. I'm guessing it wasn't that hard – an expenses-paid week in a top resort to play games with a group of guys who have all excelled in their chosen sport? OK, it was a bit mental disappearing off so quickly after Adam's arrival, but what the hell. Jenny was up for it, we had her sister to help with the babysitting, and these opportunities don't exactly come along every day. Just show me where to sign.

While Jonny took the whole thing pretty seriously (his keen sense of competitiveness hadn't diminished over the years), I viewed it as more of a holiday. I wanted to do well – of course I did, I wasn't there to make a fool of myself – but I also saw it as an opportunity to have a laugh and hang out with some interesting people. My training regime prior to departure probably best sums up my attitude.

I remembered the programme vividly from when I was a kid, Kevin Keegan falling off his bike and all that great stuff, but the person who made the biggest impression on me was the judo expert Brian Jacks, and in particular his incredible displays in the gym. Every time he was on the show he seemed to break the record for parallel bar dips. Clearly he was somebody I wanted to emulate. So how did I prepare? I jogged down to our local park with Josie in her three-wheeler, and while she played on the swings I attempted to get into shape by pounding out the dips on the kids' climbing frame. Brian's record was in no danger.

The way it worked was that they ran the events in each heat back to back, putting them together later for transmission, as if the episodes were filmed separately. In practice, this meant that once we were done – and we were in heat one – I could enjoy the spectacle of the other guys trying out their skills in football, golf, kayaking etc., before moving on to the next round. I remember particularly enjoying the cricketer Dermot Reeve pitting his wits and silky moves against goalkeeper Dave Beasant in the football trial. In his first attempt Dermot dribbled round the cones, then curled a beauty into the top corner from eighteen yards. With his next go he shimmied one way then the other before knocking the ball wide, and on his third he audaciously attempted, and failed, to lob Beasant. It was great entertainment and about a million miles away from my approach.

Stuart Pearce was in our heat, and as he was excluded from the football he was happy to hand out advice. He told me to take the ball all the way to the edge of the six-yard box, which Dave Beasant wasn't allowed to come out of, and as Dave tried to close me down I should hit the ball hard and low to his side, giving him no time to dive and save it. It worked, I scored all three goals, but at a snail's pace, a good eleven seconds behind John Regis, who won the event. Crucially, however, I was a second faster than Jonny, which meant I scored big points.

Excluding myself, one thing I noticed about the competition was the difference in mentality between the racers and the game players. For instance, the cyclist Chris Boardman, the skier Graham Bell and Jonny, were far more focused and determined than the likes of Dermot Reeve or Stuart Pearce. I guess the individual competitors have one-on-one competition in the blood, whereas the guys who perform in a team environment are less fixated on crossing the finishing line first.

Incredibly, given my attitude going into the competition, I ended up winning my heat and going through to the final. It was the 800 m that swung it for me, when I was dragged along in the slipstream of the rest of the guys, who set off at a wild pace, totally throwing Jonny, who had planned his tactics in detail, intending to pace himself, but who instead ended up being left behind. It was the first and only time I have ever beaten him in a running race.

Having had the opportunity to scrutinize my fellow finalists over the three days of filming, I knew I had absolutely zero chance of winning. Some of them were in seriously good shape, whereas I was significantly out of condition, a fact that was about to be made worse by footballer Steve Claridge. Before those who hadn't made it through to the last stage went home, the BBC laid on a party for everyone, at which Steve led me very badly astray. To say I was out of my league – by about four divisions – would be understating the situation significantly. With Steve's careful and hilarious guidance, I got hammered. He is such a great bloke to be around that I hardly noticed how much I was drinking, and it wasn't until the following morning, when I awoke with the world's worst hangover, that it hit me. Unfortunately my darling son was oblivious to my pain and continued to scream for his breakfast as I sat ashen-faced and incapable of movement at the kitchen table. Sympathy from Jenny, it hardly needs saying, was in short supply. Thank God we had a day's rest before undertaking some of the new events for the final. In the state I was in I suspect I would have killed somebody during the archery had I not had those twenty-four hours to sober up.

I was a little nervous going into the final. Having studied the various times and scores of my opponents, it was clear they were going to wipe the floor with me, even in the events I had done well in during the heats. Despite my limited expectation, I didn't want to 'do a Norway' in Eurovision and end up with 'nul points'.

I identified the 100 m as a potential saviour, not because I was particularly fast but because there were only five of us entered. Guaranteed points, and who knows, anything could happen in the white heat of competition.

'So let me get this straight,' I said to one of the officials, 'the false start rule is the same as in swimming, right? The first time someone goes early that puts everybody on a warning, and if it happens again the person who jumps the gun is disqualified.'

'That's it.'

Perfect.

'On your marks, get set . . .'

I was out of those blocks like, well, to be honest like a very sluggish ex-rower, but I'd set the stage as I had planned. We lined up again.

'On your marks, get set . . .'

Under my breath. 'Go.'

No one even flinched. They were waiting for it, and when the starter gun fired for real I was left trailing in their wake, coming in four seconds behind the winner, athlete Du'aine Ladejo. Oh well, it was worth a try.

In the end I came seventh, battling with rugby player Phil de Glanville for the wooden spoon, a mere twenty-five points behind winner Du'aine, whose acceptance speech triggered a classic one-liner from Psycho Pearce, topping off the week perfectly.

Standing on the rostrum to collect his winner's medal, and resembling an Adonis as far as I was concerned, certainly in comparison to me, Du'aine first paid tribute to his fellow competitors and the organizers before continuing, 'I'd also like to thank the team behind my success – my coach, my nutritionist, my masseur and my sports psychologist – who have been here supporting and helping me.'

At this point Psycho leaned across and whispered, 'See, Greg, that's where you went wrong. He brought that lot and all you could manage was a babysitter.' Perfect.

On the flight home I reflected on the events of the past few days and how much I'd enjoyed the experience. I'd acquitted myself adequately, with a second-place finish in the mountain biking to drag me off the bottom of the scoreboard, and I'd loved every moment of it – well, apart from the morning after the night before. If this is the life of an ex-Olympic champion, I thought, I'm perfectly happy to embrace it.

We moved out of Redgrave Place after about six months, into our own house at the bottom of a cul-de-sac, within walking distance of schools that would be ideal for Josie and Adam. It was a home in which Jenny and I were happy to put down roots and settle into a life of domestic tranquillity. The intense pain of competition, the early mornings, the altitude training, the exhaustion of the rowing machine, watching what I ate, disappearing for weeks on end, that was all in the past.

Work was going well, on my return from New Zealand I had been re-engaged by Lane4, and as far as I was concerned chapter two of my life was fully underway.

After my exertions in La Manga, however, I realized I could do with sorting out my fitness. Since I'd returned from New Zealand I had begun to let things slip. Fortunately Lane4 was the ideal environment in which to stop the slide.

I'm not a great self-starter. I never have been. I thrive in a team environment, but left to my own devices I can find it hard to motivate myself. This character trait probably sheds light on why I wasn't able to continue successfully in the single scull once I lost Harry's leadership. My results clearly showed I was drifting, and it wasn't until Jürgen pulled me back into the fold that I was able to refocus and turn things round. Similarly, if it had been entirely down to me to get off my arse and get fit I think I would have struggled, but fortunately, within Lane4 there were a number of very fit people who encouraged me.

A very good friend of mine, Austin Swain, was instrumental. Austin is a triathlete, and during our early morning sessions at Maidenhead pool, which I often cycled to, he suggested I enter the London Triathlon. I had no aspirations to compete at any serious level – my driving force was to make sure I remained active and led a healthy life – but in order to push myself I had to set goals. For the marathon in 2002 my goal had been to run inside 3 hours 30 minutes and for the triathlon my target was sub 2 hours 30 minutes, which I achieved in August 2004 with a combined time of 2 hours 18 minutes. Not bad for a first attempt. Clearly there was something left in the old bones yet.

Click.

I didn't know it at the time, but the first tumbler of the combination safe that was to swing open on that plane from Munich to London had just fallen into place.

It was spring 2004 and I had been invited to the official presentation of London's bid to host the 2012 Olympics. The event took place in the East End and was presided over by, amongst others, Barbara Cassani, then head of the organizing committee, Tony Blair, Tessa Jowell and Ken Livingstone in his capacity as mayor. It was Livingstone who captured my imagination.

Tessa Jowell spoke well, and as you would expect Tony Blair was very polished in his address, but it was Ken Livingstone who stole the show. When his turn came to speak he stepped forward to the podium with his hand in his pocket, no notes, no autocue, and spoke entirely from the heart about how fantastic it would be for people to visit London because it was such a multicultural place, capable of making every nationality welcome. With the vast number of languages spoken within the capital, he said, every country would have a support base and Londoners would relish the opportunity to throw open the doors of this great city to so many new visitors. It was clear he wasn't that interested in sport, but rather in what was good for London. As far as I was concerned, Ken Livingstone summed up why we should host the Games. That wasn't the click, however.

It came as I leafed through the wads of paperwork that had been handed out. The date being proposed for the Opening Ceremony was 27 July and given that the rowing regatta is always held within the first week of the Games that would place the finals sometime around the beginning of August. If we win this bid, I thought, I could race in London as a forty-year-old and win a second gold medal twenty years almost to the day after I won my first. I smiled at the daydream and moved on, turning my attention back to the speakers.

Click.

The second tumbler fell during a workshop I was conducting with a colleague of mine, Wil James, for seventy Honda dealer principals. It was 6 July 2005 and Wil and I were hunched over the radio in my car outside the conference centre, listening intently to the words of Jacques Rogge, live from the IOC meeting in Singapore.

'The International Olympic Committee has the honour of announcing that the Games of the thirtieth Olympiad in 2012 are awarded to the city of . . . London.'

'Yes! Yes! Yes!'

We screeched and hugged each other, totally carried away in the moment. It was brilliant news.

Back inside, the Honda delegates were buzzing. Everybody was really up for the fact that we would be hosting the Games, and questions were being fired at me about what the Olympics were really like. The killer question came towards the end of all the excitement.

'So, Greg, what does it mean for you? What will you be doing during London 2012? Will you be involved in any way? What would be your dream job?'

I hesitated for a second and then laughed. 'My dream job wouldn't be a job. It would be to compete.'

I'm not sure I really meant it, and I certainly didn't take it to heart. While I was in pretty decent shape for a working dad, the Games were still seven years away and I didn't honestly think it was a serious proposition that I could transform myself into an Olympic athlete again. Fun to imagine, but nothing more. There was a hundred times more chance that I would be watching the rowing on the television over a large and contented beer gut than that I would be sitting in one of the boats in a vest and shorts.

Click.

The realization hit me, I'm actually quite good at this rowing thing.

It was March 2006 and I was slumped in my seat, sitting in an eight on the Thames with my brother, Martin Cross, a guy called Ian McNuff, both of whom were almost fifty years old, and a bunch of others, having just come inside the top twenty in the Head of the River race. Considering our age and the fact that we had only been rowing together for a few weeks, it was a hell of a showing and way above most people's expectations.

Jonny had only suggested I join him and the 'Leg-ends', as they call themselves, at the turn of the year and I had slipped straight back into it. The previous April I had run my second London Marathon, followed by a second London Triathlon in August, and although I'd trained hard for both events I only managed to shave off less than four minutes in the marathon and went backwards in the triathlon. Those sorts of results did nothing to excite me. What was the point? I wasn't beating anybody and I clearly wasn't progressing.

Then, following Jonny's suggestion, and having barely rowed for five years, I discovered that with a lot less effort I could con-sistently produce significantly better results in a boat than I could pounding the street. It made me realize that if I was going to put any effort into sport it may as well be one for which I clearly had some natural talent.

Ian McNuff had a lot to do with my re-discovered enthusiasm for rowing. He was a peer of Martin Cross – they rowed to a bronze in the coxless four at the Moscow Olympics in 1980 – but had retired fairly young, only returning to the sport in his late forties. Ian had encouraged Jonny to put together this group of old boys, and he impressed the hell out of me. In spring 2006 we went head-to-head in a 5 km test on a rowing machine and he whipped me. I was fifteen years his junior and yet he was a stronger member of the boat, pulling 6 minutes 10 seconds or better for the 2 km ergo tests, GB standard. It wasn't even his age that was the most impressive thing, it was his results. If he was willing to apply himself and reach that level, what could I do? Surely anything was possible if I really wanted it.

Click.

Jonny, myself and a friend called Richard Wearn, known as Monster by everyone, decided to put a four together for the Visitors' Challenge Cup at Henley that year, without Ian, who had such happy memories of that regatta he didn't want to spoil them with an inevitable loss. We respected Ian's decision and he remained very much involved in our group, but to replace him we recruited a German called Jan Herzog who had rowed in the Sydney Games and was now a medical student in the UK.

Jan made a big difference. Over the course of the four days at Henley we fought our way through to a Sunday showdown with an Oxford Brookes and Leander Club boat. We lost, but as these guys were the British Under-23 team, it was no disgrace. Far from it. There we were, a bunch of retirees still capable of pushing the next generation of racers.

We had progressed significantly since the Head of the River, but Jan's arrival saw us move to an even higher level. That's what impressed me, the difference one bloke can make to a boat if he's in the right shape.

Click.

For our 2007 Leg-ends season Jonny asked a brilliant South African coach called Filipe Salbany to get involved with our eight. That decision transformed us. We evolved from a group that was pretty much self-managed, with occasional, brief chats about what we should be doing, often on conference call because work commitments made it impossible to meet up face to face, into one with hands-on direction supplied by an expert, who was the nearest thing to Harry I had come across.

In fact, Filipe had been an apprentice of Harry's, and not only were their coaching styles similar, so was the impact Filipe had on my career.

Out one morning on the Thames, Filipe called from his launch for us to stop, and drawing up alongside he explained why.

'Gentlemen, why do you pull so aggressively on your handles? Why do you feel you have to force the boat through the water? If you time your application of power properly you will glide, reduce how much you push the boat back and increase speed. It's like golf, you don't need to smash the ball to kingdom come. Think of the great Ernie Els, the Big Easy – it's all in the timing, not the aggression. There is only one of you who is actually connecting with the water effectively, so I want you to try something for me.

'Get underway, and when I call on each of you separately I want you to place your oar in the water, then let go of the handle for a moment and be aware of how it moves towards you before catching it again. I want you to experience the sensation of not pulling aggressively, instead accelerate smoothly with your legs through your stroke as the oar comes with you. You don't need to yank it. Place it in the water, accelerate and it will stay with you.

'Now go. First bow. Good. Number two, good; three, good; four; five – Greg, you don't need to do this – seven; eight.'

Later the boys ripped into me, taking the piss. If I heard the words 'teacher's pet' once I heard them a hundred times. I sucked it all up, I didn't care. The guys could have fun, for me it was probably one of the best days I'd had rowing since Harry. Filipe had reinforced in me the belief that the way in which I rowed was technically sound and made boats go faster. In so doing he made me think that perhaps I was capable of achieving more.

Filipe was full of innovations and emotion, which not only built my confidence but fired my imagination.

'Now,' he called from his bike one day as we prepared to race on the Henley course, 'I want you to row flat out for one minute. I'll call the time, then listen.'

We went for it hard and smooth. All that yanking was a thing of the past. This was rowing as it should be, as it could be again.

'That's good, but I reckon you could still have a better feel for it. Let's do another, but this time with your eyes closed!'

What?

We followed instructions and the effect was astonishing. The trust I felt in those around me soared. We didn't spear each other, we didn't screw up. Everyone knew what to do, and we did it well. We believed. There were no doubts, no weak links, and the boat flew. It was magical and exhilarating and, crucially for me, it translated into results.

At Henley we had some good races on our way to the final of what is known as the Ladies' Challenge Plate, the competition established for eights who are just off the very top international standard. On Thursday we blew the Dutch club Triton Laga away by almost two lengths; on Friday the Americans of Bantam Boat Club fell by the same margin, as did our old friends Leander on the Saturday. Something told me that Sunday's final against a very powerful Harvard team might be my last chance of a win at Henley in the same boat as my brother. We had each triumphed separately there, but never together, and I am afraid that remains the case. Harvard were too powerful, taking us by a length on the day, and while I was bitterly disappointed, I also recognized that to have seriously challenged a crew that, given the opportunity, would have been close to Oxford in the Boat Race, was a huge achievement for a bunch of old codgers. The technique was there, we just weren't fit or strong enough. Full-time work and full-time families sure get in the way of full-time training.

Out of my depth? Kidding myself? No. Talent withering on the vine? Maybe. Was I going to do anything about it? Doubtful.

I was having fun and, realistically, that was as far as I could see it going.

A highlight for me that year was when we re-enacted the Boat Race for fun – in stages, come on, four and a half miles at our age, give me a break – with two loosely-put-together crews representing Oxford and Cambridge. We persuaded Redgrave and Pinsent to become involved and we had a blast. Steve and I were in the Cambridge boat (he had once coached there and I had, well, applied there) while Matthew and Jonny wore Oxford's dark blue. For the guys like me, with tenuous connections at best, it was mostly just a laugh, but those who had actually attended the universities were ready to spill blood and guts in their attempt to win. It was as though they'd never left.

Those 'varsity' match-ups were the most enjoyable rowing experiences I've had outside of high-level competition. The thrill I felt was almost as strong as the one I feel now, because we were all technically good, mentally tough and equally not very fit. At a comparative level it was as if we were all at the peak of our form. I was participating in the sport that I love with a smile on my face for the first time in years.

I was still enjoying my work at Lane4. Outside of the family, my portfolio of clients was taking up all my energy and attention, with the end results matching the level of input. This period proved to be the highlight of my working life to date, heading up an excellent and talented team of eight, all of whom complemented each other. Having been granted a degree of autonomy within the company, I was able to steer the group in the direction I wanted, and I found the whole experience hugely satisfying.

My self-awareness of what it takes to be an effective executive coach grew almost daily. With the responsibility I had been given I knew I had to step up my performance, and I did so by building on the unique elements I could contribute in a leadership capacity; a sense of robustness and resilience. In tough times – in business, in life – I never once let my head drop and took strength from the knocks I had faced throughout my sports career, using them to cement the belief that there is always a way back. This is what I passed to my clients in our leadership sessions.

I was always open and honest about my experiences, the good and the bad. Authenticity was the key. What I gave my clients was frank advice that challenged preconceptions within their organization, helping them reassess their norms and look for more effective ways to operate.

It worked. Repeat business became a key element of the success of my portfolio, and I was supported by an incredibly dedicated team. We would talk constantly on the phone, at home, in the car, at weekends, each one of us committed to producing our individual best in order to drive the team forward. Working within that creative and dynamic group of people gave me a similar fix to the one I'd fed off during my rowing career. The mentality was the same, the drive was the same and the satisfaction in achieving our goals was equally fulfilling.

Life was good, so why even think about messing it up?

Click.

By the beginning of the 2008 season the enthusiasm of some of the Molesey Leg-ends was beginning to flag a little, not in terms of training so much as finding the time to enter competitions at the weekends. At one of the early summer regattas, to be raced on the 2012 Olympic course at Dorney, only six out of the eight could make it. Rather than parachute two new guys into the bigger boat, we decided instead to go for two fours, Jonny and I hooking up with two young, up-and-coming blokes who were the GB Under-23 pair, Dan Ritchie and Mohamed Sbihi.

As we prepared to take our place on the starting line, Dan turned to Jonny. 'Don't worry,' he said, 'I know it's tough. Moe and me will carry you two through to fifteen hundred metres.

201

You guys take it from there. I know you're pretty good at that last bit.'

Cheeky bugger. He didn't think us oldies could take the hard grind.

Moe then lent forward. 'Listen, Greg, you relax. Just set it up and let me send it down.'

He was basically saying that because I was at stroke I should set the pace but not kill myself because I had to look after my body. It felt good to know there was plenty of horsepower behind me.

The crucial element of being at stroke is that you set the rhythm, because the other guys are watching you, copying your movement. If you set a good, confident length – smooth, with quick hands, a clean connection to the water, relaxed and powerful – they will follow. But if you are hesitant, inconsistent and too aggressive, invariably that's what your crew mates will end up doing in spite of themselves, and the speed of the boat will suffer.

We began with me setting a quick pace and took an early lead, which we gradually built on, eventually pulling away from the field in the third quarter. At 1500 m we had the race won and I was able to enjoy the moment, winning on the Olympic course. Nice.

After the race, Dan and Moe's coach, Ian McNuff's wife Sue, said that she thought it was the best she had ever seen Moe row. Moe had been picked up by GB Rowing's Team Start programme, which had been introduced to identify and nurture talent at an early age. At 6 foot 8" and extremely powerful, Moe had huge potential in rowing, but at that stage he hadn't quite fulfilled it. He'd done well in the Juniors but was stuttering slightly in the Under-23 category. Since then he has come through to the GB eight and now sits alongside me in the boat, where he will hopefully realize all that potential by winning gold in London. In 2008, however, he was still very much on an upward learning curve and, according to Sue, he had moved up a notch having just rowed with me.

Perhaps I did still have something to offer.

Click.

My nineteen-year-old nephew Oli, Jenny's sister's youngest son, has just burst through the front door, deposited his rackets in the corner of the hallway and flopped down on the sofa, horizontal. He is staying with us for a year as he trains at the tennis academy at Bisham Abbey. He and his elder brother, Laurie, who plays cricket for Warwickshire, are now the sportsmen in the family.

'I'm starving,' he says, dragging himself to his feet and heading to the kitchen. 'I think I'll have a bowl of cereal before dinner. That was hard going today.'

Oli barely moves from in front of the TV for the rest of the evening, save for joining us at the dining table to eat. He's not being lazy, he needs to rest up. That's a sports person's lifestyle. I remember it well. After training all day you have to give your body time to recover if you are going to perform at the highest standards. Oli is a really good lad and I love hearing about his day, his gym work, circuits, his coaching programme and the matches he plays.

It seems like only yesterday that he and his brother looked up at me with wonder in their eyes whenever we visited. Uncle Greg, Olympic champion. As little kids they would ask me to tell them stories of my races over and over again. Now we've come full circle and it's me who's doing the asking. I want to hear everything about Bisham and the tournaments he plays in. It stirs something deep inside me.

Thirty-six-year-old dads should know better. It's a week before Christmas, it's cold, there are patches of ice on the AstroTurf and I am running around like a mad thing playing five-a-side football with a bunch of fathers from school. I should be at home wrapping presents or watching *It's a Wonderful Life*, something nice and cosy on a night like this, but instead our keeper has just tossed me the ball out on the left and I've knocked it forward with a slightly heavy touch.

Give it up, Greg, their defender is going to shield it out of play. No, wait, I can get there. Just. Go for it.

Running flat out I try to wrap my left leg around my opponent in an attempt to get to the ball before it crosses the bye-line. I think I got something on it but not much. It didn't really matter, though, because the next thing I remember is lying on the adjoining pitch. They were keen to get on with their match so I found myself apologizing and being helped to the sideline. My ankle was on fire. Not literally, but it hurt like hell. This was not good.

As the game carried on I removed my shin pads in time to watch my ankle swell.

'Greg, are you ready to come back on? I'm knackered out here, I need a break.'

'I don't think so. Sorry, boys. I think I'm done for the night. My ankle's throbbing like hell; I think I'd better head home.'

'How about you go in goal?'

'Sorry.'

I was helped to my car and somehow managed to make it to the car park exit. Left was home, right was Wycombe Hospital, five minutes away. My leg didn't feel right at all. I was in trouble. I turned right.

Getting out of my car at the hospital did not go well. I collapsed in a heap on the ground the moment I put any weight on my left leg. I clawed myself upright, grabbing the door handle for support, and managed to hop over to the nearest wall. Holding on for dear life I gingerly made my way to A&E.

Inside it was like a classic scene from *Casualty* – a kid still in his kit who had clearly injured himself playing rugby, a couple of nosebleeds, one guy with a packet of frozen peas clamped to his head and a drunk woman screaming obscenities. I made it to the desk and explained what had happened.

I was called through after about an hour, helped onto a bed and lay there as the doctor examined my leg. I was determined not to squeal as she manipulated my ankle and then sent me through for an X-ray, which revealed a minor break. Before they put the plaster on I called Jenny.

'Hi, it's me, I'm at Wycombe Hospital.'

'Who's hurt themselves?'

'Er, me.'

'You f****** w*****!'

'Sorry, honey.'

We were meant to be hosting a Christmas party in less than a week and we were way behind in the preparations. This was not going to help.

Having my ankle plastered was worse than I could have imagined. I had to lie back with a V-shaped cradle under my knee, which was OK until they asked me to straighten the leg so they could finish underneath. The pain was excruciating and sweat leaked from every pore as I desperately strained my thigh muscles in a futile attempt to control the involuntary shaking. Something was really, really not right.

By then one of my football mates, Ken, had arrived and he drove me home, kindly offering to sort out picking up my car later. It was pretty late by the time he helped me through my front door, and after a brief explanation of what the doctor had told me, I bum shuffled my way up the stairs and into bed. Sleep was impossible. I tried everything, including counting to a hundred and holding my breath, but it was useless. At 4 a.m. I woke Jenny.

'Honey, my ankle's fine, I can barely feel it, but my knee is killing me and it's getting worse. I think I'm going to have to go back to the hospital. Can you call Ken and ask him to give me a lift, he won't mind.'

Back at a much quieter A&E I explained to the nurse what the problem was.

'Mr Searle, before we proceed can I ask if you have any money?'

'Er, no, not on me. Why?'

'Well, then I'm afraid I can't supply any additional ibuprofen.'

'I think this is going to take a bit more than a couple of pills. I know you're the doctor and everything, but I think there might be something else wrong. I'm usually pretty good with pain and this is really bad.'

Eventually Ken convinced them to take another X-ray, looking a little further up my leg, and that's when they found the real damage, a fracture of my tibial plateau, which is where the shin bone comes up to the knee. In my case the break was right at the top of the bone, as if someone had smashed the blade of an axe down on it. If my ankle was a one-out-of-ten injury, this was a seven.

Suddenly I went from requiring basic painkillers and a decent night's sleep to emergency surgery. In an instant my treatment room was transformed into something resembling a battlefield. It wasn't quite *Saving Private Ryan*, but it was pretty dramatic. A morphine drip was quickly found and plugged straight into my arm – that helped a lot as by this time I was suffering the most severe pain I had ever known – while doctors and nurses flew back and forth preparing me for an ambulance trip to Stoke Mandeville hospital, where they would perform the required procedure immediately.

This isn't going to ruin our Christmas.

I don't know whether it was the drugs talking or me wanting to be seen as a bit of a hero, but when I came round after the operation, with screws holding my leg together, I was determined to be out of there as quickly as possible. Nothing we had planned was going to be cancelled. Two days later, on a Saturday afternoon, Dad picked me up and took me home to a house full of our friends enjoying mulled wine and mince pies. A couple of hours later, having wished everyone a Merry Christmas and waved them goodbye, Jenny and I were at the Lane4 fancy dress party. I was Mr Bump.

The madness continued and I could no longer blame it on the morphine. We went to Jenny's family for Christmas dinner and we drove straight from there to Paris for New Year, where I challenged our host to a race. I was going to crutch my way across the snow-covered park by the Eiffel Tower and back again while he ran three laps around it.

What the hell was I trying to prove? That I was invincible? Or that despite the severity of my injury I wasn't done yet?

Click.

Back at Lane4 in January I was working with Nestlé on a two-day workshop, explaining a question-based method of coaching people based on what is known as the GROW model. I offered to be the guinea pig, with the clients asking the questions.

'What's your *goal*?'

'I want to go skiing in April.' I was still on crutches.

'What's the *reality* of achieving that goal?'

'Well, I've had a bad break in my shin plus a lesser fracture in my ankle, so it isn't going to be easy. But I don't believe it's impossible.'

'What are your *options*?'

'I will set myself a tough training schedule which I'll undertake as soon as I physically can. If I stick to that I'll be skiing by my target date.'

'What's your *will*?'

'I am one hundred per cent committed.'

The group looked at me as though they believed it was my mind rather than my leg that was the real problem. I'm pretty sure not a single one of them thought it was possible for me to be slaloming down the Alps within three months. What they didn't understand was that having set myself that very specific and measurable target, I was prepared to do whatever it took to achieve it. From a seemingly impossible situation I was experiencing the same level of motivation I'd had when I was at my peak as an athlete. Up until that moment, when the resolve to go skiing crystallized and I saw what was required to make it happen, I had been drifting in a sporting context, with no specified goal. Now I had a purpose.

The holiday was a huge success. I ended up snowboarding rather than skiing – which was probably even crazier given that skis at least offer some ankle protection – but to me the important thing was that I had faced a serious injury and once more overcome it, despite my age. Thanks to the long hours I'd invested in Marlow Club gym I emerged on the other side of my setback in a better place, active, strong and ready to get back in a boat with renewed determination. I felt I was going somewhere. I just didn't know where.

Would I be bidding for a second Olympic gold twenty years after winning my first if Martin Cross hadn't telephoned me in May 2009? I'm not sure, but I have my suspicions. As I said, I am not exactly the best of self-starters. I had flirted with the possibility of making a comeback in those quiet moments in the middle of the night when you lie awake and try to imagine your future, but every time the thought sneaked up on me I dismissed it. There were too many obstacles and too many difficulties to take the notion seriously.

Did I have it in me to bridge the still enormous chasm between my current level of fitness and that required of an elite athlete? And even if I could make the grade physically, would anybody in GB Rowing even consider me? Would Jürgen? Did I want to risk setting myself up for a humiliating fall? Would I be regarded as nothing more than a bloke facing a midlife crisis and trying to rekindle his youth? Could I face the havoc it would wreak on my stable, happy life? What would it do to my marriage? Would it be fair on Josie and Adam?

No, with so much blocking my path, the thought of a comeback in May 2009 was a pipe dream, and a private one at that.

Then Martin called.

He had been engaged by FISA to provide commentary on the upcoming World Cup race in Banyoles and wondered if I'd be interested in helping him out.

'Sure, why not? It sounds like fun.'

It's impossible to say for sure whether Martin would have joined the dots and come up with my name if the first race of the season hadn't been at the location of my gold-medal triumph in 1992. To me, however, it was another example of how winning that coveted prize changes your life for ever.

Click.

Martin and I watched the semi-finals together to get a feel for the event, with Martin offering excellent advice on what would be required from our commentary the following day, then we drove back to the GB team hotel where he was staying. I had been booked into somewhere different and Martin wanted to drop off his gear before taking me on there. As Martin and I walked up the steps to the front door, the British team manager David Tanner appeared.

'I'm sorry, Greg, but I'm afraid you'll have to wait outside. You are media now and I've imposed a ban to avoid any distractions. No exceptions. You understand, I'm sure.'

Like hell I did. Martin had been granted permission to stay there because he and David were friends, but David's dedication to discipline meant that courtesy hadn't been extended to me, to the extent that I wasn't even allowed inside the hotel lobby. At the time I thought Tanner's decision was ridiculous. He knew my history as well as anybody, and he must have known that the last thing I would do was jeopardize the chances of any of the rowers by pestering them with questions. If the press were regarded as 'them' surely I was one of 'us'. That's what I'd thought anyway, up until that moment. Now I wasn't so sure.

As I was sitting on the steps waiting for Martin, Matt Langridge, the stroke in the GB four, wandered over for a chat. Christ, I thought, he looks strong and fit. Compared to me anyway. We knew each other vaguely, through occasional encounters at the various summer regattas in which I'd been rowing recently. We also had Matt's coach in common, Filipe.

'Greg, how's it going? I hear we might be seeing a lot more of you soon. The word on the street is that you're hitting the comeback trail. That's great. We could do with an old head around here. But you'd better get a move on, time's not on your side.' He was laughing, but something in his tone said he might not be joking.

'Yeah, well, you never know. Do you think they could fit my Zimmer in the boat?'

'For you, anything. We can even arrange for some Horlicks at the end of the races.'

'Now you're talking.' I patted my stomach. 'I might just need a few workouts first, though.'

It was light-hearted banter, but there was more to it than that. Had someone been quietly sowing some seeds? Filipe perhaps? And was it such a ridiculous notion? Matt was treating me as something of an equal. We had immediately established common ground and it felt good, as if he was accepting rather than ridiculing me.

Click.

The final race of the regatta was the men's eight, in which the British boat won bronze, behind the Italians who took the gold.

With my commentary obligations over I made my way down to the landing stage to enjoy the atmosphere, and there I bumped into my old sparring partner from Atlanta, Raffaello Leonardo, who was a member of the winning Italian team. Raffaello seemed delighted to see me, and after we shook hands and spoke for a short while he introduced me to some of his crew mates. It was clear my popularity amongst Italian rowers had not diminished, because before I knew what was happening I was being ushered onto the podium to have my photograph taken with a number of the guys. I was quite taken aback by my reception. Having been absent from the rowing fraternity for so many years I had been quite nervous about hanging out with the current crop of rowers, but in that instant my fears were swept aside. Rather than being an outsider, forgotten and irrelevant, I was clearly still a legitimate part of the upper echelons of world rowing. This was my world, so why had I been hiding from it for so long?

After that Spanish experiment Martin asked me to join him again at the two remaining World Cup races, the first in Munich and the second in Lucerne. Over those weekends we spent a number of great evenings together as he introduced me to life on the media side of the sport, but somehow it never completely captured my imagination. In fact, the high point for me came well away from the microphone when Martin persuaded Empacher, who were exhibiting in Munich, to allow us to take a double scull out on the racecourse on the Saturday evening before the finals. It felt good to be on the water, rowing the course that some of the world's best oarsmen would be competing on the following day. This is where I belong, I thought.

Then came Poznan and the World Championships, where my resolve and confidence were put to the test.

I arrived at the Polish lake half-baked, which wasn't like me. I hadn't put the effort I should have into my role as colour commentator. My heart wasn't in it, but that's no excuse. You turn up ready or you don't turn up at all. If you're injured you don't race, if you race you're not injured. If you have a job to do, you do it to the best of your ability. That's how I have always lived my life, and yet for some reason in Poznan I let myself slip.

Each day at breakfast I would avoid eye contact with the other hotel occupants, many of whom were the FISA delegates responsible for organizing the event. At the very least I should have known some of their names, if not what they actually did, but I hadn't bothered to find out and I felt embarrassed.

'Morning, Greg, it's great to have you here with us. You are just what we need, young blood coming through. You must join us later for a glass or six of red,' they would joke, 'and a big fat cigar if you're up for it.'

No thank you, I would politely decline. I wasn't one of them.

In Poznan I was to be sidekick to David Goldstrum, a veteran of his profession, while Martin commented on different races. David likes to talk, and while we didn't exactly clash, we didn't see eye to eye all the time either. He is one of those commentators who loves to spend hours in their room trawling through the record books in order to produce startling facts the following day. When the time came he could reel off the ages of each of the women in the Ukrainian eight if required, and even if it wasn't, or explain in detail what the Dutch sculler had told him about her approach to training. Me, I managed to mix up the names of the two women in the GB pair. I knew one was called Liv and the other Lou, but which way round was beyond me. Still, in comparison to my knowledge of the lightweight scene, I was an expert on women's rowing. Perhaps I had never quite got over the fact that 'my boat', the coxed pair, had been downgraded in Olympic terms in favour of these little guys.

I know I was never fully on the ball during those Championships in terms of my research, but I could have contributed useful insights into the racing and strategies that were being played out in front of us had I been given a chance to get a word in edgeways over David. That, however, proved to be beyond me much of the time, and on the odd occasion when I succeeded in interrupting David the atmosphere in our commentary box turned decidedly frosty. In one race he even turned off the mics to reprimand me for talking over him.

I was floundering in an environment in which I felt uncomfortable and out of place, and to hide my embarrassment I decided the only thing to do was to act like a holidaymaker and have some nights out. Not a smart move when you've got to be sharp in the morning, but in a roundabout way I guess it led me to where I am today.

'Come on, mate, let him in. I know he's not looking too special at the moment but he'll be all right. Give him a break, he's just won a gold. I'll look after him. Here, will this help.'

I was standing outside a nightclub in Poznan talking to the bouncer on my second to last night in the city, or so I thought. At my side, requiring considerable propping up, was Alex Partridge who, along with Matt Langridge, Richard Egington and Alex Gregory, had just become world champions. Feeling somewhat out of place I found myself tagging along with their celebrations, during which Alex had managed to knock back most of a bottle of sambuca. Most rowers tend to be more or less teetotal in the months before big races, then when it's over they go for it. Alex had been leading from the front until the pace eventually caught up with him.

Having emptied the contents of his stomach on the side of the road, however, he caught a second wind and we decided the bright lights of the disco were for us. The €10 note I slipped the doorman did the trick and that's pretty much all I can remember of the evening. As for the next morning, well, I'm still trying to forget that.

As a thank you for looking after him so well, Alex invited me to be his guest at the GB team's end-of-championships party the next day, which was hosted by their sponsors Siemens.

'Tanner isn't going to be too thrilled if he sees a non-team member like me there,' I told Alex.

'What does it matter? Everyone will be too hammered to care or even notice who's there. Come on, it will be a laugh. You never know what might happen.'

Click. Click. Click.

NINE

THE COMEBACK

Sixteen minutes 56 seconds.

I can still feel the ache in my arms and legs as I make my way north to Nottingham. That was tiring, but I'm pleased. I did the 5 km test earlier in the morning at home on my rowing machine, and the time, 16 minutes 56 seconds, is a decent performance on which to build. I enjoyed the session, pushing myself through the pain barrier, and I want more of it. More of that sensation of having driven myself to my limits. It wasn't easy, I haven't extended myself like that for a long time, but then again, I haven't had any reason to. Until now. I have a lot more agony to go through, but it's not beyond me.

It's 2 September 2009 and I am driving to my two-day workshop with Nestlé Cereal Partners, turning over in my mind all the things I'll have to do before calling Jürgen. Jenny and I spoke briefly about my big idea yesterday evening on my return from Poznan, but what with playing with Josie and Adam, handing out the presents I'd brought back and checking I had everything sorted for work, we didn't have the opportunity to go over anything in detail. She was excited and supportive, but there's so much more to discuss.

Get myself in shape.

When are the British trials? The beginning of October, or the end? Do I have time to train, to hit the 6 minute 10 seconds qualifying time for the 2 km ergo test that I know I have to make to even be in with a shout?

I have to speak to Jürgen.

How will this work with Lane4?

Sponsors?

Where is my single? And my blades?

Seriously, where *is* my single? That's a good question. It's been a couple of years at least since I've had it out on the water; it was when my friends Bob Tucker and Will Castle were visiting I think. We took all the kids down to Higginson Park in Marlow to feed the ducks. I remember now, they persuaded me to have a paddle that day for old time's sake. They borrowed a double from Marlow Rowing Club and I collected my boat from the scout camp and outdoor activity centre at Longridge, by Marlow bridge. That's where it is now, I'm sure of it, on those wooden racks outside. God I hope it's in better nick than the last time, when it was covered in mud and bird shit, with an old wasps' nest crumbling in the shoe!

It was a fun day with Will and Bob, rowing back and forth along that stretch of the river while the kids played in the park. It didn't end so well, though, when I rowed over to where the kids were throwing bread in for the ducks and, for a laugh, started to splash about a bit, daft Dad like. I lost my grip on one of the oars, and as I leaned out to retrieve it I rolled right over, taking an unintended dip in the Thames. Not exactly Olympic-standard oarsmanship. And to add insult to injury, when my head bobbed back up, I wasn't just looking at the amused faces of Josie, Adam and the others, but at the steely gaze of Sir Steve Redgrave! Well, his statue anyway, which had been erected there after the 2000 Games in Sydney.

Must do better, Greg.

The more I turn these issues over in my head, the more excited I become. I've got to speak to Jenny. Now. I've got to know how she feels. It can't wait until I'm back home.

I make the call from the car phone.

'Honey, it's me. Sorry, I know you're busy, but we've got to talk. This thing, this comeback dream, am I mad? I want it, I want to make this happen. I can do it, I'm sure, but I need to know what you think. Is it too much? Is the cost too high? It's all whirling around in my mind.'

Jenny can't get a word in. It's all coming out in a torrent. I can sense her smiling at the phone as I speak. She's heard me like this before, but not for a long time. I take a breath and she jumps in.

'Greg, Greg, listen. Calm down. Let's talk it through. It's a big step. You need to think about it in practical terms. Can we afford it for one thing? And what about Josie and Adam? I know what this entails, remember. You will be away for about a hundred days a year and they will miss you. And how do you think they'll feel about not having a real family holiday until 2013? That's a long time for them, Greg, and they will grow up fast. You know as well as I do that there is no way you will be able to take time out if you are really serious about this.'

'I am, but you are right we won't be able to get away, not properly and I will miss them badly. But maybe it will be like when I was a kid, just starting out, when Mum and Dad came to the races. That could be our holiday. OK, it's not a beach but it can be fun. And I'll be able to get home in the day time more. I can pick them up from school when I'm in the country. How'd you think they'll feel about all that?'

'I think if their dad is rowing in a big race for his country, they'll love it. It's not just them I'm worried about, it's you. How will you feel about missing the family?'

'It will be hard, I know that, but it isn't for ever. And I want to make them proud of me. As for money, I was thinking, I can continue to do some stuff for Lane4 and maybe I can find some sponsors. I know a few people through Lane4 and outside. That's possible, probable even. I think so anyway. Isn't it?'

'It is. We can make it work, we can plan. You've got contacts, if you do this, people will be interested. You just need to make it happen. We'll be OK. But these are all side issues, things we can control. For me, Greg, there's really only one issue you need to think about. Do you feel in your heart that you can make it? Only you can answer that question. What I can't face is the thought of you putting yourself out there and ending up reliving the disappointment of Sydney. Do you believe in yourself? Really?'

She's right. Sydney. That's the shadow that sometimes creeps up on me in those quiet moments when no one else is around. Jenny understands that. Sydney 2000, where my rowing career apparently came to an end. It has never felt right. It isn't a good place for my story to have finished. If I take this chance, if I make the leap today, maybe I can eventually close my rowing story in the way I believe it should have ended all those years ago, with another gold. This is the last ever chance. This is the moment. Do I believe in myself? That's all she wants to know. She's not picking holes, looking for problems, trying to find reasons not to put us through this, and God knows there are enough of them. All she is asking is if I believe in myself.

'I can do this, Jenny, I know I can.' As I say the words, I feel a lump forming in my throat, I feel my eyes welling up. 'It will be huge, making a comeback. I realize that. It will change everything from now until the Games. I don't know how it will end, but I've got to go for it, Jenny, with you next to me, all the way through to our Olympics. One thing I promise you, though, whatever happens I will enjoy the journey. It won't be a waste.'

The tears are flowing now.

'OK. Good. That's what I wanted to hear. I know what you get like when you're determined to do something. I know you will do everything to make it work. Let's make this real, Greg. The Olympics will be huge, and I'd rather you were putting your heart into that than working your arse off for Nestlé or someone! I haven't heard you like this for years. It's like you've been reignited. We'll be right next to you. But I've got one condition. And I need you to do this for me or I can't go through it. Promise me you'll do it.'

Oh God. She's having second thoughts.

'I promise.'

'Pull over, you idiot! You're in no fit state to drive!'

I made it to Nottingham in one piece where, following that conversation with Jenny, my comeback trail began in earnest in an almost deserted hotel gym with a few easy 500s on their rowing machine and some bench presses. This was the start of the quirky little programme I put together for myself, integrating work, rowing and conditioning. I gave myself three weeks to get into shape before contacting Jürgen to discuss whether this mad idea could actually become reality, or whether it was just a fairytale.

My day would kick off at 6 a.m., when I would get up with a spring in my step, keen to head down to Longridge before the family were awake to take my scull out on the Thames. This was the only place I could train really. Understandably, I wasn't allowed access to the British team's rowing facility; Molesey was an hour away, which was too far to go every morning, even though I'm sure they'd have had me, and I wasn't ready to join Leander. So Longridge it was, where I would drive to the pot-holed car park, change beside the car, then scrabble through the undergrowth of the scout camp to find my boat. When I first started out there the autumn sun regularly shone, but it wasn't long before the snow arrived and the sessions became really tough.

Right from the beginning these weren't pleasure trips up and down the river. My mindset had totally changed. Instead of enjoying the freedom, the quiet, the glistening of the water, the sights of the riverbank, as I had on those rare occasions over the past two or three years when I'd taken my boat out, now I was focused, aware of my arms, my legs, my back. For the first time in years I was thinking seriously about rowing.

The left blade is digging. The right blade is coming out too early. I've got work to do.

I set myself a target – of course I did, that's what I do. I wanted to get in 10 km each morning before returning home for breakfast with the kids. Compared to what I do now it was relatively pitiful, but it was a big step forward. It hurt, but it was a pleasurable pain. Being back in the seat of my single was where I wanted to be.

Gym visits had to be fitted around my Lane4 schedule. If I was working from home Jenny and I would go to the local Marlow Club together, where she, along with other mums taking advantage of their kids being at school, would do leg curls and aerobic work, while I lifted increasingly heavier weights, working on my rusty power-clean technique, and invariably collapsing in a sweat-drenched heap while the other club members looked at me like I was mad. It was hard not to feel self-conscious.

If I had an office day I would try and make the gym before returning home in the evening, but if I was away on client work, it was more often than not impossible to fit in a meaningful session. Those *Rocky*-esque days of the early nineties were back with a vengeance.

Building my muscles and power was essential, but it would have been pointless if I couldn't translate that into decent ergo performances. The 6 minute 10 seconds cut-off time that I would be required to meet at the all-comers trials in Boston, Lincolnshire, was foremost in my mind. If I missed that, everything would be in vain.

At home I used a Concept2 rowing machine that the manufacturer had given me back in 1997 after my sculling bronze at the World Championships. Pounding out 5 or 10 km to build endurance and then pushing myself over the all-important 2 km distance. In those first couple of weeks, the qualifying time seemed like a pipe dream. I just had to remain confident that the speed would come.

While weight training was often impractical when I was on the road, there was no reason that travelling and staying in hotels should get in the way of my ergos. I would pack the old Concept2 in the back of the car and set it up in my room, where I would fit in forty-five minutes at the end of the workshops and ahead of any evening activities.

On 24 September I was once again in Nottingham with Nestlé Cereal Partners, at that same gym, but this time there were no easy 500s. This was serious. I had marked 26 September as the day to call Jürgen. Time was running out.

It was a two-day workshop, focusing on NCP's strategy for the next three years. At the end of day one I stood up and gave a potted history of my career, including showing the Barcelona race, then I talked a little about my personal goals, how I had set myself a three-year plan to win a gold medal in London.

Up until that moment I had spoken only to my family about what I hoped to achieve, and Jenny, Jonny and my parents had been incredibly supportive. Jonny's only concern had been that I might run the risk of over-committing myself and make things difficult at home. When I reassured him that Jenny and I had spoken at length about the potential pitfalls and pressures and that we were confident we could make it work, he only had one further comment.

'Go for it.'

As for Mum and Dad, they were excited, and more than a little surprised, when I broke the news.

'Greg,' Dad said to me as he shook my hand, 'rowing has brought your mother and me an enormous amount of pleasure over the years. We've been around the world following you and Jonny and we've loved it. There is not a sliver of doubt in my mind that you won't make this happen, that you won't succeed, and we'll be reliving some of those wonderful moments once again. We're proud of you.'

While speaking openly about my ambitions for 2012 in Nottingham didn't quite constitute earth-shattering breaking news, it caused quite a stir amongst those in the workshop, and everyone was keen to quiz me further over a couple of pre-dinner pints of beer.

'Thanks, but I'm afraid these days I tend to only do pints of orange and lemonade. And anyway, I'm going to hit the gym now. Today's a big day for me. If I don't crack the qualifying time on the rowing machine then the whole thing will be over before it's even begun. It's now or never. Wish me luck.'

As the bulk of the group disappeared off to the hotel bar, three fit-looking guys hung back. 'Mind if we tag along, Greg? We'd love to have a go at racing you if that's OK.'

'Sure, why not.'

'If this is going to be a spectator sport, then count me in as well.' This was my co-presenter, Jeanette Wilkner, head of HR at NCP and the person who'd hired me, having seen my Lane4 work with the main Nestlé company over the previous couple of years. It was Jeanette who had recommended to the Cereal Partners board that they engage Lane4 to facilitate their strategy planning and we'd been working together since the beginning of 2009.

Jeanette had rowed at Cambridge in her student days, which was one of the reasons we got on so well and performed effectively as a team. In fact, it was Jeanette who was to become pivotal in helping me overcome one of the barriers to my comeback by introducing me to her marketing department, which in turn led to a critically important sponsorship deal. Over the next twenty minutes, however, she would play a very different role.

'Absolutely, let's go.'

Having these three blokes join me wasn't exactly what I'd envisaged. I had planned on being very focused, and now I was beginning to feel a bit pressured. 'We don't have much time before dinner and I don't want to be late. A highly tuned athlete like me needs his food,' I joked to relieve some of my tension as we made our way to the gym. This was a big moment and I needed to keep loose and relaxed.

Maybe this could work to my advantage after all, I thought. I set up two rowing machines, one for me and one for my new rowing partners.

'How about this. I've only programmed your machine for 1500 m but mine for 2000 m. Why don't you do 500 m each, then jump off and let the next guy take over. Let's see who gets to the finish first.'

They beat me, not by much, but it didn't matter. Having them alongside actually helped as I love to race. By the time the last guy finished I was something like 100 m from the end, blowing hard, very hard.

'Come on, old man, why are you slowing down?'

Jeanette was leaning right into my face, giving me some good-natured stick to drive me on.

'Does it hurt too much? You're past it? You don't have it any more. Just give it up now.'

No chance. I threw everything I had into that final push, my T-shirt sticking to my back, stained dark with perspiration. My mouth was dry. I could barely see the screen in front of me as sweat stung my eyes. My legs began to shake. I can do this. I'm not past it.

Six minutes 8 seconds.

Time to make that call.

*

'OK, Greg,' Jürgen said once I'd outlined briefly what I wanted to discuss, 'let's get together and talk. Meet me at Caversham tomorrow.'

'Great, thanks. Er, just one thing. How do I get there?'

The following day, glancing at Jürgen's directions scribbled on a pad lying on the passenger seat, I found myself driving down a country lane. Turning right onto a newly built road, I stopped the car for a moment. The sign indicating the way to the Caversham gates gives a clear indication of where the power in modern-day rowing lies. It read 'Grobler Way'. I was about to become a convert.

Caversham hadn't existed in my previous life, but it's now the headquarters of British rowing, a state-of-the-art facility opened in 2006 for the exclusive use of GB rowers. It comprises a 2000 m rowing lake and one self-contained building consisting of a boat house full of very nice boats, a gym, an area with rowing machines, a couple of changing rooms, a cafeteria, plus offices and a meeting room.

As I drove up to the complex I stopped my car again. Ahead of me was a huge sign that brought a wry smile to my face. Here we go again.

'The Redgrave and Pinsent Rowing Lake'.

I met Jürgen in the small, cramped meeting room, with the flip charts stashed in the corner, a television screen attached to the wall and the floor space almost entirely filled with a hexagonal table at which we sat across from one another. I explained what had brought me to my decision, and what I'd been doing over the past few weeks. I looked into his eyes and he looked back into mine. He was assessing me.

'Have you thought about coaching?'

'I'm not interested in that. I'm serious about doing this as a rower. That's the only option as far as I'm concerned.'

'OK, I can see that. Now let me tell you where I stand. I select people on merit. If you are good enough you will be in the team. That's all that matters. You need to prove it to me, Greg. No one is too young or too old. But understand, if you are just the same as someone younger, then he makes it, not you.'

'I get it.'

No special treatment then. Good. That's the way it should be. I don't want any. He hasn't told me to forget it, though, that I've got no chance. In fact, he's much more receptive and warm than I had expected. I can make this happen.

Jürgen's reaction was an important boost. We'd had our issues in the past, over his training methods, the Empacher boat and, probably most significantly, the fact that I turned my back on him and Leander in 1992 when Terry Fuckwit insisted on wearing his black hood. Back then, with Steve Redgrave saying some positive things about me, Jürgen almost certainly wanted me to join his group, but I opted for a different route throughout most of the nineties. I'd chosen loyalty to one club, Molesey, over naked ambition and I hadn't regretted it. In football terms I suppose I'd been a bit like Ryan Giggs, sticking with Manchester United for his whole career rather than jumping at more lucrative offers from elsewhere.

Yet there I was, almost twenty years later, with cap in hand, knocking on his door, hoping for a chance to 'play for England' under coach Grobler. The prodigal son had returned and he'd been made to feel welcome.

Since that first meeting in Caversham, Jürgen and I have grown close and our relationship has been excellent. I've done well under his guidance and if he asks me to jump I absolutely ask how high. I like to think that he sees I've brought something that was previously missing from his team.

What do I bring to the table, in addition to rowing, that I didn't bring before? Or, to put it another way, what is it I have now that other people in the team don't? What additional traits does

Jürgen see in me? I don't think it's maturity in the sense that I can handle the pressure and others can't. Putting it in a rugby context, I'm not the guy who gathers his team-mates together under the posts when the opposition have just snatched the lead with five minutes to go and gives a calm speech about how we have to keep our heads and keep doing what we are doing and we'll score the winning try. I might have some of that mentality, but others certainly have it as well.

No, I think the thing I have is an appreciation of the bigger picture, of what an opportunity it is to be an athlete now, because I've had it and lost it, and now I have it back again. I also understand what it used to be like, when we didn't have Caversham, when we didn't train three times a day because we had work to go to. Rather than viewing tough, hard training as a bit of a drag, an unpleasant and painful box that has to be ticked, which in my view is the mentality of failure, my attitude is to embrace it, take it on and do the best I can. However hard the programme might be, it only has one purpose, to enable each member of the team to win a gold medal. I hope I make that obvious in everything I do within the team environment. If my attitude is clear to those around me, then perhaps some of it might rub off. The same goes for how I react to being coached. I've become more open and receptive this time round and I believe it's important to demonstrate this. If I can change my technique after all these years, then others ought to be able to as well.

Normal life didn't stop just because I'd come up with this madcap idea of becoming an Olympic athlete again. In addition to work, there were other commitments that had to be met.

I have a cousin whose son was a member of a rowing club in Bideford, Devon, and my brother Jonny and I had happily agreed to pay a Saturday visit to name some boats and give a little talk. With a late morning arrival required, we had to set off early, which meant there was no time for training before we left. Not a problem, how long could a naming ceremony and a short talk followed by a light Q&A take? I was certain I'd be home in time for a decent ergo session before settling down in front of the *X-Factor* with the family.

Not exactly.

We arrived on time, and after the formalities were over some of the parents asked whether it would be OK for a few of the kids to row in boats with Jonny and me. Sure, delighted to. I climbed into one quad and Jonny got into another and we were each joined by three kids. After the first 500 m out and 500 m back it suddenly went from a 'few' to every kid in the club wanting a go. We must have gone up and down that stretch of water a dozen times, which took up most of the afternoon. It's a good couple of hundred miles to Bideford from Marlow and there was no way I was going to make it home in time to fit in any training. With only a couple of weeks to go to the trials in Boston, I began to feel a little twitchy.

The refreshments that had been laid on came to my rescue. A quick exit would have been inappropriate, so while everybody was milling around chatting I decided to take advantage of the rowing machine that had been set up in the middle of the room so some of the kids could try it out.

'Would anyone mind if I hog this for sixteen minutes or so?' I asked my cousin.

'No problem. As long as you don't mind an audience.'

The 5 km ergo is probably the most unpleasant test you can do. In a long 20 km session you get a sore arse and your muscles are tired at the end, but it's boredom as much as anything that gets to you. There is no gritting of teeth as you struggle to keep going. With the 5 km there is, and a whole lot more.

It's a long-distance sprint at 2 km pace virtually the whole way, only for two-and-a-half times longer. It kills you and it's hardly something you'd want to put yourself through in public, but with the trial looming I had little choice. I put personal dignity to one side and got on with it while those around me sipped tea and nibbled on scones. Maybe the *Rocky* analogy doesn't work after all. I don't think that sort of thing happens very often on the mean streets of Philadelphia.

The following week Jenny's comment regarding the kids' holidays was very much on my mind. We had planned a weekend away to Cornwall with two other couples and their kids, and I was determined not to cancel. I didn't want my Olympic ambition to compromise family time, or at least for it to do so as rarely as possible.

We had a lovely time, the early autumn weather was kind and we enjoyed a spot of surfing, pub lunches and afternoon walks along the beach, kicking a ball about or stopping for a game of cricket on the sand. I couldn't abandon my regime entirely, though. Along with all the other gear we took with us, I managed to squeeze my ergo into the car, and in the mornings, as the others went off on cliff walks, I would set it up in the car park and do 20 km while my friends and family were enjoying the spectacular views.

It was a juggling act, but it was one I was getting good at. I just hoped it would pay dividends.

On a cold, wet early morning towards the end of October 2009 my mate Wheelie and I were strapping our single sculls onto the roof of my car and preparing to drive to Boston for the trials. As I watched him tie off the boats and climb into the passenger seat I felt pleased he was there. Wheelie and I had been in World Championship squads together in the late nineties, but it was only in New Zealand, during the America's Cup, that we had become close friends. He is three or four years younger than me and exudes boundless enthusiasm and positivity, which that morning gave me the shot of extra energy I needed as I prepared to take my first steps back into competitive racing after an absence of almost a decade.

Wheelie was based in Cardiff where he worked as a pharmaceutical rep, but he had kept up his rowing and when I told him I was planning a comeback, beginning with the Boston trial, his response was immediate.

'Why don't we do it together? I'm not letting an old codger like you take all the glory. I'm in pretty good nick, let's show them how it's done.'

'You're on.'

The first stage of the trial was held in a huge sports hall in the Boston leisure centre, where seventy big, strong hopefuls, ranging in ages from eighteen to, well, me, were milling around registering when we arrived.

There were some familiar faces as I stood waiting my turn to complete the necessary forms, but none of them were amongst the rowers. It was the administrative staff and coaches that I recognized, people such as David Tanner and Steve Gunn. They were my contemporaries, not my fellow competitors.

Along with name, age, height, weight and which rowing club you were affiliated to, one of the questions on the registration form was, 'Name of coach'. I wrote Harry Mahon and handed it back to the guy who was processing the new arrivals. He read it then looked up at me.

'Didn't he die nine years ago?'

'Yes, but he's still with me when I am sculling.'

My DIY training regime seemed to have paid off when, in the afternoon, I pulled 6 minutes 6 seconds fairly comfortably in the 2 km, placing me something like twenty-third in the rankings at the end of the first day. Good enough, but well behind Wheelie who came in tenth, with a time of 6 minutes flat.

I bumped into David Tanner soon after the test and mentioned that I felt quite proud to have gone under 6.10 given the limited amount of training and preparation I'd been able to put in. He looked at me and said, 'I'll tell you when you have done something to be proud of.'

Right. Thanks for the support, David.

I realized then what I was letting myself in for. He was probably just trying to motivate me but it made me feel that the man in charge didn't understand what made me tick. If I was going to pull this off I was going to have to learn to soak up a lot of stuff I might not like.

I smiled at David. 'OK. I look forward to that.'

A few minutes later I found Wheelie sitting on a gym mat along with all the other guys who'd made the cut, waiting to be addressed by Jürgen. 'We might be old enough to be their dads, but we've both still got it, Greggles!' he laughed. 'And I bet they won't be as smart as us when it comes to race time – this is going to be good.'

Once everyone was settled, Jürgen spoke to the assembled group.

'Well done on making it through the first stage. Anything is possible from here. There are no names on any seats for the Olympic team. No one is too young and no one is too old. You might have noticed already that Greg Searle is here.'

Gee, thanks Jürgen.

'Greg won a gold medal in 1992 and he's back trying again, with as good a chance as anyone else. Race well and I'll see you tomorrow.'

Lunch for Wheelie and I was enjoyed amid the very civilized surroundings of a large department-store restaurant on the out-skirts of Boston, where alongside the local blue-rinse brigade we tucked into a nice lasagne, jacket potato and salad. In contrast, on our way there we'd noticed some of the other all-comers, most of whom were probably students, making a beeline for a local burger bar while munching their way through a packet of Jaffa Cakes just to keep their hunger at bay. Two very different worlds were going to clash on the water the following day.

After lunch, Wheelie and I went for a quick paddle to familiarize ourselves with the course, before chatting up the locals at Boston Rowing Club, who allowed us to nab a couple of indoor racks so we'd have clean boats and warm, dry shoes the next day.

'We're staying one step ahead of the game, Greggles. They might have youth, but we've got nous.'

Sunday was the real test, a time trial in our single sculls. We set out in the order established on the previous day, and as number 22 set off I hung back, adopting some wily old tactics such as stopping, adjusting my gate and sorting out my feet, to ensure there was a nice gap between the two of us. A minute rather than the twenty seconds allocated.

I felt confident that I would go well in the trial and was likely to catch the guy in front. I knew that if I had to row through his wash or steer around him it would slow me down. As I wasn't going to get another shot at this I wanted to give myself the best possible chance to succeed. In fact, I caught him anyway, and the next bloke. I'd gone well, I just didn't know how well until we were on our way home.

Wheelie took the call. It was from his coach in Wales, who'd been helping out at the trial. It turned out Wheelie had done pretty well, but had narrowly missed out on making the grade. As for me, I hadn't just gone well, I'd won the whole thing. On the basis of what I had achieved over the weekend, I was the best of the all-comers.

Christ, this is really beginning to happen.

Wheelie was brilliant, disappointed not to have made it to the next stage but delighted for me.

'Bloody fantastic, mate. Well done. You've still got it, you canny old bastard.'

That probably summed up how I was feeling, a deep satisfaction that whatever magic I'd once possessed was still there. After all these years, I hadn't lost the ability to row, and row fast. Prior to the trial I'd had very little idea what to expect. Fitness-wise I was OK, my ergos had shown that, but had the sport moved on in my absence? Were the coaches teaching new and better techniques? It was possible. I couldn't know until I tested myself in a competitive environment. I'd done that and come out on top. But as well as satisfaction that I'd passed my first big test, there was a degree of relief.

Three or four of us from Boston received weekend invitations to go to Caversham and train with the GB team scullers. On each visit I made sure I performed to the best of my ability, doing everything asked of me on both the machines and the water, and hoping Jürgen would notice. There was no special treatment, my past was just that, the past. Now I was simply one of the group, finding whatever spare peg was available in the locker room, keeping my head down, trying not to annoy anyone, following the programme that was set for us, taking advantage of the excellent facilities and working hard. I had a lot of catching up to do.

Having said there was no special treatment, the fact that I was a known face was an advantage as I didn't feel so much of an outsider. It was Matt Langridge again who stepped up, just as he had on those hotel steps in Banyoles.

On maybe my second trip to Caversham I bumped into Matt as I was preparing to put my single scull into the water.

'Greg, great to see you.' He looked genuinely pleased. 'So it's true, you're making a comeback. Good.' He raised his eyebrows in mock horror. 'But shit, I don't fancy your chances in that.' He was pointing towards my decade-old boat. 'Listen, Jürgen's got me in a pair at the moment, so why don't you borrow my single? I don't need it for now. I think you'll notice a difference. Unlike that old thing, it's not been carved from the trunk of a tree to start with!'

That was good of Matt. He didn't need to lend me his boat but he was keen to help out, to give me the best chance possible of making an impact. I felt as though he was saying I belonged there.

I accepted his offer gratefully. Ten years in boat manufacture is a generation if not more, and the improvements were tangible, helping me to remain there, or thereabouts, in the training I was involved in throughout November and December.

How I would fare in race conditions was yet to be seen, and it wasn't until the following February that I would have an opportunity to find out. A proposed pre-Christmas trial was cancelled because of the weather, which in retrospect probably helped me, as those extra couple of months allowed me to make up for a lot of lost time.

This was a hectic period in my life. I was working hard at Lane4, while increasing the intensity and regularity of my training in an attempt to stop the GB guys from disappearing out of sight in terms of their fitness. In between I was trying to keep sane and continue to function as a family man.

Christmas was important. The previous year I'd sort of messed it up with my broken leg, and I didn't want the kids to miss out on all the usual fun and games this year, like Dad being able to join them playing with their new toys or going for a Christmas Day walk before lunch, all the usual stuff. I did manage to slip in a tough 5 km ergo in the morning, though.

When I mentioned this to one of the British guys a couple of months later he thought I was mad.

'A five k on Christmas Day! You're nuts. Doing a two k is pushing it if you ask me. I try and avoid five k at the best of times. They're killers. But to do one through choice! At Christmas!' He laughed. 'If you ask me, you need professional help, Greg.'

'Well, I had to work off all the mince pies somehow.'

*

Towards the end of the year I addressed my situation at Lane4. If I was going to realize my ambition of making the GB team for the summer regattas it was clear I couldn't continue in full-time employment. By then I had begun to sound out potential sponsors to plug the inevitable financial hole that would result from cutting down my working schedule. My friend Keith Wishart, whose kids went to the same school as mine, had already provided some cash and was introducing me to some great contacts. In addition, Nestlé Cereal Partners had indicated they would come on board, which was a huge confidence boost – I realized I had to make the jump now or it would be too late.

First I spoke to Adrian Moorhouse, outlining what I thought was possible and practical, and he was very supportive. That was one definite advantage of being involved with a company whose roots are firmly based in sport, and Olympic sport specifically. Adrian fully understood the powerful motivation that was driving me.

'You know I would love to have you continue full time in the business, Greg,' he told me as we discussed the various options, 'but if I'm honest with myself I know that if I was in your position I would go for it.'

The deal was struck, I would drop to one-third salary and one-third client days, which worked out at a manageable thirty days in the calendar year. Another obstacle had been addressed and overcome, and I got off to a cracking start in January when I flew out to LA to work with BT Operate for a week. With travel included as client time and an intense workshop over five or six days, I'd clocked up almost a quarter of what I had committed to before the year was a month old.

The February trial was a flat-out regatta in which I was competing against the GB scullers, and I beat the guy who was the team's spare. This meant that of the British squad who had been sculling in Poznan the year before, the six who had actually raced were ahead of me, but I was faster than the reserve, a result that secured my ticket to the team's Portuguese training camp later that month. For my first trial in over ten years, and given the fact that the LA trip had taken a week out of my water-based training schedule, I was pleased with my performance. I was in the mix, which at that stage in the comeback trail was realistically the best I could have hoped for.

If Jürgen was impressed he hid it well. 'Good, Greg, but there's a long way to go. Keep sculling for now. This is not decision time.'

Portugal was tough, physically demanding and an enormous step up from what I'd undertaken up until that point. I was knackered the whole time, but I coped. Just.

The days began with a long water session, 24 km usually, then 20 km on the rowing machine followed by an additional 16 km on the lake in the afternoon. The camp had one primary goal: to build as wide a base as possible of Jürgen's pyramid of fitness. I was starting from a position well behind the rest of the pack, which meant I tried extra hard to prove myself in each training session.

In my training group was Alan Campbell, the fastest sculler in the country and Britain's only other single sculling World Championship medal winner after myself back in 1997. Being out there amongst the big boys, like Alan, was a massive challenge, but it was where I wanted and needed to be and I acquitted myself well. While I knew I wasn't a threat to Alan, I think I might have had him and his coach a bit worried, but more importantly for me I was keeping up, not embarrassing myself and not breaking down. Crucially, I was pulling decent numbers in the ergos, comparable to what I had been achieving ten years earlier. That gave me the confidence to know that I could train to an elite level and not fall over. Speed on the water would follow, I was sure, as my technique, fitness and race sharpness continued to improve.

The Portugal trip was another critical step along the way and my performances were such that on our return home I made a seamless transition to become pretty much a full-time member of the team, while continuing to juggle my remaining Lane4 commitments.

I was now a regular not only at Caversham, but also at the Bisham Abbey sports training facility, which meant one thing: heavy-duty weightlifting was now back in my life big time. Bisham was a million miles from the Marlow Club I used to train in. There, Jenny would be next to me engaged in light arm curls to tone and generally raise her level of fitness; here, I was alongside guys lifting bars with weights that looked like car tyres on the end of them.

The weekly routine was punishing. Bisham for a morning session of monster weights, Caversham for a long row, followed by lunch, then another rowing session or an ergo in the afternoon, five days a week. Saturday was Caversham for two rowing sessions and Sunday one rowing session in the morning, from which I often had to rush off to referee Adam's football at 10.30 a.m. or attend a swimming gala with Josie.

I was just about managing to keep all the various balls in the air.

The first of May was circled in red in my diary. This was the last day of a three-day trial at Caversham, at which Jürgen was going to make his final boat selections for the World Cup regattas over the summer. Everything rested on that trial.

Before then, however, I had to negotiate a further training camp in Varese, followed immediately by an important trial in Belgium, the last before final selection, where any remaining dead wood would be cut out.

The timing of the camp wasn't ideal as it fell during the kids' Easter holiday, so Jenny and I decided to make a bit of a thing of me leaving, try to make it exciting by bringing Josie and Adam to the airport to see me off. We didn't try that again. As far as I was aware the pair of them were fine, holding it together and waving enthusiastically as I disappeared through security, but apparently the moment I was out of sight they both dissolved in floods of tears. As Jenny told me later, she had just about calmed them down by the time she got to the car.

As in the February trial, the scullers who had competed in the 2009 World Championships beat me, but this time so did the team's reserve – by a couple of feet. At least I was way ahead of another all-comer, a guy from Molesey who was miles back in ninth.

My battle with the reserve had been close, but nonetheless it was a disappointing result, if not wholly unexpected. I chose to view it as their youth allowing them to take a greater leap forward rather than me taking a step backwards. What was clear, however, was that I wasn't on the brink of forcing my way into that group. I suspect Jürgen had known that all along. Even way back he had never really been interested in me as a sculler, but before he made any decisions he had to see I still had it in me to compete.

Immediately after the Belgian trial, Jürgen sat me down at a picnic table by the course.

'OK, Greg, I am very pleased with your progress. I can see that you are hungry and dedicated and committed. And I have seen you can train, you have proved your fitness. But it's also clear you aren't what I think we need for the sculling team. To me, you are a rower, you always have been, and now I want to see how you perform in that environment. I want to see you with one oar rather than two. When we arrive back home you have a couple of days off and then I want you at Caversham ready to row. You have ten days before the May trial. Show me you belong in the eight. Make me pick you. If you perform, you are in; if not, it's the end.'

No special treatment.

Ten days to prepare for perhaps the most important trial of my career. Ten days to switch from sculling to rowing. It wasn't long, but I knew there would be no second chance. I could either give up or go for it. Stick or twist? No contest. Twist. I'd give it everything I had in the days available and see if I could beat the odds.

The trials were to be conducted in what is known as seat races, during which twelve guys compete for the eight seats in the boat. Hodge and Reed were already secure in the pair, and the trials for the four were conducted separately.

Over the ten days prior to the trial, Jürgen had placed the twelve contenders for the eight into three fours and we trained in those groups, an A boat of four guys from last year's World Championship crew, a B boat, where I was, and a C boat, strong rowers who had as good a shot as anyone at securing a place.

The seat races were a series of ten 1500 m contests, with rowers moved between the three boats after each race in order to assess which combinations worked best. In the first race, the A boat beat the B boat by a second. I was then swapped with one of the guys from A. The C boat would stay the same this time. We then raced again, this time A beat B by a second and a half. Based on that, the assumption was made that I had made the boat go faster by half a second.

The whole premise of the system is that no one knows who will be swapped next, so everyone goes as hard as they can in each race, hopefully providing a fair reflection on performance levels within a racing environment.

It was nerve-racking but I loved it. To me, that is what rowing is all about – the drama of racing – and I found it exciting and motivating. This was exactly what we'd been missing all those years ago: real team competition for places, transparent and fair.

It brought out the best in me, which eight months earlier, when I'd been necking shots in a Polish brewery, would have seemed impossible. I didn't recognize that behaviour any longer. The man who looked at himself in the mirror on the evening of 1 May would never act like that now. He'd travelled a long way and was now a member of the British eight for the forthcoming World Cup season, nineteen years after he'd last raced internationally in the event. I'd made it.

Nineteen years. That was a long time ago. Some of the guys I was now rowing with weren't even at school then. If it had been the prodigal son's return when I'd reunited with Jürgen, this was Dad turning up and insisting on dancing at the youth club disco.

Over the course of that 2010 summer season I was very aware of the dangers of a potential parent-child relationship developing between me and the rest of the crew. To operate effectively, as I had learned to my cost in 1996 and 2000, it's essential to work as a unit, and while I recognized certain unique aspects that I brought to the table, such as an unremitting enthusiasm for even the toughest training session, it was critical that these did not in any way set me apart from the rest of the guys. When my inclusion in the GB team was announced there had been enough attention focused on me as it was. That was perhaps understandable, given the fact that I had 'retired' so long ago, but anything else that marked me out as not one of 'us' would become a problem.

In 2010 there were no such issues.

We kicked the season off with a win at the World Cup regatta in Bled at the end of May, which was fantastic, but we didn't allow ourselves to become carried away for one very simple reason – neither the world champions Germany nor the silver medallists Canada were there. That said, the victory was still very important, for a couple of reasons.

Firstly, the eight received a lot of attention going into the race, partly because of my comeback. I was keeping a video diary for the BBC and that guaranteed a fair bit of exposure, which I don't think the rest of the guys in the boat minded because it placed the boat firmly back on the map after a disappointing 2009 season. If we had messed up, however, questions might have been raised over whether the media coverage was proving detrimental. That could have been the first sign of a wedge being driven between me and the rest of the guys. Secondly, and more importantly, with four crew changes since the previous season there was considerable interest in whether the new additions had been wise choices. Bled proved they were.

OK, Germany and Canada were absent, but we did defeat the Dutch and the Poles, who had been ahead of us in the 2009 World Championships. That was tangible proof that we were moving in the right direction. Overnight the victory propelled the eight from being the lowest-ranked boat in the GB team to parity with the others. That was critical to our self-esteem and gave us a strong identity. The key question was, just how far in the right direction had we come? The remaining two World Cup races, in Munich and then Lucerne, provided the answer.

The Germans won them both, ahead of the Chinese and the Australians respectively, with us in third. And to ram home the point, in Munich we were murdered, six seconds behind the German boat.

We still had a lot of catching up to do before the World Championships in New Zealand.

A mid-September afternoon at a training camp in Italy. This morning we had a good session out on the water and now the eight of us, plus our cox Phelan Hill and the two coaches, John West and Christian Felkel, are sitting under umbrellas, shading ourselves from the late summer sun and discussing our progress. John leads the conversation.

'OK, guys, listen up. We've had a good season so far and it can get better. As of tomorrow there are exactly fifty days to go before the final on Lake Karapiro. You have the capability within you to win gold there. But whether you do so or not will not be decided on 7 November, it will be determined over these fifty days. If you truly want to become the first British World Championship gold-medal-winning eight you have to make it happen right now, today, and every day until the race. It's no use just showing up in New Zealand and pulling as hard as you can. You will have lost long before then. So how are you going to make it happen? It's down to you and no one else.'

'We must act like gold-medal winners.'

'Every training day needs to be perfect, a gold-medal day.'

As my team-mates warm to John's theme with these comments, a phrase comes to me. This is going to be about more than merely how we train. 'In everything we do over the next fifty days we need to demonstrate gold-medal behaviour.'

Everyone seems to like the sound of this. John steps in again. 'So what are gold-medal behaviours then?' From there the ideas come thick and fast.

'Always turn up on time.'

'Treat each other with respect.'

'Have honest conversations.'

'Look each other in the eye when we talk.'

'Offer help when it's needed, before it's asked for.'

'Don't talk in the boat unless we're stationary and everyone can hear.'

'From the moment we leave pre-training chat, Phelan is in charge. Whatever he says goes. No back chat, no dissent, no second guessing.'

It's coming from within, there's no sense of anything being imposed. It's liberating, it feels good, as if we're making progress. We're setting our own agenda, drawing the lines that can never be crossed if we are to become World Champions. This is what we need. This is the difference. *This* is gold-medal behaviour.

We set our own target, to win gold by breaking the world record. Everything we did from then, and still do, is benchmarked against winning in the time of 5 minutes 17 seconds, two seconds faster than anyone has ever gone over 2 km.

All our sessions are built around rowing at 5.17 pace. For instance, if we are undertaking four sets of 250 m, two will be at race pace, 100 per cent, i.e. so 39 seconds, which is virtually an eighth of 5.17. Then we will do one off the start, which has to be a bit quicker, so that is 104 per cent, then finally one absolutely flat out, faster than we will ever reach in a 2 km race, 110 per cent, the maximum pace we can achieve.

Over longer distances, say a steady 16 km, the coaches still want to keep us honest rather than drifting around looking at the scenery, so they will dictate a pace of 74 per cent, and if we fall off that and lose concentration, Phelan will pull us back.

Every session, every distance, everything is geared to hitting the 100 per cent mark on race day, the day we must perform.

This goes beyond merely gold-medal behaviour, this is world-record behaviour.

The fifty days went well. There were no scheduled competitive races but we were constantly involved in internal competition, racing the other GB boats, each of us looking to attain our own 100 per cent pace. In a head wind, that might be impossible, but if our eight hit, say, 96.3 per cent and the four hit 96.1 per cent of their benchmark speed, we 'win'. That level of competition kept everyone focused and, judging from our results, we were going well by the time we arrived in New Zealand.

Winning our heat against the Australians, who earlier in the summer had defeated us in Lucerne, was a significant boost to our confidence. We were rowing faster. We could take the Germans. It also meant we avoided the repêchage and progressed directly to the final, giving us a distinct advantage over everyone else, except predictably Germany, who also made it straight through. To defeat them we were going to have to pull out every trick in our bag and perform at our absolute best. We had it in us, we just had to deliver when it mattered.

The day before the final John and Christian called a team meeting. It proved to be one of the most extraordinary meetings I've ever attended.

We kicked off with the transactional details, the head stuff rather than the heart stuff – timings, warming up, how the day would unfold, the actual plans for the race and all that – led by Phelan, who does a very professional job. Facts, figures and clear thinking are his thing, which isn't surprising given that his day job, from which he's taking a sabbatical, is at the Treasury.

Then we move onto the emotional bits. We'd held such meetings regularly before races and had benefited from a number of different transformative exercises, such as shutting our eyes as Phelan made the calls and visualizing the race ahead. This is different. This is a huge occasion and John has another plan.

He draws our attention in a very relaxed way. 'Here's something I've been wondering. Why do you row? Why do you come every day and do this?'

Awkward silence. I don't want to be the first to speak, jumping in like I know it all. I'm not that guy, so I hold back. Let's see what the others say.

Someone pipes up. It's pretty good stuff and it gets the ball rolling.

'I like winning races, I always have.'

'I hate losing.'

243

'I want to be an Olympic champion.'

My turn.

'I want to be happy when I die.'

That's got everyone's attention.

'I believe there are only so many opportunities in life to do something that you can be proud of. I am going to die one day, I know that, but before then I want to have done everything as well as I can to make those special things happen. Rowing has given me a lot of incredible moments and I'm not ready for them to end. Tomorrow can be another one. That's why I row, that's why I do this. If I can look back when it's all over and say that this had been a great experience, that I've tried as hard as I can, then I'll be able to die happy.'

My words seem to linger in the air before hitting home. It triggers something. We start to talk about what being here really means to us, why it matters. We are creating an incredibly powerful emotional connection. I can feel the level of trust soar.

'I was bullied as a kid.'

It's our strokeman Dan Ritchie speaking and he has tears in his eyes.

'I was a swimmer at school. A good one, but one of the coaches picked on me, constantly undermining me and telling me I was no use. He once pinned me against a wall and punched a hole next to my head. To intimidate me. Towards the end of my two years at that school he didn't even acknowledge my existence. The last thing he said to me was that I would never be a world champion or make it in anything. The world is made up of losers, he told me, and you are one of many. I am here to prove that fucking bastard wrong and I'm glad I have the chance to do it with you guys.'

He is struggling to get the words out now.

'I feel closer to all of you than anyone, apart from my family and my fiancé. In fact, you are family. I mean that. I really enjoy rowing with all of you.'

Dan isn't the only person in the room crying when he finishes. We each talk to him about what he has just said. He has opened a door for all of us, and everyone reveals what tomorrow's race means to us as individuals and as a team.

We're going to do this for ourselves, but crucially we are also doing it for each other.

The following day every member of that boat knew exactly what we were going for – the gold – and why we were going for it. It's impossible to assess fully what difference these things make, but I can say from my experience in high-performing teams that what we had there was the most powerful connection I've ever known. At last I was truly able to understand what had happened on that lake in Sydney when the French pair called the names of their kids.

We took it out hard, but Germany took it out harder. They seemed to move quicker than us in the first 100 m and there was nothing we could do about it. By 250 m they had about half a length. We knew this might happen, but it wasn't what we wanted. As we settled into the race our boat was quicker than theirs. For the next 1500 m we clawed our way back, rowing well, digging deep. We were tough and strong, looking to make every stroke count, to move us an inch closer to being back on terms. With 250 m left we drew level. We pushed with everything we had, moving the rate up, but we didn't have quite enough to finish the job. There was just over half a second in it on the line. But that's all it takes. We had silver, not gold.

I had mixed emotions. I was bitterly disappointed at coming in second, but at the same time we'd fought back strongly against the World Champions, proving beyond doubt that we could be talked of in the same breath. If we could get stronger and move away from the start quicker, then we could win. On the day, they raced better – by a fraction – but as a demonstration of how far we'd travelled it was a major statement. We weren't out-classed as we had been four months earlier in Munich. Most importantly of all, our crew had gelled in a way that was sure to deliver over the coming two years.

I have always been extremely proud of the bronze I won in the 1991 Vienna eight. What we had in that boat was extraordinary and the connections continue to this day. We still have the same respect and trust in each other. That 2010 boat felt the same. I was convinced we would have an amazing future together, and if the only thing that dented that optimism was the fact that I'd missed out on a gold medal by the narrowest of margins, well, I could live with that. Something far more momentous had occurred over the course of that season.

Jenny was with me in New Zealand, and after the regatta we had a few days' holiday back in Sydney, Australia, which proved to be a very cathartic experience. The morning after I'd lost in 2000 and Redgrave's four had won gold, Matthew Pinsent went off to be interviewed by Nicky Campbell on *5 Live* from the top of the Sydney Harbour Bridge. I really liked the Nicky Campbell show and I would have loved to have been the guy he was talking to at the summit. But I wasn't. It got to me at the time and a decade later I was happy to exorcize that particular demon by taking Jenny up on to the bridge following my return to medal-winning form. We bought the official photo taken of us up there and it's still the screensaver on my computer. I see it every day. Sydney no longer casts its shadow over me.

Looking back on that 2010 season, the victory in Bled in the opening race takes on an even greater significance for me now, although I didn't realize it at the time. It's the only race I have won so far in my comeback. Since then I have had to accept that I will rarely again experience the thrill of winning, that adrenalin hit, because in training it's virtually impossible for me to do so. The rest of the GB team is now so strong that realistically my aim is to keep towards the top half of the group. For me this requires an extreme amount of mental strength. I love winning and I need to believe I will do so when it matters, in an eight, in London in 2012, but to get there I won't be able to enjoy many first-across-the-line moments. Instead my reward has to be internally driven. I feel proud of myself everyday and recognize my personal little successes against my own benchmarks. That's what keeps me going.

It didn't take long to get back into family life after my time in New Zealand. Jenny and I headed straight from the airport to the Wycombe Swan Theatre, where Josie was performing in a street dancing show, and the following morning I went into the kids' school to hear her playing flute at assembly. Having been away for more than a month and having missed out on various school activities there was no way I was going to miss another one. Regardless of jetlag I was there with Jenny in the audience as a proud dad enjoying his daughter's musical achievement. But there was a surprise in store.

Following a nod of encouragement from his head teacher, Adam was suddenly on the stage in front of everyone, clutching my silver medal. This had come out of the blue and I was only told later that he had pleaded with Jenny the night before to be allowed to sneak the medal into school for a special show and tell.

'My dad is a rower. He was in a race. And he came second!'

His teacher prompted him: 'And what was the race, Adam?'

He concentrated for a moment, then a huge smile spread across his face as he announced to the school, 'It was the World Championships! Out of the whole world, my daddy was second!'

The thought had never struck me before. Until that moment both my children had only ever known me as Dad, who *once* did something quite cool. Now they see me as Dad who *is* doing something quite cool.

Jenny squeezed my hand and smiled. My eyes were wet.

*

On 15 November 2010 I sat down to update by goals for the coming year.

> Really do this thing?
> Win gold in London 2012.
> Be a *total* legend.
> How am I going to achieve these goals? Physically, technically, mentally?
>
> **Physically:**
> Lift bigger and better in the gym. Use the heart-rate range to check in training that I'm actually going as hard as I should, not drifting.
> Keep injury free.
>
> **Technically:**
> Efficient and effective. Let the boat flow.
>
> **Four key words on how I row:**
> Long
> Connected
> Relaxed
> Hard
>
> **Mentally:**
> Don't be afraid to be emotional.

Looking at this list now, there are three aspects that strike me. The first is that I moved my original goal on a step, from 'Be a legend' to 'Be a *total* legend'. In 2009 there was an element of dreaming about becoming a legend. It wasn't arrogance, who am I to say who qualifies as a legend and who doesn't, instead it was a form of personal shorthand – to achieve my Olympic goal I had to make changes to how I was conducting my life. I wanted Jenny and the kids to be proud of me, to be there when I picked up my very last gold medal. To do that, to realize that dream, I understood I had to change my ways. I had to act like a legend.

In November 2010 I recognized I had to push myself further. It goes back to the 'quite fancying winning another gold' after 1992. That wasn't strong enough. You have to stretch yourself continually, or at least I do. So I set an even more challenging behavioural target. Be a *total* legend. We'd won silver in New Zealand. OK, but we needed to do better if I was to achieve what I have set out to achieve, and that meant I had to perform better.

Second, 'Don't be afraid to be emotional.' That had been a big thing for me in 2010 and it remains so today, although I haven't always hit it spot on. It's a reminder that what I am doing is fun, I should enjoy it, but also that it matters, and that I should let that show, too. It's an amazing opportunity I've been given; I've worked hard for it, and I want to show up every day with a smile on my face and make the most of the journey I am on, even on those occasions when it's incredibly hard.

The flip side is also important – it matters. So if I am not happy about any aspects of our preparation, I speak up. I do something about it. I've learned that it's OK to wear my heart on my sleeve – for the good bits and the bad.

Then there are the four key words I wrote down. These were alive and real to all of us during the 2010 season; they had evolved over the summer, culminating in us buying into rowing long, connected, relaxed and hard. They became trigger words, more shorthand, which everyone understood: do things today that others won't, so tomorrow you can do things that others can't. Row like you are the best in the world.

It worked, the improvements we made were real.

Then in 2011 we began to drift.

TEN

IN AND OUT OF FOCUS

I have never once questioned the decision I made to stage a comeback, but there have been some dark moments when I have asked myself whether I'm going to succeed.

One of the worst came at the trials on Dorney Lake in February 2011. I had worked hard over the winter, I was feeling fit and doing everything that Jürgen asked of me; but at the trials I came worse than last. I was in a pair with Tom Broadway and we didn't make the A final. That was gutting. Reaching the A final at least indicates you are in the top twelve rowers and your position within the team is probably safe. Instead, we found ourselves in the B final where we were beaten into eighth place by two blokes from Oxford University. They were very good rowers, as can be seen by the fact that one of them is now rowing with us in the 2012 eight and the other, an Old Hamptonian, became president of Oxford University Boat Club, but that was little consolation. The lowest any of the GB team members should ever rank is seventh. I couldn't understand it. I thought I was training well, Tom had won silver with me the previous summer, and suddenly it all seemed to be falling apart. What was going on? Had the years eventually caught up with me? I didn't think so. Physically I was strong, I knew that, I just wasn't rowing well.

I refused to panic, that would achieve nothing, instead I tried to assess rationally how I was feeling. What *was* the problem? I had to reassure myself that it had nothing to do with my age. Yes I had experienced a moment of doubt during the race when my legs had been screaming and the young students would not give up their chase, but I dismissed it in the cold light of day. I hadn't suddenly turned into an old man. As I know well, you don't become a champion overnight, and equally, you don't suddenly become a has-been in the same time frame. I realized this was about how I adapted to changing seasons, how I coped with moving from winter training into racing. It wasn't something I had done for a very long time and I needed to find my own way through the transition.

Over the winter most of the work we do is low intensity in terms of the boat, around eighteen strokes a minute as opposed to competitive rowing, which is up at about thirty-six, double the frequency. Then as the various trials approach and the season begins in earnest we shift gear, focusing on more intense water-based sessions of less than ten minutes flat out or four-and-a-half minute races where you have to push hard the whole time. I had to relearn how to make the adjustment, to refocus on my technique and remind myself I wasn't rubbish. And I had to do it pretty quickly. There's no point being the king of training if you don't perform when it's race day.

It's all related to belief amongst your peers. Putting in performances during trials that match what you've been doing in training demonstrates to everyone that you are a trustworthy, reliable member of the team, a bloke who can do the business. If you don't perform on the water, regardless of your ergo scores, doubts will be raised in people's minds. Is he the man? Can he perform when it matters? That's why it's critical to be able to transfer your hard winter work onto the lake.

I had a long way to go.

The next stage in the selection process, following that February trial, was what is known as a 'matrix'. In terms of my rowing, this proved to be the lowest point I have experienced in my comeback.

The matrix test was meant to consist of seven bowsiders and seven strokesiders, of which I am one (my oar is on the right-hand side of the boat), undertaking a series of fourteen pairs races over 1500 m. In this instance our numbers were reduced to twelve following an injury to one of the strokesiders, which meant a bowsider had to drop out to even things up.

The purpose of a matrix is to provide detailed information on the relative speeds of the rowers on each side of the boat. This is critical data for the coaches to work with because rowing at strokeside or bowside are not interchangeable disciplines and they have to be able to determine separately who the most effective guys are on the right and on the left. There are a handful of people who can shift almost seamlessly between the two sides, but for the majority the conversion takes at least a year to master.

Probably the simplest way to demonstrate the difference would be to take a look at my hands. The blisters and calluses on my right hand are in the palm, and on my fingers on my left, because that hand has to reach out further to grasp the oar. The opposite would be true for a bowsider.

On arrival at Caversham on the first day of the matrix we were greeted by Christian Felkel, holding two baseball caps with six numbered slips of paper in each. I drew number five, which meant that for the first race I would sit behind the number five bowsider in the pair. At 9 a.m. the race went off, all six boats giving it their all over the 1500 m course, with the times recorded for each. All the strokesiders then moved up a boat for the next race in an hour's time, so I joined the number four bowsider, who remained in his boat for all six races as the strokesiders moved in rotation.

Six flat-out 1500 m races is a gruelling test for everyone and the whole process was repeated the following day, this time with us strokesiders sitting in front and staying in the same boat, with the bowsiders moving from one partner to another.

The times for each race are recorded and at the end of the two days each rower has two sets of cumulative times, one for when you are at stroke (i.e. at the front of the boat – the day you remain in your seat while the others rotate) and one from when you are sitting behind, in the bow seat.

The trial was conducted over a Friday and Saturday in late February and we were all still in the dark as to the results when we squeezed into Jürgen's meeting room at Caversham on the Monday morning. I'd enjoyed the two sessions, they were hard work and exhausting, but I felt it had gone OK and I was in an upbeat mood as we settled down to hear what Jürgen had to say. I wasn't expecting to have won the battle of the strokesiders, but at the least I suspected I would be sitting somewhere around the middle.

By way of preamble Jürgen praised all our efforts and determin-ation. That was nice to hear, but seconds later my mood plummeted when he handed out the results. I was stunned to discover I was the worst of the strokesiders. Looking at the piece of paper in my hand with everyone's times recorded I could see immediately that generally whoever had rowed with me had come in the bottom half of each race, and had done well not to be last.

I might be making the results sound worse than they actually were – I'd delivered in a few of the races – but whichever way you looked at it Jürgen wasn't giving me good news. Using the information he had gathered, he then announced that he was putting together various training pairs in the lead up to the final April trials, which represented the most critical date in the selec-tion calendar. Even at that late stage, if you didn't perform you could be cut, while outsiders still had an opportunity to break into the team. The dream could end right there, and I would now be approaching the trials on a major low.

The pairs had been worked out not merely on the basis of partnering the winning strokesider with the winning bowsider, the second with second etc. Instead Jürgen had taken a broader view of what combinations he thought would work best together. It transpired that I had done less badly, though still not well, when in the stroke seat, and Cameron Nicol had done the opposite. In addition, when we had raced together with me at stroke we'd come in third, so Jürgen put us together thinking, I presume, that we would complement each other.

I was happy with Jürgen's decision. Cam and I are both physically strong, we fitted well together in a boat and we get on very well. We both have plenty to say, but more importantly we listen to each other. I was also delighted by the fact that we were going to be coached by John West, who knows how to get the best out of me. For his part, I think John was genuinely pleased to be coaching us. He saw our raw potential and gave us the confidence to believe we could be the dark horses in the pack. We'd both had good winters, were strong on the ergo and in the gym; all we were lacking was the subtlety to turn that into pairs speed.

We started out well – I could sense small daily improvements, which was encouraging – but when we arrived at our training camp in Italy I was suffering badly from man flu (really, I was ill). It was the first time in the comeback that I had been properly laid up. I missed a couple of days training, and when I came back Cam and I had to take it very easy. This proved to be the golden key that unlocked the door to much of the pace I'd been missing since the winter. Physically I couldn't do a lot of the work Jürgen was asking the rest of the guys to do, so instead Cam and I concentrated on short recovery sessions, during which I focused on how the oar felt in the water, how smoothly I was picking up the load and how to suspend my body weight effortlessly rather than using my muscles to wrench myself backwards each time I took a stroke. It was like being with Harry again, when he asked me to pretend I had weak arms like his. The only difference was, this time I really did. But the speed was coming as our partnership began to click into place.

It was during this training camp that I rowed with Cam to the stretch of water where, back in 1992, after I'd suffered a crisis of confidence following a bad session and a fall-out with Jonny, I had experienced the most awesome rowing session of my life. Being there again reminded me of what I was capable of.

While Cam and I were operating separately from the rest of the team, we had the opportunity to try out a few different options. At one stage Cam explained to me how he liked to approach the first stroke of a race. It was a slightly different technique to what I was used to, and when I gave it a go it was a bit of a disaster to begin with, as it made me feel extremely unsafe and wobbly in the boat. I was willing to persevere, though, and after twenty minutes or so of intense practice I found myself mastering a way of starting that I'd been afraid of for two decades. It struck me as I rowed back to the landing stage afterwards that although I might be old in years, it was essential I remained young and open-minded in my head. If I was going to succeed I had to find ways to be receptive to change. And I was learning. We employed Cam's start for the rest of the time we rowed together.

Under John's supervision we began to turn things around, I rediscovered how to row efficiently, how to get out more than I was putting in. As a result our boat began to move fast at the higher rates, and once I felt well enough to rejoin the main group we arrived with a lot more speed. In a few sessions Cam and I produced training pieces that were quicker than anyone else, including Andy Hodge and Pete Reed, the reigning World silver medallists. Confidence was returning.

We returned to the UK for the trials on Dorney Lake. If we did well there all the previous tests would be forgotten. First there was a 1900 m time trial to seed the semi-finals. Cam and

I attacked it, but with the efficiency and subtly we had learned while I was weak from flu. Now that I was strong we strode down the course and were rewarded with the fastest time. In our semi-final, we were beaten by Hodge and Reed in a tough race, but we were never in any danger of being overhauled by the boats behind us. Consequently we secured a second-place finish that put us through to the A final. For me that was critical, given what had happened back in February.

For the following day's final we stuck to our approach – controlled, efficient rowing – and although at around 1000 m there was a moment when I thought that if we push hard here we could challenge the leaders, I was also aware that we needed to focus on defending our position. We crossed the finishing line without troubling the eventual winners, but that didn't really matter. More importantly for us we had maintained control of the minor places and finished in a very pleasing third.

Given that only a few weeks earlier Cam and I had both failed to shine in the matrix and now we were performing near the top of the team has led me to question the weight given to that form of testing. Demonstrating you have the ability to jump from one combination to the next doesn't appear to me to be a particularly relevant selection criterion. That's why it tends to be used only as a last resort, I guess. I think Cam and I proved that it's more representative to allow combinations time to train, to establish efficient and effective methods of working together, and then race hard against others who have been doing the same.

What made the difference over those weeks that Cam and I trained together? The fact that we enjoyed rowing with each other was important, as was our determination to improve on our previous results, but I also believe an additional element was that I was older and wiser this time round. I understood the value of being open to change and new ideas, and I'd been able to implement them to good effect. In my mind the disappointments of the matrix were now a distant memory. I was firmly on the front foot again and looking forward to the challenges that lay ahead.

The crew for the eight was changed for the 2011 season. Based on a session of seat racing that we held directly after the Dorney trials, Jürgen introduced two new guys to the boat. I knew my seat wasn't in jeopardy when myself and another guy were included with Hodge and Reed and the coxless four for a separate session, away from the others. I was involved in a seat race with Ric Egington from the four, and although he beat me, ensuring I wouldn't be moved into that boat, being regarded by Jürgen as one of the top eight rowers in the team was another major shot in the arm for my confidence.

As for the re-jigged composition of the eight, it was a mixed blessing I would say.

Our boat was certainly faster, but the introduction of Noddy (Nathaniel Reilly-O'Donnell) and Alex Partridge, who are both pretty vocal, changed the dynamics within the crew. That wasn't a bad thing in itself as all crews need a mixture of different characters, but the key question was how quickly the new line-up would gel. Crews change regularly; it's how you deal with it that's important.

There was another element to this shifting landscape that for me had an even greater impact as we moved into the summer: John West was chosen to coach the four, which meant Christian was now on his own with us.

Christian is an excellent coach in his own right, and over that season he did a very good job, but nevertheless I believe we lost something essential when John moved on. Together, they represented one of those occasions when the whole is greater than the sum of its parts. Two excellent coaches making an even more brilliant double act, complementing each other in a classic good cop, bad cop manner. Christian was the good cop – a lovely bloke, very encouraging and happy for the guys in his boat to take a lot of personal responsibility – while John was more demanding; he would tell us what to do as opposed to asking our opinions on what we wanted.

In John's absence, I believe we began to lose focus. In many ways it reminded me of when Harry was forced to take a step away during my single sculling days. I knew where that path led.

Not that you would have known in the early days that storm clouds were gathering.

There was a good feeling in the air as we trained hard at Caversham in the run-up to the first World Cup race in Munich. There was a positivity in the boat, with guys, particularly the younger ones, stepping up to the mark when previously they had kept their heads down. With John's departure the crew was given its head a bit more than before and this seemed to bring out the best in my team-mates. In many ways they appeared to be filling the hole that John had left.

Prior to setting off for Munich we held what is called a speed order test, where every boat within the GB team race on the same day, with everyone looking to hit 100 per cent of their target time. The night before the test, each of the eight received an email from our crew mate Moe Sbihi. In his note, in which he made it clear just how much the coming months meant to him and how we were all in this together, taking on the world, and how we were going to succeed, he signed off as 'Wolfpack member No. 5'. That's how we saw ourselves, a tight, ferocious pack that was going to hunt down our opponents mercilessly.

It proved to be the high point of our unity.

The speed order test had gone well and we arrived in Munich with high hopes that we had not only made up the 0.6 seconds from New Zealand, but that we were now fast enough to beat the Germans.

We weren't. Although there were some mitigating circumstances.

The organizing committee of the regatta decided to test out the procedure that will be employed for the Olympic Games if poor weather conditions result in significant differences between the lanes in the heats. Choppy water, strong winds and driving rain could make one side of the course either completely unusable or put the boats drawn there at too much of a disadvantage for a fair race. In such circumstances, if there was a risk that any race would be affected in this way the result would be decided on the basis of a time trial. Fair enough, but in Munich the situation was a little different. With only nine entries in our event, instead of the two fastest boats qualifying automatically for the final, with one eliminated and the others fighting it out in the repêchage, they decided to use the time-trial results as a means of seeding the heat, with everyone progressing through to that stage.

Perhaps we were naïve or over-enthusiastic, I don't know, but when the starter lowered his flag we rowed with 100 per cent intensity, going out very hard. We won by about a minute, which is an enormous margin, and there was good reason for it. Everybody else paddled the course, thinking the whole thing was a bit ridiculous and deciding to save themselves for the knockout heats and semis, which were only three hours later.

As top seeds we were up against the fourth, fifth and eighth boats based on the time trial, and this included the Germans, who were still relatively fresh. They beat us by about a length and qualified direct to the final, whereas we had to row the repêchage the following day. We won that race, but it took a lot out of us.

Lining up for the final, our bodies had already been through three hard races compared to the Germans' one, and it showed. Once again they beat us by about a length, with us scrambling for second ahead of the Poles and the Dutch.

Silver was not what we'd planned on coming home with, but on the positive side we'd had a huge workout and held up pretty well. Surely that gave us a great platform from which to launch our campaign for the rest of the season. You might have thought so, but unfortunately that wasn't the case. Instead of building momentum, we began to unravel.

The second World Cup was also scheduled to be held in Germany, but because of an outbreak of nasty food poisoning, which was eventually traced back to some bean sprouts, the GB team decided not to enter. This suited our eight pretty well because we would have been under-strength, with Dan Ritchie suffering from appendicitis and Alex Partridge distracted by the imminent arrival of his baby.

As a substitute, Jürgen decided to put on a 'fun' regatta at Caversham to keep our competitive juices flowing. It was the turning point of the year, in the wrong direction.

Day one saw the eight broken into two fours, which raced against the coxless four and a scratch four that comprised the pair and the spare pair. In that race of four fours, it was very close between the coxless four and the scratch four, and between the two boats from the eight. Disappointingly, however, our battle was being waged a good two lengths behind the leaders. That wasn't how we wanted to be seen, and that was the best bit of the weekend for us!

The following day we raced as an eight against a boat made up of the other two fours from the previous day. This is the one that mattered, we told ourselves as we lined up. The Wolfpack owns this particular stretch of water today.

They spanked us, by two lengths.

Yes, we were still without Dan and Alex, and yes we'd rowed OK against a scratch boat that defied logic and somehow managed to fly, coming close to the world record, although admittedly assisted by the wind, but nevertheless it was shattering. In those two days I think we lost our confidence and struggled to recover.

Christian called a team meeting. It was painful. Where the crew had so recently been united, with new leaders coming forward and contributing when required, now there was a void. Christian asked us how we felt and no one spoke, no one seemed prepared to say what they really felt. There was a clear lack of leadership and I didn't know how to address it.

After that meeting, we began to splinter into smaller groups, all desperately fishing around for answers, with no one finding any. Had John West been involved, I think he'd have taken us by the scruff of our necks and demanded we resolve whatever issues had crept into the boat, but that wasn't Christian's style. He was more hands-off, intending to let us work out the problems ourselves. We failed.

Alex would make a suggestion. Sometimes I'd agree with him, but often I wouldn't. I'd offer another possible solution and Noddy would come up with a third. Not one of us seemed capable of successfully communicating the point we wanted to make to the rest of the team. Meanwhile, Moe withdrew into his shell.

I felt I was being pushed and pulled in different directions. Should I shut up and keep my own counsel, or speak up and try to move us forward in the direction I felt, because of my experience, was the correct way to go? The pressure began to show.

During one training session I felt that Christian wasn't being very clear in delivering his instructions from his bike on the towpath, while others in the boat were talking and challenging our cox Phelan, which was definitely not the gold-medal behaviour we'd agreed upon. As we drifted to a virtual halt, the bickering continued. I had to speak up: 'Let Phelan do his job. Whatever he says, let's just do it.' Then I shouted over to Christian, 'We don't understand what you want from us. Please give us clear direction!'

'Why don't you shut up, Greg.' It was one of the quiet guys in the team, someone who hardly ever loses it. 'Why does it always have to be you with the last word!'

I clammed up immediately, really quite upset, and as I rowed back to the landing stage in silence I could feel the tears of frustration in my eyes. I wanted to make a difference; I was trying to help, but somehow I was getting it wrong.

The incident unsettled me because it struck at the very essence of my comeback. I was no longer wedded to doing things my way. Instead I was far more open to listening to what Jürgen had to say and implementing his action plans with 100 per cent commitment. And there I was in the eight trying to help us find a solution, which I would willingly have backed and supported if we could have found it, but my team-mates thought my only concern was to have the last word.

The Wolfpack was running the risk of disintegrating.

It's the eve of the Henley Regatta, June 2011, and the Germans are in our backyard.

We've managed to claw back a fragile unity in the boat over the past week or so, and now Alex Partridge is pulling us closer together as he addresses the team meeting on the evening before our first heat.

'Guys, the next couple of days are huge. We won't race here next year. We all know that. It's too close to the Games. So this is our last chance to prove ourselves on home water before the Olympics. We are not going to let ourselves down. Our families are here, our friends are here, and for some of us this moment will never come again. Retirements, heading off down different paths, we don't know what the future will bring. What we do know is that over the next few days we can perform at the highest level in front of those we love. Let's do it. Let's make them proud.

'The Germans are here and we're going to beat them. They are not better than us. We all know that. Last time we screwed ourselves by sitting on the start line with too many hard races under our belts. This time everything will be even.

'This time we can do it. This time we *will* do it.'

We smashed the Australians, the World Championship bronze

medallists, in our heat. We raced well, as a unit, and for the first time in many weeks I felt the Wolfpack was re-forming. It didn't last.

Fragile unity I called it, and fragile things are easily broken. I began to hear the whisperings of discontent almost immediately after that heat against the Australians. It was small things, niggling things, which began to pull us apart again. The fact that Dan had gone off on his own to secure some tickets for his parents, who had hardly ever seen him row, took on a disproportionate significance. I thought it was an entirely reasonable thing for him to have done, and had things been going swimmingly no one would have noticed or cared. But as it was, with the cracks in the walls of our boat merely papered over, Dan's actions upset a few of his team-mates.

'Where is he?'

'Why is he not focusing?'

'Doesn't he care about the final?'

The reality, of course, was that the unrest had nothing to do with Dan, and everything to do with our internal insecurities. Given our collective state of mind, it was remarkable we performed as well as we did.

Once again the Germans jumped us at the start. We stuck at it hard and hung onto them well, staying within three quarters of a length for the first third of the race, at which point they steered on top of us, forcing us to battle through their wash and making themselves very difficult to row through. The umpire warned their cox to be careful and he was; he never quite went too far.

There is no doubt that we were beginning to draw them in over the last 500m, and had we been in lanes I honestly believe we could have snatched it, but as it was their cox continued to push the edge, keeping us in their wake, and they beat us by a length.

A week later we were in Lucerne for the final World Cup meeting before the World Championships in Bled at the end of August.

The overriding emotions in the boat were anger and frustration. Whatever else happened, we were determined not to repeat the mistakes of Munich and Henley. We were going to beat the Germans this time.

Unfortunately, with this goal fixed so strongly in our minds, we forgot to race the other boats.

We lost to the Dutch in the heats, a crew we had consistently beaten, and beaten well, over the previous twelve months. We started the race poorly, allowing the Dutch to stay with us in the early stages, and although we managed to pull away in the second half of the race, we never quite buried them and found ourselves in a scrappy dogfight over the final quarter. With three strokes to go I felt we were about to row through. We had the power and the intensity.

'You've got them!' Phelan shouted.

In that brief moment of joy and relief I think we lost one per cent of our intensity in the last few strokes. You can't help yourself when you think the race is won. But it wasn't. We lost and I was pretty pissed off at Phelan for making the call too early.

'You lost us that fucking race!' I raged, but in truth I was angry at myself as much as him. We had the talent, so why couldn't we produce the results? My frustration at being unable to answer that question bubbled constantly just below the surface and it didn't take much for me to erupt. I wasn't alone. Our fragile unity was on the point of shattering entirely.

The loss to the Dutch forced us into the repêchage, where we came second behind the Polish crew, the same guys we'd comfortably rowed away from in Munich only a month earlier. That was probably our lowest point of the year results-wise, although we did qualify for the final, which meant we were still alive, just.

There was a lot of head-scratching on the Saturday night before the final. Our confidence was wafer thin. As I made my way from room to room to speak to my crew mates individually, checking the temperature of the team, I was greeted with a variety of emotions: confusion, frustration, anger, but very little positivity.

There had to be some way back. There just had to be.

At the team meeting that evening Christian was uncharacteristically incensed.

'What the hell's been happening out there? What do you think you're doing?'

He then opened the meeting to the floor and was rewarded with a mixture of silence from some of the guys and outrage from others at what was going wrong. I listened to it all and when it was my turn to voice an opinion, I simply said, 'I don't want to use up any of my airtime to talk about the Poles or the Dutch. I want to talk about the race tomorrow.'

Christian moved on round the group, giving everyone a chance to speak if they wanted to, before changing the tone of the conversation and steering it back to the race the following day.

'OK, now let's think about the final. Greg, what's your opinion?'

I'd come prepared. I'd brought the notebook I use to jot down the key points that are raised in our various team meetings, and for the first time since coming back to rowing I very deliberately set out to lead the meeting by speaking up rather than purely by example. That wasn't what I went into the eight wanting to do, but I did it because I felt I had to, given everything else that was going on. If no one took control I was convinced we'd end up where we'd already been too many times in recent weeks, with everybody gassing around and nobody landing on anything in particular.

'OK, here's what I think. We're close to the Germans and to everybody else, and we haven't shown our best yet. So let's focus on getting the basics right. We all know how to row. Let's clear our heads and keep it simple – place the blade and leave the handle out there; think legs, legs then backs, hands in and out at the same speed and relax to place the blade again. Tomorrow we need to start well, then do a good transition into pace. We must not let the stroke rate drop, each of us must be individually tough to make that happen. At 1000 m we pick it up, with 500 m to go we make sure we are focusing on our own boat, not looking around. In the last 250 m we blast it. Bang, bang, bang, home.'

There was total silence in the room for a moment, before Christian broke it. 'Unless anyone else has anything to add, that's it then, isn't it? That's what we've got to do tomorrow.'

I slept much better that evening, and the following day we had a very good pre-paddle, with everybody on the same page for the first time in many weeks. In the race itself we got bronze, pipped to silver by the Dutch in a photo finish – they had avoided the repêchage and had therefore raced only once before the final – and just ahead of the Americans. Germany won, 1.8 seconds ahead of us, the same gap as in Munich and probably a fair reflection of how both boats were performing.

Given where we had been, I was reasonably happy with that second Lucerne medal of my career. The Dutch were improving, that was clear, we just had to make sure we improved more. As for the Germans, well, at least they weren't stretching away from us. We'd manned-up when we had to and fought our way out of a slump. I suppose we left Switzerland in pretty much the same state as we'd arrived, but hopefully having learned something along the way.

It was a relief but it wasn't good enough. With altitude training to come, plus two and a half weeks in Portugal, concentrating on speed work and acclimatizing to the heat, I hoped we'd be in far better shape by the time we arrived in Bled for the World Championships, where we had to be interested in only one colour: gold.

On race days in Bled, as we arrived at the boat park half the crew would go off in one direction to check their bags while the other half went directly to the GB rowers' tent for something to eat. It wasn't that we'd fallen out, we just weren't making any effort to stick together. We were an eight, but we weren't acting like one. It might have been better if we had actually had some major disputes, because then at least it might have drawn attention to the behaviour we didn't like rather than keeping our mouths shut and not addressing the issues that were causing a problem. I discovered after the final that some of the behaviour they didn't like was mine.

Those World Championships were the first time Josie and Adam had come abroad to see me compete. They had a wonderful holiday with Jenny, my parents and our lodger Lindsay, swimming in the lake, visiting the castle and generally loving being around all the activity of the event. I tried to see them as often as I could, popping to the hotel where they were staying for a hot chocolate before their bedtime and then sitting up with Jenny for a while. It was only after the championship was over that I discovered this was seen as a problem by the team. In our debrief a couple of the guys told me they were bothered by how much time I spent with my family. No one said anything at the time and it wasn't as though I was missing out on group activities. At best four of the guys might be off having a coffee in town together, while two of the others went for a walk and another went off to his room on his own.

In hindsight, I can see that spending time with my family might not have appeared very crew oriented, but in reality that aspect of our boat had broken down already. Once again, had John West been there in his role as bad cop I don't think it would have happened. He would have insisted that the eight stick together, regardless of whether mine or anyone else's family was in the vicinity. Christian's attitude was the polar opposite, more adult-to-adult, but I think we acted like helpless kids and failed to step up when we needed to. He was happy for us to do what we wanted as long as we were fresh and ready to get going each morning when it was time to deliver.

Despite our lack of unity we were committed, we all trained hard, but each time we raced at Bled the start determined the outcome, with the Germans taking an early lead to which we failed to respond. This was one of the key areas on which we weren't unified and it's something we still have to address. I felt our tactics for the first half of the race didn't add up and I said so. We knew they'd fly from the first stroke, but we still set out to go as fast as we could for the first 500 m and then only to fade by one second in the second 500 m. Unfortunately, these two goals are at odds with each other. I felt we should either go out as hard as we could, or look to minimize the fade. Trying to do both was confusing and left us about a length behind at halfway.

What I believe we should have done to address the problem was to go very, very fast in the first 500 m and risk the consequences in the second 500 m, because in every other encounter we'd had with Germany they had already killed us by the halfway mark, before we'd even decided to properly engage in the race. It was a repeating script and we weren't changing our part in it. Normally I would advocate that we should row our own race and not become distracted by what the other boats around us are doing, but having been consistently beaten by the Germans in the same manner every time, surely this was the one occasion when we ought to adjust our thinking. By blasting the first 500 m we would at least still be in the race, and if we could hold it together in the second 500 m we could trust our training and ingrained pattern of racing. It's not as though we would have just stopped rowing in the second half!

To my mind, the way we raced that final, sticking to our well-worn plan, handed Germany victory. Yes, we were very gallant in our attempt to catch them, but it was never going to be enough. We had set a target for gold and we came home with silver. Whatever way you try to spin it, and there were positives to be found and areas that we could identify as requiring attention, the season ended without the prize we all wanted. In many ways it had never really got started. So what went wrong after all that positivity I'd felt in New Zealand?

One of the problems was that I personally felt like our needs weren't well looked after. We were given what felt like the worst rooms in the hotel for some reason, and when I challenged this my complaint appeared to be dismissed out of hand. It felt like my opinion ranked very low in the overall priorities. It took me straight back to David Tanner at the Boston trials in 2009 – 'I'll tell you when you've done something to be proud of.'

That sort of approach definitely brings out the worst in me as I really don't like being treated that way and find it insulting rather than motivating.

This attitude aside, principally I believe it was the disconnect within the eight in 2011 that caused the most damage. In a later training camp someone described the 2011 season and having too many chiefs and not enough Indians, and I can see why people thought that.

Christian was trying to encourage us all to speak up, but with no one to moderate the discussions, we often slipped into petty, childish, fractious behaviour. I was as much to blame as anyone, half stepping up and half taking responsibility, and in so doing I found myself becoming one of 'them' (the management and coaches) instead of one of 'us' (my crew mates). That was definitely one of the downsides of my decision to lead the discussion in Lucerne, and I found it an uncomfortable position to be in.

In 2010 I had been one of the Indians, performing alongside the rest of the guys, but in 2011 I ended up becoming 'Daddy Greg', which resulted in the rest of the eight forming little groups I wasn't invited to join. As Moe brilliantly put it, 'In 2010 you were like a cool Uncle Greg, watching our backs, looking out for us, but letting us get away with stuff. Then in 2011 you became an annoying father figure. But to be fair, we had become difficult adolescents.'

It was the one issue I'd been desperate to avoid in 2010, and by allowing it to creep into 2011 I believe I contributed to the fact that we didn't progress as well as we should have.

What was most infuriating was that if I could have had the mandate then I feel certain I could have made a really positive difference to the way our team behaved. I've worked with some much tougher crowds in a corporate setting, but then I was always in a lead position. Within the GB rowing team that was never the case, not even in Lucerne, and therefore most of the time I had to leave things to run unchecked. That said, I'm not sure there could have been any practical way to reconcile wearing those two hats within the team, and having to make a choice between them is a simple matter. Above all, I am a rower. I suppose if I really want to know whether I've got what it takes to wear the other hat, well, I'll just have to apply for Jürgen or David Tanner's jobs in a few years!

Given the fractured nature of our challenge over that summer, as I said in my interview with the BBC after the final, the fact that we managed to come home in second place was a silver medal won rather than a gold medal lost.

Our situation wasn't much improved as we geared ourselves up for 2012 after a three-week break following the World Championships. Jenny and I had planned to fit in a week's holiday together over that non-rowing period while the kids were at school, but having been away so much over the summer, and having enjoyed spending what little time I had managed with Adam and Josie in Bled, I decided I'd much rather stick around at home that week, taking the kids to school in the morning and hearing about their adventures over dinner in the evening.

I loved that week, I managed to switch off from rowing and the problems in our boat and felt refreshed and very much up for our first training camp, which would kick off the most important ten months of my rowing career. Unfortunately, it didn't take long for us to slip back to where we'd been over the summer. The camp was in Seville and during one team meeting I told everyone I'd heard Clive Woodward speaking a couple of weeks earlier, and how impressed I'd been with a lot of what he'd said, in particular about the media and Twitter. I suggested we should be careful not to write anything critical or derogatory about each other on any social networks because I couldn't see how that would help us win the Olympics.

Some people seemed to agree. 'Mmm, yeah OK, I get that.'

Others were more reactionary. 'For fuck's sake. I think we're clever enough to know that. We're not stupid.'

Once again, despite the best of intentions, I'd transformed myself into a pseudo team manager, telling the guys how to behave without a recognized and accepted platform from which to do so. Instead of holding back and chipping in positively from the floor as someone else led the discussion, I'd pushed myself too far to the front.

I was increasingly aware of these issues as I sat down towards the end of 2011 to assess my goals from the previous year. I could sense that those tiny fault lines that had existed in 1996 were threatening to reappear. That had to be avoided. As the winter drew on I continued to train with Cam in our pair, but I didn't want our closeness to create a potentially negative wedge within the team. To combat this I made a conscious decision not to team up with Cam during every gym session. Instead I hooked up with whoever happened to be available, whether he was the youngest or one of the guys I was particularly competitive with. It was important, I realized, to demonstrate that I was more than happy to rub shoulders with everybody and become a fully-fledged member of the team again.

*

In late November I hit a bit of a low. I wasn't performing as I wanted to and it caused me some concern. No special treatment. Jürgen had made that clear. I would be in the boat on merit or I wouldn't be in the boat at all.

The problem arose during one of our early trials. There were supposed to be nine pairs racing, but due to a bout of illness there were only four boats, including Cam and I, and Cam was suffering. He had picked up a nasty bug and was on a short course of antibiotics. We came third out of the four in the first race and didn't participate in the final head-to-head because the doctors insisted Cam had to rest. He'd said he felt sort of OK, but in reality he looked a bit spacey and he wasn't as strong as normal.

I only mention the fact that Cam was ill to set the scene. It's how I reacted that's important. On one level I was pleased with the fact that we were there at all, since so many others had pulled out. We had showed up and raced, that was important. We had grit, but we'd still lost to people I didn't want to lose to. That wasn't good, and neither was my performance.

In the boat I'd felt very tired. I was giving it everything, but I just couldn't make it happen, so I overcompensated, stepping away from my normal calm performance. It was like, 'Shit I've got to give it more', rather than, 'Keep calm, row as you do normally. You're going well, you know what you're doing.'

When I'm rowing I want to be confident and on top of it, always thinking, Yes that was a good stroke, and retaining my poise, which is critical in any sport. When you are on form you have all the time in the world. There's no panic. Confidence allows great footballers to find space on the pitch that otherwise doesn't exist. Rowing is exactly the same, you want to be in control of what you're doing, but in November I found myself snatching at my oar, allowing the blade to tear through the water as it entered. Long, connected, relaxed, hard? I'll give myself hard, but as for the other three . . .

A few days after that disappointing trial we were off on our travels again, to altitude training in Sierra Nevada, Spain, where myself and the rest of the eight received a much-needed confidence boost, laced with a strong dose of concern over our seats in the boat.

Jürgen was giving a talk, setting out his current thinking for the forthcoming season, and the Olympics in particular. He showed us some graphs, which illustrated that in the previous World Championships the gold medal in the pair was won by the New Zealanders in 99 per cent of the world record time, in comparison to the British victory in the coxless four, which was achieved in 96 per cent of the world record. As the guys in the four digested this information you could see them shifting uncomfortably in their seats. What Jürgen was basically saying was that it was easier to win gold in the four than it was in the pair.

As a result of this, he explained, he had decided to alter the team's strategy by moving our best athletes into the four, thereby making it our number one priority. This meant that Hodge and Reed would be dropping the pair and be in contention for two of the seats, with the other two places also up for grabs.

He then continued by looking at the eight. The Germans had won gold in Bled in 97.5 per cent of the world record time and we had come a close second. As a result he saw our event as another strong candidate for Olympic gold, provided we strengthen the composition of the boat. Whoever dropped out of the four would almost certainly be moving into the eight, and there could be additional changes given that we had a strong young contender in the team as well. It was a tremendous feeling to know that Jürgen believed the eight could become Olympic champions – but only if you actually had a seat in the boat!

Every trial between then and April was going to be critical.

The first on the schedule was December in Boston, where Cam and I pulled things together a bit after the disappointments of

November. We came in fourth out of the five boats racing and would probably have been at least one place higher had I not been a little too clever for my own good. I was steering and got greedy, attempting to cut one of the bends on the course too tight. Instead of buying us valuable seconds, I crashed us into an overhanging tree on the bank. Not my finest hour.

While the magic Cam and I had enjoyed on Dorney Lake back in April seemed to have deserted us, on a personal level I felt good. Despite the November hiccup I'd had a successful winter, training well and maintaining my focus since Bled, aware that in the past I had allowed my race-mode mentality to recede too far during the off-season. With Jürgen having explained his plans to us – although we were sworn to secrecy – there was absolutely no place for a slow, sluggish start this year.

The matrix that Jürgen arranged pre-Christmas was my first big assessment to see if I was on track. Despite my reservations concerning the effectiveness of these tests in the selection process, I appreciate how useful they are in presenting the coaches with a snapshot of how each of their rowers is performing. From the first race to the last I rowed aggressively and hard, ending up absolutely knackered at the end of it, but delighted with my second-place finish on the stroke side, ahead of Ric Egington, who had previously always beaten me. My comeback felt very much on track.

Then it all came crashing to an abrupt halt.

Over Christmas Jürgen set a cross-training programme for us to follow, including ergos at home, cycling, running and gym work. Christmas Day itself was clear, but on Boxing Day the schedule stipulated an hour's run, which I would have to fit in while visiting my parents. I didn't mind, I know what it takes to become an Olympic athlete: dedication, self-discipline and an eye for the finer details that give you the edge and make you perform to the peak of your ability. I was going to follow Jürgen's programme to the letter, to prove to him when we returned to Caversham after the holiday that I had the necessary attributes in spades.

'Dad, can I borrow a pair of your running shoes? I forgot to pack mine.'

I don't have a runner's build, and at the best of times I don't look particularly graceful pounding out the miles, but in Dad's slightly-too-small trainers my gait was even worse than normal. Jenny, who was walking with Josie around the loop I'd mapped out for myself, commented afterwards that as I passed the two of them I resembled a stumbling giraffe rather than a fleet-footed gazelle.

My back was aching after the run but I dismissed the discomfort as nothing more than the result of wearing the wrong footwear. I'd had twinges before and nothing came of them. I could see no reason why this should be any different. Later that day we went to Kempton Park to watch the King George VI chase and as Kauto Star glided his way over the fences, with our money riding on his nose, Josie and Adam were keen to get a better view of the finish line.

'Come on then, up you get. I can manage one of you on each of my shoulders.'

As I stooped down for them to clamber on I spotted Jenny shaking her head. 'I don't think you should, Greg, not if your back's sore.'

'But Jenny, I'm stronger than I've ever been.'

'Even so, why take the risk.'

She was right. The following day my back was significantly tighter and more painful, and although I tried to continue with Jürgen's programme it wasn't going well. I began to grow increasingly nervous that I might have a real problem.

'It's because I'm not out on the river,' I explained to Jenny when she asked how I was feeling. 'If I'm not rowing my back always stiffens up. And all this cycling just makes it worse.' I wasn't sure who I was trying to convince.

We reconvened at Caversham on 2 January and I went straight out in an eight, but I was a passenger for the entire session. At the end, as we were lifting our boat out of the water, I couldn't even bend down to help, and made a token contribution at best in carrying it back to the boat house.

As soon as I'm back out on the water regularly it will loosen up. Nothing to worry about. The following day I decided a light ergo session before training would help. I couldn't even sit on the seat.

Shit.

I spoke to Jürgen, trying to make light of it, and he agreed that I should skip training and have a word with Anne Redgrave, the team doctor. Just in case.

'I'm not sure, Greg,' Anne said after examining me. 'This could be disc-related. I'm sending you for an MRI immediately.'

'We're due to fly to South Africa in a few days' time, I'll be OK for that, won't I?'

'Let's wait and see.'

I went to a place in Weybridge for the scan, where I'd been once before when I first broke back into the GB team. I'd undergone an MRI then, which was intended to be used as a baseline should I encounter any future problems. Like I was now. Comparing the two scans revealed some good news. My back had undergone some changes over that two-year period, but it appeared I wasn't suffering from a major disc problem. There was nothing torn or bulging. What was clear, however, was that there was significant wear and tear, the full extent of which it was impossible to assess. We would just have to see how I responded to treatment.

South Africa was out of the question. An overnight flight, followed by two weeks of intense cycling, which is a major part of that training camp, wasn't going to work for me. To be honest, that wasn't the worst news I could have received. Following my accident in New Zealand, coupled with what had happened to Jenny's brother, competitive cycling isn't very high on the list

276

of activities I enjoy. If there was one camp to miss, this was it. Provided I was fighting fit on the team's return then I couldn't see that a great deal of harm would have been done.

That little meeting room at Caversham has been witness to some of the pivotal moments in my second rowing career. It was where I first met Jürgen to discuss the reality of my comeback, it was where the magnitude of what I was trying to achieve came crashing home to me after the matrix trial, and in January 2012 it was once again the venue for an extraordinary moment.

Jürgen and I were sitting at the table with Anne as she explained what the MRI scan had and hadn't uncovered and recommended that I shouldn't travel to South Africa. I sat in silence as Anne spoke, scared of how Jürgen would react to my first physical setback since he had agreed to consider me rowing again.

He nodded as Anne finished her summary of my condition. 'That sounds very sensible. There is no point in potentially aggravating Greg's back at the camp when he could be here receiving treatment. I agree he should remain at home.' He then turned to me. I will never in my life forget what he said next.

'Greg, I am really happy with you. What you have done in the last two years has shown me enough that I know I want to select you for the Olympic Games.'

I could barely breathe. Had he really just said that? I couldn't sit on an ergo, let alone row at the moment. Seconds ago I'd been worried he might have thought I was beginning to show the first signs of decline, and now he was telling me I was in the team. I was going to the London Olympics.

He expanded. 'It's OK for you to stay here while we're away, get yourself right, and when we are back we'll get into pairs. I want you to recover and be strong again. You still need to make the final in the trials and that is what I want to see.'

'This is an amazing moment for me, Jürgen.' My voice trembled as I shook his hand. 'Thank you.'

Jürgen then went on to explain his intentions in greater detail, which he would also share with the rest of the team in South Africa. It was all to be kept a secret until the official announcement in April. He had pre-selected an elite eight people for the Olympic squad, of which I was one, along with Hodge and Reed, three of the guys in the current four, and two others from the eight.

Knowing that everything I had done over the past two years had been enough made me feel very special. I had realized part of the dream that I'd first scribbled down on a plane from Munich to London. But only part of it. Being in the team wasn't enough. I wanted to win. And to do that I had to overcome my back injury.

On the day the rest of the guys were touching down at Johannesburg airport I was lying face down on a couch in Harley Street as a specialist called Keith Bush, who I'd been sent to by Anne Redgrave, stuck a big needle in my coccyx, giving me an epidural cortisone injection. That afternoon I was on my bike in the living room at home, the following day I was out sculling. The transformation was incredible. My prospects were looking very rosy indeed.

Five days later the wheels came off my recovery. The pain returned.

There's a bus passing and it's making the walls shake. Violently.

Oh look, there's an old school friend. Hello! Hey, it's me, Greg.

I want to go and speak to him but I can't get up. My arms, they're so heavy.

I'm drifting, floating away, the light around me is dimming. I understand I'm dying. But that's OK, I've had a good life.

No wait. I can't die. I can't. I'll miss the Olympics. I must come back. Come on, Greg, you can do this. Come on, Greg . . .

'Come on, Greg, wake up. It's finished. You can sit up now.'

I recognize the voice. It's Keith Bush, the specialist who's helping me with my back. I'm lying face down on his couch with my shirt off. As I haul myself to a sitting position I can feel a sharp pain in my lower back. It feels bad, really bad. I'm confused. What's happening? What has he done? It must have been worse than he's letting on. I stare at him.

'You've operated on me, haven't you? You put me under and operated! Tell me the truth! What's going on? You and Anne, you've been hiding something from me. It's all over, isn't it? I am never rowing again.'

The room begins to spin. I'm losing focus.

'Calm done, Greg. It's all fine. Take some deep breaths. Good clean air. You'll soon clear your head. You're just a bit confused. Give yourself a moment to come round properly. I think you might have gulped down a bit too much laughing gas. Small breaths I said, but I guess you've got those big lungs. Don't stand up yet, I don't want to put my back out picking you off the floor. Wait until you feel better and then we can have a little chat.'

It takes a minute or two to pull myself together. That was one weird dream. It's strange the things that come to the surface when you're out of it. They're the things that are worrying you, I guess.

I'm sitting at Dr Bush's desk, with my mind back to normal, as he explains that the procedure he's just performed on my back, involving twelve separate injections, has gone well. I remember exactly where I am and what I'm doing here. As I leave the office, convinced that I haven't in fact been operated on, I'm aware of how sore my back is following the treatment. I hope I didn't embarrass myself as Dr Bush was pushing in the needles.

As we shake hands at the door, I have to reassure myself. 'Er, just one last thing. How was I with the injections? Did I do OK?'

He smiles and pats me on the shoulder. 'Yes, Greg, you were very brave.'

That visit to Harley Street took place over three weeks after the pain in my back returned, a month after I'd had the cortisone injections, which clearly hadn't fixed the problem. I explained to Anne Redgrave as soon as my back was causing me trouble again that I was struggling. She'd looked worried.

'OK, well, it looks like we'll have to try something else. You take it easy for the next week and once Jürgen is back from South Africa we'll discuss options with him.'

That wasn't an easy conversation. I think Jürgen had expected to see me almost back to normal, and instead we were sitting in that small meeting room again, with Anne outlining how the first level of treatment hadn't worked and recommending I undertake a second stage of injections, called sclerosing.

'It is a bit like burning the tendon to cause a build-up of scar tissue, which then strengthens the weakened area,' Anne explained. 'A series of sclerosing injections, a dozen in each session, will cause an inflation of the tissue in Greg's back, which in turn will react and strengthen itself. Doing nothing at all is an option, but I wouldn't recommend it. We'll be living on a knife edge the whole time in case Greg breaks down, which is a distinct possibility if we ignore this.' She then turned to me. 'It will hurt at the time. Sorry, Greg. And it will set you back in the short term, but after three doses a week apart, we should see long-term improvement.'

I looked at Jürgen's face as Anne spoke. It was a picture. This was not the news he'd been hoping for, but he nodded in agreement.

'OK, that is clearly the best approach. You will need to train in between the injections, Greg, and make sure you don't lose any fitness. Then I'm sure you will be ready for the training camp in Portugal at the end of February and final trials.'

I knew that if I wasn't significantly improved by the time we went to that training camp, my place in the boat could be in jeopardy. These injections had to work, and I had to keep training.

That was a difficult period for me, from mid-January onwards. That first cortisone injection had to be out of my system completely before I could begin the sclerosing treatment, which meant that my first session with Dr Bush wasn't until the first week of February. Up until then, I just had to tough it out.

As I was worried that riding my bike would aggravate my injury, I decided to continue rowing as best I could. I was awkward and uncomfortable in my single, and at times the pain in my back was quite intense, but I definitely felt better doing something as opposed to nothing. If I didn't keep training as best I could I would have too much to catch up on before the season started, even if Dr Bush did manage to cure me. Weighing up the two options – taking positive steps or sitting around on my sofa all day feeling sorry for myself – there was only one way forward as far as I was concerned.

Putting things in perspective, on a scale of one to ten, before Christmas my back was an eight or nine, then over the holiday and into the new year, when it became too painful to row, I would say I dropped to a two. The cortisone injection probably pulled me back to six, a level at which I could bumble along, but as that wore off I dropped down again to a four.

Once I began the sclerosing treatment, and was able to train harder, things started to improve, but it was slow. After each set of injections I could do nothing the next day, then some light work followed by a couple of days of rowing, two days of hard sessions, then it was time for the next injection. On my second visit to Dr Bush's Harley Street office I tried to limit my intake of laughing gas. I succeeded, to an extent. I had another weird trip, but it definitely wasn't as far-out that time. By my third and final round I'd mastered it.

The first half of February was frustrating because I was unable to perform as I wished. When my team-mates were required to do one of those gruesome 5 km ergos it was decided it would be a mistake for me to join them, but I wanted to do something, so Jürgen asked me to do 3 km instead. It was important for me to show that I was giving my all within my limitations, to reaffirm that I was a guy who could be relied upon to give everything possible. Maintaining trust within the team was crucial at this stage of the year. Trials were approaching, seats were soon to be allocated, and the Olympics were looming large.

In mid-February I received some much-needed reassurance from Jürgen. The spate of illnesses that had occurred at the December trials had deprived him of the opportunity to assess everyone fully. As a result Jürgen decided to instigate an additional trial session in February, from which I was thankfully excluded. Instead, Jürgen asked me to accompany the other seven pre-selected guys for a few sessions in an eight while the rest were assessed. I felt very proud and privileged to still be in that elite group, despite my recent setbacks. It proved Jürgen's faith in me hadn't diminished, even though I was a bit of a passenger. That didn't matter. What Jürgen seemed to be telling me was that provided I still made the final in the March trials, that was all he was looking for at this stage.

For the Portuguese training camp I was once again paired with Cam, and our first week together went OK. We weren't exactly setting the world on fire, but as I was still in recovery mode and Cam was trying to accommodate me by making the pair as comfortable as possible, I was fairly happy with how we were going. I was beginning to find more movement and slowly getting to grips with rowing effectively with my 'new' tightened-up back. Now that all three sets of sclerosing injections were behind me, I gauged my back had improved to a six on the one-to-ten scale.

Unfortunately for Cam, as I improved he took a step backwards, suffering a rib injury which required him to return to the UK for treatment. At the same time we lost another member of our squad, Noddy, to some heart problems, which resulted in me being paired with Tom Ransley for the rest of the trip and into the critical March trials.

'As long as you make the final in the trials that is all I will need.'

I know Tom pretty well, having rowed with him in the eight for the past two years. He's a different character from Cam, much quieter and with a less-refined rowing style. I say that with absolutely no disrespect. Tom is a big, strong guy who can pull incredibly hard and can make a boat go very fast, he just wasn't involved with the sport from an early age, only taking it up at university, and as a result his technique can come across as a little rough. Being paired with Tom was good for me. As I still wasn't back to my best, he could act as the engine of our boat and I could control the steering and balance. We dovetailed well.

The March trials were held at the Olympic course, and we stayed at the Oakley Court hotel in Windsor, where we will be billeted for the Games. This was the first occasion we had been there as a team, and it was one of those moments where London 2012 moved a little further into focus. This was real, this is what life was going to be like in August, and we liked what we saw, right down to the river taxi that would be transporting us to Dorney to avoid any traffic problems. There was a clear sense that planning and organization had been well implemented to support the work we were putting in.

For the trial itself, we started off with seeded heats comprising five boats each, two progressing straight to the final while the others would battle it out in the repêchage. Unsurprisingly, Tom and I were not well seeded, and as we looked at the line-up we reckoned it was highly unlikely we would place in the top two. We made a decision. Who says old dogs can't learn new tricks? With the events of the previous year's Munich regatta still raw in both our minds, where we had expended too much energy too early in the competition, we decided not to repeat that mistake.

We discussed the options with our coach John West and came up with a plan.

'We'll row hard to 1000 m, at which point I will assess whether we are realistically in with a chance. If not I'll give you the call and we'll take it easy over the second half of the course. Agreed?'

'Agreed. There's no point in knackering ourselves for no reason. If we can't do it in the heat, we'll do it in the rep.'

With the trials being conducted at the Olympic venue they had attracted a fair bit of attention and it was with a degree of embarrassment that Tom and I paddled home a full minute behind the other boats in our heat. That's a long time for family and friends to wait to cheer you across the finishing line. Even so, we knew it had been the right thing to do. At the halfway stage it was clear that we weren't in the hunt, and as making the final was of vital importance to us both – for me to prove myself to Jürgen and for Tom to guarantee himself a place in the forthcoming seat race, which would determine who was in and who was out – having to endure a sheepish wave to those who'd come to support us was a price worth paying.

The plan worked.

In the repêchage we qualified for the final in second place with a little bit in hand. The following day we gave it our best shot and were in contention in the final at the 500 m mark, but in the last quarter the field pulled away from us and we came in ten seconds behind the winners but not adrift of the fifth placed boat. The result was largely immaterial, however, with both of us having achieved what we set out to. It had been a positive few days, with my back not only holding up but actually continuing to improve as the last hurdle in the selection process approached.

Jürgen was keeping his cards close to his chest, leaving the rest of us with nothing but guesswork, supposition and conjecture to occupy our minds in the run-up to the seat races on which everything depended.

I had attained the recovery benchmark he had set me, making the March final, and while that gave me confidence that my place in the team was safe, Jürgen never 100 per cent confirmed anything to me. I understood why. While we could all make educated guesses as to what he was thinking, based on what we thought we knew – Hodge and Reed moving to the four for instance, and myself and the others being given a pre-selection nod – nothing was absolutely certain. And that is the way it should have been. There were clearly two, perhaps three, seats in the eight still up for grabs, with two of the previous year's four potentially moving in, and others knocking at the door.

In such circumstances it was essential that everyone conducted the final round of seat races with the mindset of twelve guys fighting for eight seats. That way each race would be completely honest, with everyone giving their all, and allowing Jürgen to make fair comparisons. If I had known, for instance, that I was definitely in the eight, mentally I might have switched off in one of the seat races, which could have been a disadvantage to whoever had been swapped into my boat.

Not that anybody needed to have worried. Given what had happened since that Boxing Day run at my parents, I was determined to show, in no uncertain terms, that I was back. The four I was in won every one of our races, which gave me a great deal of confidence that Dr Bush and his needles had worked their magic. I was back up to seven on the scale and I was convinced there was better still to come.

Once again we were squeezed into that meeting room awaiting Jürgen's announcement.

The manner in which Jürgen had swapped us around a couple of days earlier in the seat races had provided the final clues as to who he was assessing. I hadn't been shifted once, which was a strong indication that I was in. In my reading of the situation nothing had changed since the last time I had sat there with Jürgen and he had told me of my pre-selection, provided I could demonstrate my fitness in the March trial. I had done that; I had ticked the boxes that had been asked of me.

Based on what we had witnessed during the seat racing, however, the guys who were walking a tightrope between success and failure in the eight were Cam, Dan Ritchie, Tom Ransley, George Nash, James Foad and Will Satch. I was feeling particularly concerned for my two buddies, Cam and Dan, both of whom had faced a difficult time over the previous weeks. Cam hadn't participated in the seat racing, as Jürgen felt he wasn't sufficiently recovered from his rib injury, while Dan had been nursing an Achilles problem for some time, which had held him back. During the seat racing both Dan and I had been seated at stroke in the two fours that had been involved in all the swapping – Dan and I had remained static, which indicated that he wasn't being given an opportunity to be assessed against me. The omens didn't bode well for my friends.

Another place being contended was between Tom Ransley and George Nash. In the seat racing it had seemed very close between George and Tom and I wasn't sure what Jürgen was going to say. Guys like Tom, powerhouses who don't necessarily adapt immediately into new boats, often perform relatively poorly within the strictures of the seat-racing system. But if they are selected for an eight and given a couple of weeks to train with a stable group, they can come through and shine. These are the decisions Jürgen is paid to make.

The atmosphere was highly charged as we filled the tiny room while Jürgen sat thumbing through sheets of paper. Experience of similar meetings had told us this was not going to be a swift process. Those with jangling nerves would have to endure Jürgen's protracted delivery, which could potentially last up to thirty minutes before reaching the critical announcement. He had a manner of presenting his decisions which can kindly be described as measured, and he had no intention of deviating from it. Each person would receive individual feedback, which tended to go something like this.

'So, Greg, you have had a tough time. You had a great winter and I was very happy. But over Christmas it was hard. But I am glad to see you got sixth place in the pairs trials. That was good. Yes that was good. I was impressed with your rowing at stroke in the seat racing. So it's clear you still have the competitive side. I know you're coming back. So, last not least, I am happy with what you have done.'

Then he would move on to the next guy. Whilst it was good to get the individual feedback, we all wanted to cut to the chase.

Eventually the moment arrived, and it was as I had anticipated and my friends had feared. Cam and Dan were out, as was Noddy. In came Stan Louloudis, who had been in the spare pair but had been making huge leaps forward over the past months. Ric Egington and Matt Langridge from the four also joined us. During the seat racing Tom Ransley and James Foad had proved they still deserved their seats ahead of George Nash and Will Satch, who would now race as the pair.

I felt for those who didn't make it, especially Dan and Cam. Having been on the train, as Jürgen would say, it's very difficult when you're asked to get off! But I couldn't dwell on the misfortunes of others. We had our new line-up for the forthcoming season. And for the Olympics, I hoped.

There are never any absolute guarantees. Injuries can happen, form can disappear, those were my worries as we flew off to Italy soon after Jürgen's announcement for the final training camp before the World Cup season began in Belgrade. For me, the camp was all about two things: concentrating on bedding down with my new crew mates and ensuring my back continued its recovery. Ibuprofen was still a daily necessity, as was a routine of stretching and strengthening exercises separate from the rest of the guys. The possibility that I could break down at any moment, that I could prove to be the weak link, was never totally banished from my mind as I lay on my bed at night, thinking back to that brewery in Poznan and forward to Dorney Lake in August.

I accept now that such concerns will be a feature of my life, right up until the dream comes to its conclusion. Whatever that may be.

So, how am I feeling?

Italy went well. My back is now probably an eight and I am working hard to move on another notch. If I can make nine, I believe I will be performing at gold-medal standard.

And our eight? We feel strong, positive and united. The dysfunctionality of 2011 has disappeared. In Italy we travelled together in a minibus so small it was barely able to accommodate us all, and it was perfect. We ate together, laughed together, focused together. Once more we are all reading from the same page.

We've got each other's backs again.

That's gold-medal behaviour.

ELEVEN

IF NOT US, WHO?

Wednesday 1 August 2012.

6.35 a.m.

The Olympic gold medal will be won or lost in just over six hours.

I've been awake since around half past five, watching the minutes count down on my alarm clock to 6.30, the time I have set myself to begin this final day of my comeback.

Now I'm looking at myself in the mirror. Who do I see? From almost exactly twenty years ago Brian Miller's words fill my thoughts.

'Who is your real opposition? Who stands between you and the gold medal?'

The answer remains the same. It's the person staring back at me.

I'm not worried about the man I see there. I feel ready. My back is strong, a recent training camp in Portugal has gone well. We've been concentrating on the technical elements of rowing that will make us go faster; short sharp bursts of acute pain rather than the chronic hurt of lengthy rowing sessions. Physically my body has responded to everything that I have asked of it. Yes, I am ready. All I can ask now is that in a few short hours, when I return to this room, I will look at that same face in the mirror and know that I gave everything I had to win our race.

Our preparations have not been perfect but following a disappointing World Cup series over the summer and injuries in the boat, in Portugal everything seemed to come together at exactly the right moment. I know as a crew we have reached the stage where we are capable of racing better than ever before.

My mind turns to last night's team meeting where we each spoke about what we thought we brought to the crew, and reinforced each other's beliefs with positive affirmation. I smile to myself as I remember a particular moment when tears sting my eyes and I struggle to speak.

I am talking about Moe and the contribution I believe he makes to our boat and I recall 2008 when he and I rowed together and won in a coxless four on the Eton Dorney course. After the race, Moe's coach Sue McNuff said she had never seen Moe race better. Four years later we are still together, on the same course, drawn in the same lane, this time aiming for Olympic glory. Through tears and a fast-tightening throat, I try to tell Moe and the other guys that rowing with him back then gave me the confidence to know I could still perform at this level and I now believe it is our destiny to finish the job, to win a gold medal with him sitting behind me.

I did manage to compose myself enough to discuss what I believed I brought to the table.

'I understand how to finish an Olympic final,' I explained. 'I did it once in 1992 and in 2000 was on the receiving end of others who dug deeper than I did. It comes down to the final 750 m. You can do whatever you want up to that point but it is the last segment of the race that decides the winners and losers. That's when your heart, and your mind, and your body must come together like never before. That's what each one of us will experience tomorrow.'

Following that discussion, John West sat us down to watch three race videos. The first was Jonny, me and Garry in 1992, the second was the GB men's eight victory in Sydney, where they won in a manner similar to our own game plan: to set out hard, trust in the men around us, and hang on with everything we have to cross the line first. The final race was the coxless four of Pinsent, Cracknell, Coode and Williams, another slugfest right to the very end where British bravery once again saw them home.

Three GB gold medal performances, all close, all informative, all inspiring.

Following the 1992 video, John asked me to talk about what our mantra had been going into the final.

'We had one phrase that resonated above all others. "If not now, when? If not you, who?" It was right for us then and it's right for us now. In 1992 sitting on that start line we realized that the next six minutes would change our lives for ever. Whether that was going to be the ultimate change for the better was down to us and nobody else.'

John spoke again. 'Somewhere there are nine Olympic gold medals sitting on a tray destined for nine guys who tomorrow will be sitting in a boat. Those nine men are in this room now.'

Finally one of the eight from Beijing made his contribution. He too had suffered Olympic disappointment four years ago, narrowly missing out on the gold medal to Canada, but he had learned from the experience. 'We never led the race. We didn't give ourselves a chance to win. That is not going to happen to us tomorrow.'

Following a breakfast of Shreddies at our team hotel we board the river boat, which David Tanner has arranged to transport us to the course. It's a slice of home advantage we are happy to enjoy. Most of the rest of the rowing teams are being housed in accommodation at the Royal Holloway campus in Egham, requiring a shuttle bus via the M25 to deliver the athletes to Eton Dorney. It is a good piece of work by David to secure this hotel in Windsor for the team. Such seemingly small positives can make a huge difference.

We arrive at the Olympic course through the main entrance at much the same time as the first groups of supporters. As we walk through the gates there's a moment when the milling crowd stops to applaud as we walk past, some enthusiastically waving Union Jack flags. This morning I didn't think it was possible to be lifted any higher than I already was. I'm wrong. This is a truly memorable, wonderful experience. That 2009 drive up to Boston in the rain with Wheelie seems in equal measures a lifetime ago and only yesterday.

The surges of adrenalin and emotion continue. I now realize there may be no limit on how high the British public are going to lift me today. During our pre-race paddle, a 4 km loop of the course up to the start and back, we pass the grandstands that line the banks towards the finish line. They are already beginning to fill and the reception we receive sends a shiver down my spine and goosebumps along my arms. When we cross the finish line for the last time before the race itself the cheers ring out as though we have just won gold. Incredible. I want that one more time.

Just before we set off for the paddle, John spoke to us. 'I know you will be feeling nervous. That's OK. But out on the water now, let's not worry that this is the Olympic final. You all know what to do and you all know you can do it. Go out there for your paddle and confirm to yourselves you are the best rowers in the world. Because you are.'

Standing back in the boathouse afterwards I echo his words. 'Guys, with those crowds cheering us I know I felt nervous, we all did I'm sure. But look at it this way. That pre-paddle was perfect. It felt amazing sitting in that boat with all of you. We've seen we can use those nerves positively once already today. They'll reappear in a few hours, let's use them again to have a brilliant race.'

There is time to kill now before our final team meeting at 11.30 and I make my way to the dining area to grab something to eat. I am not exactly hungry, my stomach is in knots, but I know I should have something. I force down a bagel and a banana. I can't face anything more substantial.

Nerves. They are inescapable, but sitting here now, quietly watching the other rowers, coaches, Olympic officials going about their day, I'm not going to let the nerves consume me. I will never be here again. I'm going to embrace every emotion, every feeling.

I know I can perform under pressure. This isn't new. I have never buckled in the past and I'm not going to do so today. I know my body will perform. The hours of training to ensure that are behind me. I'm not afraid. I allow myself a moment to look into the possible future.

God Save the Queen, playing for us.

Jenny, Josie and Adam standing, tears of joy and pride in their eyes.

The aftermath . . . the British public joining in our celebrations, inspiring a new generation and giving my grandchildren a story to tell long after I am gone.

I smile and drag myself back. Such images are the output. I must pull myself back to the necessary input. To achieve those dreams, those outcomes, I have to nail the process goals first. I can do that. I know I can row hard and I know I can row well. We have a race plan. John talked us through it last night. We all signed up to it and I believe in it. It's been born of experience and belief.

We know the Germans are going to start fast. We also know that in an eights race you have to get in front, and once there you have to stay in front. We have committed to each other that even if the Germans get away quicker and lead through the 500 m mark we will row past them. We will lead this race. We will break them. We will destroy their composure, pulling apart their ability to stick together when it matters. We will ask the mental questions they are not used to, forcing them in turn to ask physical questions of themselves. The only thing we do not know is whether they will have an answer. We will be strong in the second and third 500s and rely on the amazing crowd in the last stage of the race to bring us home.

Experience and belief.

The experience.

Our training camp in Varese in April had ended on an incredible high. Set against our world record benchmark time we hit 92.1 per cent in the final time trial, the best of all the British boats, men and women, heavyweights and lightweights. The men's eight was the quickest crew of the GB team. Exactly where we wanted to be. Then Stan Louloudis, our new strokeman, injured his back.

Three days before we flew out to Belgrade for the first of the three World Cup meetings the decision was taken to leave Stan at home to rest. It was a minor blip we told ourselves. He would be returned to full fitness by the time we arrived home.

In Serbia we won our heat but a look at the relative times after the race revealed that at the half-way mark we were a good couple of seconds slower than the German boat in their heat. That left us with a decision to make for the final. With the late change in our crew it was going to be tough to win but we still wanted to go for it. If we merely stuck to the tactics we had employed in the heat the likely result would be that we would lose to the Germans in exactly the same style as we had so often in the past. That cycle had to be broken. It was time to write a new script.

Here was an opportunity to change the pattern of racing and see how they held up when not in control the whole way.

We smashed it out of the start and as everybody else settled into their rhythm we just kept it going, driven on by wild shouts of excitement and bellowing war cries from within our crew. While it may not have been conducive to producing a victory over the full 2 km, it was exhilarating. At 1000 m we were leading as we had set out to do. Then reality came home to roost. We were rowing aggressively but not efficiently and in the third 500 the Germans came through to take the lead, leaving us with very little in the tank and fighting to defend our second place. Despite having to take silver again we learned something that day. We had the raw speed, what we had to work on was sustaining it.

We arrived home in a positive frame of mind. From a personal perspective I was pleased that I had committed myself completely in the race; I had tried my best, and I think others in the crew had learned a bit about themselves. I liked the fact that the style of racing we adopted had taken us right to the edge physically and we found something extra beyond where we had been before. We'd always known we could row well, now we knew that deep within us there was more than we had ever previously shown. And we had got there without one of our most talented rowers.

A week later we tried to put Stan back in the boat. It didn't work. In Varese we had been flying, but in that first training session with him once again in his seat, when we upped the intensity level after about twenty minutes he broke down, which came as a blow. What had at first appeared to be a relatively minor setback was now looking significantly worse.

In the run-up to the second World Cup race, in Lucerne, Jürgen decided to push us incredibly hard physically. He had taken the decision that it was far more important to worry about the Olympics in two months time rather than the next race in two weeks. Those sessions hurt like hell. I felt like I hadn't recovered fully from Belgrade and found myself falling from the rowing machine in a heap and taking a bit longer than usual to get up. I wasn't alone, everyone was struggling. But I understood that this training was going to deliver us physically to a place that would see our boat through that third 500 when it mattered most, and I was willing to put myself through the pain. I confess, though, that during those weeks I had moments of feeling my age.

Given Jürgen's decision to concentrate on power over technique the result in Lucerne could probably have been predicted. In the final we started well, kept with the Germans, and in the third 500 rather than fading we came on strong, pulling virtually level with the leaders and giving us a moment when we thought this was it, we're going to beat them for the first time. But they responded in the last quarter as we slightly fell away, second again. But we had pushed them hard.

In Belgrade we had performed well in the first and second 500s but failed in the third; in Switzerland we had delivered the first, second and third 500s drifting only in the final segment.

We were learning. We knew we could go fast but now we also knew that the speed was something that could last. The question was, could we maintain it for long enough?

Lucerne offered one more insight into what might happen in London. It was there that the Canadians, the Olympic champions, first started to show as a serious threat, breaking the world record when we raced them in the heat. The conditions were conducive to a fast time and it was worrying that we did not make the most of them.

On the day of the heat there was a significant tailwind, which we failed to deal with effectively. When you row with the wind in your face, helping you down the course, you have to make sure to get hold of the boat quickly because the stroke feels a little shorter, but we were not getting our blades in the water fast enough. It was something we knew we had to work on back at home because on the Olympic course at Dorney rowing with a tailwind is a regular occurrence. Another worry.

The third and final World Cup event in Munich featured a much depleted field with the German, Canadian, Dutch and American crews all failing to turn up for various reasons. We didn't turn up either, although we were there.

Lukewarm is probably the most charitable way to describe our performance. We won the 'race for lanes' convincingly against the Poles, Australians and Ukrainians but in the final itself, well, we missed our opportunity. Even in the warm-up I could sense we weren't quite up for it. As the German TV boat came past we were lined up in our boat having a 'comfort break', with one guy standing and a few cocking their leg over the side. This isn't unusual in itself but as we laughed at the uncomfortable situation I watched the Polish crew row past, focused, intent, shouting encouragement to each other as if they were about to go to war. What happened next was probably not a surprise.

We staged a re-enactment of the bad old days: a slow start, quickly dropped, and then a desperate attempt to claw our way back into the race, eventually coming home behind the Poles and Australians. Not a good way to end our World Cup season.

The one positive I managed to take from Munich was that all the indications pointed towards a very tight Olympic final. Countries that we should have beaten had defeated us and while it was true that we had been off on the day of the race, it also demonstrated how fine the margins were between success and failure. Being one per cent down on our A-game had cost us a length of speed; the reverse was also true. If we could find an extra one per cent, with Stan back in the boat and through better rowing, we could be ahead of the field.

The experiences that would lead to our game plan for the final mounted up as London 2012 eventually arrived on our doorstep.

Friday 27 July 2012 was a much anticipated day, with London hosting the Opening Ceremony to welcome the world and show off Britain at its best. With that taking place across the other side of the capital, and running late into the night, attendance was impossible. Instead our women's team arranged our own version at the team's hotel, marching through the gardens in our white suits with Katherine Grainger carrying the nation's flag. I'm afraid when this was suggested I was one of the detractors who thought the whole thing a bit of a waste of time. Surely we had more important things to worry about? I was wrong.

Following the procession we were treated to a mildly amusing welcome speech from David Tanner, who took on the role of Queen for the evening, declaring the games officially open after we had witnessed Matt Wells, a member of the British team since the Sydney Olympics, hold an Olympic torch aloft (unlit) and then ceremoniously lower it to ignite (with a lighter) our own Olympic flame (a candle), which we kept burning throughout the duration of the regatta.

Re-framing became an important part of my, and all the eight's, Olympics. We had managed to take something positive out of the disappointment of Munich, and found ourselves having to do so again following the outcome of the draw for the heat which saw us competing alongside both the Canadians and Germans, together with the Dutch – how the supposed seeding allowed that to happen is beyond me. The impact of our poor performance in Munich may have been greater than we thought at the time.

If we could have chosen who to race in the heat it would certainly not have been both those boats. Only one crew would go through to the final, with the remaining three from each of the two heats fighting it out in the repêchage. A more favourable draw could very well have seen us qualify direct but given who we were up against we chose to view it as either a first chance to beat our nearest rivals and recognize we were fast enough to win the Olympics, or, if we did not prove victorious, a means to find out what we were up against and have time to do something about it. In addition, if a second race was required it would offer an opportunity to undertake another high-pressure row with Stan, who thankfully was back in the boat, his back working well enough.

A narrow defeat by the Germans left us contemplating the second of those two reframing options.

In a rehearsal for the final, we took control of the repêchage from the start – fastest in the first 500, fastest again in the second and in control for the whole race. In the third and fourth 500s the other boats did come back at us but we never felt in any danger of losing. Had we required it, we believed our cox Phelan Hill would have taken us up to another level. We had controlled Canada and made a clear statement, we felt, that the gold medal race was now down to us and Germany.

Experience and belief.

Experience had shown us that all-out attack was the only way to beat the Germans. The belief part, that was simple. All I had to do was look at the guys I was rowing with.

Alex Partridge in the bow, someone so competitive and whose mind is so active that at times he reminds me of myself at my worst – or best – because he wants to win everything all the time. He can easily feel the world is against him and that's when he seems to perform at his best, on a mission to prove himself. There's no better person to have in your boat when that mission is to finally defeat your great rivals in the only race that matters. Alex's mind races when he's fired up; he's passionate and it's critical we keep that fire burning without over-cooking it. I've been very aware of this whenever I room with him. If we end up talking rowing just before sleep I'm careful not to make any outlandish statements about what I think we should be doing, because although I can then say goodnight and be out like a light, Alex will lie awake for hours turning over in his head what I've just said.

James Foad has been in it with me for the whole journey. James is a tough, quiet competitor who rows very well and always as hard as he possibly can. He's not one of the biggest guys physically but he is very solid, reliable and trustworthy.

Tom Ransley, quite a complex character, is strong, with an ability to dig incredibly deep and take himself to another place, which we will need in the closing stages.

Ric Egington has the capacity to be the most physical rower in the world. He's big and incredibly powerful and it's the job of the guys around him to keep the rhythm of the boat smooth so Ric can do his work. If Ric is comfortable he has the ability to row the boat like he's on an ergo, using his awesome raw physicality.

Moe Sbihi, who sits behind me, is big and rangy, with lungs that let him perform at altitude better than any rower before him. Moe has had to learn to use this size effectively and to push himself to new levels. He's achieved that, although I still believe there is more to come. He seems young and this is his time to deliver. He has the power and technically he's now rowing better than ever before.

Matt Langridge is someone I look up to as a great rower with immense natural talent combined with strength and power. He knows his own mind and though I'd often like to approach our training differently he's not going to be easily swayed. He believes in himself and he believes in what we are doing. I'm very happy to follow his lead.

Stan Louloudis, a born winner. He's a natural physically and technically, and though he may be young he has a maturity our crew badly needs. Another who reminds me of myself when I was twenty. I like that.

Finally our cox, Phelan Hill, the brains of the operation. He makes sure everything is in order. In the boat he's in charge. There's no second guessing any more. As a team we talk enough before and after our sessions, but on the water we are all on the same page, executing the plan that Phelan lays out for us. It boils down to sensible basics. We are no longer trying to over-complicate things as we have in the past. We know how to row hard when it matters and using simple cues Phelan keeps us focused on the different elements of rowing well, ensuring we are tuned together to do the things we need to. It's that harmony on the day that will make or break the gold medal hunt. We still use the key words from 2010 – long, connected, relaxed, hard – but we have now added a fifth, 'together'. That's what is going to make the difference.

11.30 a.m.

We're sitting in a circle on a balcony at the back of the Eton Dorney boat club. We feel good. We feel ready. John is speaking, telling us that this is our moment.

'Tonight you will look at yourselves in the mirror and know you gave everything,' he says. I look around the guys and with one hundred per cent certainty I know that each one of them, each one of us, is going to lay everything they have on the line in one hour.

11.55 a.m.

We're in the boat, paddling behind the grandstand, heading towards the start line. Above the roar of the spectators urging on Helen Glover and Heather Stanning, who I desperately hope are winning in the women's pair, I hear a child's voice ring out. Two voices.

'Go Dad!'

I glance to my left and spot Jenny, Josie and Adam. They've slipped away from their seats to give me one last lift. I give them a slight, secret smile and allow my thumb to come off the oar for a second in positive acknowledgment of their encouragement. Just like in 1992 I have family in the boat with me again.

12.25 p.m.

Lane 2 on the start line. A momentary thought skips across my mind. The wind has been flicking around all morning. A cross wind from my left, but will it be cross-tail or cross-head? I'd been hoping for cross-tail, confident that we have resolved our issues in such conditions. But it has settled now. Cross-head.

I'm disappointed. Now the crews on the near side of the course have a slight advantage thanks to the bank providing a degree of shelter. The middle lanes – heat winners Germany and the US – will have less benefit but the Canadians, who secured lane five over us on the toss of a coin, are sitting on the sheltered side of the course.

I put the thought out of my mind almost the moment it rears its head. For the second time today I hear Brian Miller's voice. 'Concentrate on controlling the controllables.'

I slip into the routine I have followed for more than twenty years, helping to control my nerves and normalize the situation as best I can. It starts with reaching down to grip my right ankle, I can't explain why. Normally I would be touching my lucky Hampton rugby socks, the same ones I've worn for every major race since my school days, but unlike in Barcelona, Atlanta and Sydney, the Olympic marketing machine has banned anything in the boat that isn't official. Concentrate on the controllables Greg.

I breathe deeply, from my diaphragm, centring myself, relaxing.

I reach further down into the boat, to my foot stretchers, confirming one bolt is tight, then a second and third. Now on to the riggers – fourth bolt tight? Yes, and fifth, sixth, seventh, eighth and ninth. Always nine. I am a fifteen-year-old kid again, checking his equipment before the race commences. This will all have been done a hundred times by others prior to this moment, but I don't care. It's my responsibility to make sure everything is as it should be. I've always done it. I'm not stopping now.

The nerves are building. Another breath from my core, long and deep.

I think of Josie at the start of a swimming race, picturing her standing on her block surrounded by other kids. A whistle is blown and she leans forward. 'Take your marks, go!' She dives in, swims with everything she has, and climbs out of the pool at the far end.

What nerves was she facing? Massive, but she dealt with them.

I see Adam going out to bat, waddling to the crease in oversized pads and a helmet that rattles around his head. He must have his heart in his mouth as he prepares to face a bigger boy bowling a hard cricket ball straight at him. Yet he does it.

Now here I am sitting in a boat doing something I have done for more than twenty years, surrounded by the best seven rowers in the UK. My kids handle their situations. I can handle mine.

I notice a cameraman on the landing stage. He's focusing his lens on lane one, the Dutch, then moves on to us. From more than a mile down the course I hear a massive roar as thirty thousand spectators see the image he's relaying on a large screen in front of them.

He continues down the line. A moment of calm, one last Olympic breath before the starter begins his sequence.

'Netherlands.'

'Great Britain.'

'United States.'

'Germany.'

'Canada.'

'Australia.'

'Attention.'

We bury our oars in the water.

I look at the red light. Two, three seconds remain.

Green light. Buzzer.

Pull!

Five hard strokes to get away.

Concentrate on making the next fifteen long. We've been

working on this since the heat. Press out the finish of each stroke to move the boat a long way every time. Maximum distance per stroke.

'Patience!'

'Poise!'

'Composure!'

Phelan is reminding us to focus. Adrenalin tries to cheat you into wheel-spinning strokes, short and fast. Row hard. Row well.

A minute in and I am beginning to hurt. I really don't want to mess this up. I can't stop now though. I'm here.

The years between 1992 and 1996 flash into memory. Before Barcelona I never interrupted a 20 km ergo. After Barcelona I began to take breaks, to stretch, rehydrate. I know where that led. I'm no longer that person, not now, not today. Since making my comeback I have never once stopped at anything. I push through to the end. Always. Today is no different.

Keep going Greg. Row hard. Row well.

Passing the 500 m mark, Phelan calls. 'Second place. A canvas behind the Germans.'

That's OK. Eight feet. We're with them, moving well.

Now we dig deep. Now we push on. We've agreed we will not cruise. Keep pushing. Keep pushing. This is where we give ourselves the chance to win.

'You are moving. You are moving on the Germans.'

'Halfway. Half a canvas.'

We can do this. We can hit the front.

Phelan makes the call.

'If not now, when?'

More.

'Greg, do this for Josie. Do this for Adam.'

My deepest emotions rise to the surface. I push like never before.

'You are leading the Olympics!'

The wall of noise hits us at around 1500 m. The crowd are in the boat with us, driving us on.

I can no longer hear Phelan. My muscles are screaming, ears on fire. I fix my gaze on Matt's back, moving with him. My focus is my body now. Nothing else matters. The pain in my arms and legs – that's my world. Every second of resistance I feel means I am doing my job with that stroke. I am moving our boat on to the finish line.

Place. Push. Pain. Resistance. Release. Connect. Engage. Place. Push. Pain. Resistance.

I'm in unchartered territory. Everything I have done since Poznan has been building to this unknown minute and a half. 500 m to go and it's impossible to know what they will consist of. We have given everything. We're leading the Germans, the Olympics. Now I am in total darkness. My brain is closed to everything except rowing long, rowing hard, rowing together.

Yet still I feel the crews either side coming back.

With twenty strokes to go I sense one last thing. Up to then we've been controlled and aggressive. Now we're ragged. I must row well. We've switched to autopilot, rowing at an unconscious level. Where is the finish? I know we are not quite together but surely the end must be close.

Beep.

The race is over. I hear noise, cheering from my left. Our boat is silent. I don't understand. Beyond the noise I can see the digital scoreboard.

1. GBR. 2. CAN. 3. GER.

We've won. So why aren't we screaming with delight?

My stinging eyes clear, focus sharpening.

1. GER. 2. CAN. 3. GBR.

The landing stage is a scene of devastation. Some of our guys are still in their seats, bent over their oars, head in hands. Others are stretched out on their backs, too exhausted to feel anything. One or two are hunched down in despondency, crying.

I try to speak to each of them. Like my team-mates, I'm disappointed, desperately so. But I also know that winning the bronze is important. Fourth is an empty place. To be able to stand on the podium, in front of this crowd, is recognition of what we have achieved.

We gave ourselves the opportunity to win. There are no regrets.

We forged a well-aligned, happy boat. Could we have been emotionally tighter? Like Jonny and me in 1992? Like the French in 2000? Could we have done more to hold it together at the very end? Maybe, maybe we could have practised our sprint finish more under pressure, maybe we could have taken more time to hurt ourselves in blistering finishes. Sure, Jonny and I did that regularly, on the ergos, when we would approach Molesey boat house after a hard session, even racing Slovenians on Banyoles days before our 1992 final. But that's not how this rowing crew of eight strong characters has been built.

Was it possible to have done things differently? I have worked with such good people at Lane4 and I know how a team can connect at a deeper level. I think we could have been more aligned and able to change for the better, but not this time. That isn't the way John, Christian and Jürgen work. I knew when I came back that I would take Jürgen's way or the highway and his approach has not let me down. We came within a few strokes of Olympic gold on a foundation of controlled, efficient, strong rowing and incredible physicality. It took us so close. The sum was greater than the individual parts, no question.

Would I have taken a different approach had I been in a position to do so? Probably, but at what cost? In 2011 I made myself an outsider to the crew and in 2012 our new key word was 'together'. I'm sure I'd have broken things down had I gone against the grain at this stage.

There were times when I had a desire for us to become the greatest team there has ever been through my eyes, but I soon realized that it was more important that we became the greatest team there has ever been through nine pairs of eyes. That's the journey we've been on and it's been a good one. No regrets.

On the pontoon where the medal ceremony is about to take place, Matt calls us together in a huddle. I'm pleased it's him who is going to have the last word, not me. At this moment, I am one hundred per cent one of us, not one of them. I don't need to speak.

'Guys, we did our best. Each one of us should hold his head up high. Let's enjoy this moment. You don't want to regret in ten years that you didn't make the most of the next few minutes. There are thirty thousand people supporting us and we owe it to them to show we are proud of what we did, what we achieved, and the country we are representing.'

Matt's correct. This is a special moment. We are all about to receive an Olympic medal in front of our home crowd. It is not gold, that's gut wrenching, but it's an Olympic medal.

I smile when I see who is conducting the presentation. FISA president Denis Oswald, the man responsible for cutting the coxed pair after Barcelona, leaving us unable to defend our title. There's an irony there somewhere but I am too tired to work it out.

The medal feels heavy around my neck, like it means something. It does; it's proof for me that the past three years have been worth it. I spot Jenny and the kids in the family stand in front of the podium. Josie and Adam are in floods of tears. Happy or sad I don't know, but seeing them makes me well up too. Happy or sad? Proud.

The German anthem rings out and I listen with respect but my gaze is firmly on our own flag as it rises above me. Just as the music ends and the applause begins to die down I catch sight of Mum and Dad, in the very back row of the stand. I'm reminded of my grandfather, watching his sons play sport through the school fence. In the same way my father doesn't want to be in the show or steal any of the limelight. But he wants to be there. Thanks Dad.

What's he doing now? He's acting out a rowing action and pointing to the far side of the course, to the main stand. Even with the world watching I'm still his son and he's still my father, offering advice and instruction. We've planned to go over anyway, to acknowledge the incredible support we've received, but it is a welcome reminder. Thanks again, Dad.

As we prepare to stow our boat after thanking the crowds for everything they did for us, John West calls us together one last time. 'No one, no one could have given more of themselves. You can all look yourselves in the eye and know you gave your best. You didn't get out what you deserved. With that wind I thought you didn't have a chance, but you still took it on. You still went for it and every one of you should be proud of that.'

I finally meet up with Jenny, the kids and my parents in the family area. There's no room for upset and tears here. I'm happy and they are taking my lead, laughing, hugging, kissing. Excited.

We did it. All of us.

Jenny laid on a party at home that afternoon. The house was decked out in bunting, Jonny was there, Mum and Dad, a few friends from the present and from the past. Will had even flown in from America. Everyone was celebrating our success and the dedication we had shown as a family. The toasts were made with champagne, my first sips of alcohol in months. I hadn't missed it, but it tasted good. To me it signalled I was moving on.

Later, at a dinner in Marlow I gave a speech thanking everyone for making my dream first a possibility, then a reality. Each person in the room had contributed, from friends helping to look after the kids when I had been away from home so much, to Mum,

Dad and Jonny who had made me who I am and Jenny who had allowed me to be who I wanted.

I felt very honoured to be standing amongst them.

Josie and Adam then followed with some words of their own. Adam was funny, making us all laugh with stories of me at home. Then Josie stepped forward, a sheet of paper in her hand from which she read. It was her 'After the Olympics' list, compiled for me.

'Get a dog.'

'Go on a balloon trip with Mum.'

'Have a touring holiday in America.'

'Play more cricket with Adam.'

'Take Josie swimming more.'

The Olympics give, but they also take away. We all understood that right from the beginning. But it's over now. I've got some catching up to do. I can't wait to get started.

The following morning the man in the mirror looks back at me and smiles.

1992 had been about family.

2012 had been about family.

The future is about family. It starts today.

If not now, when? If not us, who?

ACKNOWLEDGEMENTS

This book would not exist, my story would not exist, without the support and encouragement of many people. It is impossible to name everyone, these acknowledgments would run for pages and pages if I did so. My sincere thanks therefore go to all those listed below, and for those of you who I have had to omit for reasons of brevity, I hope you know who you are. I am grateful for everything you have done for me.

Mum, Dad, Jonny, Jenny, Josie and Adam. For everything.

All the Searle clan for their support, especially cousin Peter for being there with me in 1992 and again twenty years later.

Also Jenny's family, the Hickmans, for welcoming me into their lives, and Laurie and Oli, for the roles they have played even when they might not have realized it.

Lindsay, who came to lodge with us and ended up being a great help to Jenny and the kids while I was away from home for so many long stretches of time.

At Hampton School the guys I rowed with in the eight and Martin Cross and Steve Gunn for creating an environment where champions are inevitable.

Everyone who sat alongside me in the Junior GB Team.

The World Championship eights I rowed with in 1990 and

1991, and especially Garry Herbert who played such a key role in guiding Jonny and me across the line in the gold medal position in Barcelona; Brian Miller, for helping me believe, Jim Walker my housemate during those years, and Ben Hunt-Davis with whom I shared my twenty-first birthday.

Tim and Obby in 1994.

Will, Bob and Dodge in 1997.

Everyone at Lane4 especially Ade, Graham, Hutch, Dominic, Austin for his unshakeable support, and Jonny Z, Mike Hurst, Wil James, Liz Campbell, Paul Jewitt-Harris, Jennifer Quinton and Shona Horseman.

Ed Coode in 1999 and 2000.

Ian Walker with whom I had the privilege of sharing my incredible America's Cup adventure, and Mark Covell who first gave me my break to enter the world of sailing.

Wheelie, Josie's godfather, who has joined me throughout my journey, has shared his enthusiasm every step of the way and given me support when I most needed it.

All our friends from the Spinfield School gates, especially Jackie and David Veitch.

All our friends at the Wycombe District Swimming Club, especially Nicky and Glenn Mathews.

The Molesey Leg-Ends, for the fun and for keeping me in a boat.

The people who are no longer with us and who won't read this, though I hope they knew what this meant to me and what they did for me: Granny, Jenny's father John, her brother Keith, my Aunt Trish, my cousin David and Harry Mahon, the magician.

My comeback would have been impossible without the support of sponsors and believers. You have all made a huge contribution. Keith Wishart, Martin Ryan, Ben Wilson, Jeanette and Andrew at NCP, Roel at BT, Nikos, everyone at Concept2, especially Alex; everyone at BMW who backed me, Daryl at Coca-Cola, Paul at

Canvas Holidays, Siemens for their support of British rowing and the great work of those at UK Lottery.

Jürgen Grobler of course, for his belief in me, for taking my madcap idea seriously, and for what he has done for rowing in this country generally; John West, and Christian Felkel.

All the medical support team, especially Sally and also Juliet for helping look after my back.

Everyone I had the honour of rowing with in those eights of 2010, 2011 and 2012, especially Cameron Nicol and Dan Ritchie.

David Wilson who believed in this from the beginning and who helped me produce the book that I wanted.

My agent Kate Shaw who also believed in me right from the beginning, and that I had a story worth telling.

My publishers Macmillan, who had the faith to back this project, and especially the work that Jon Butler, Cindy Chan and Katie James have put in to ensure I am proud of the book you find in your hands now.

Steve Redgrave for his support and belief throughout my comeback.

All the rowers, at home and abroad; I've loved competing with you.

And finally, all of you, the people who have cheered and supported me and British rowing for so many years. Without you our sport wouldn't be the same and I would not have experienced the highs and the lows that have shaped my life and which I have been fortunate enough to write about in the pages of this book.

Thank you all.

Greg Searle
8 August 2012